Boston Observed

To four immigrants who found their way to Boston

James Leslie Gerrard (England)

Mary MacLeod Gerrard (Prince Edward Island)

Julius Sjöberg (Sweden)

Johanna Nelson Sjöberg (Sweden)

my grandparents

Boston Observed

by Carl Seaburg

This Town of Boston has a history. It is not an accident,
not a windmill, or a railroad station, or cross-roads
tavern, or an army-barracks grown up by time and
luck to a place of wealth; but a seat of humanity, of
men of principle, obeying a sentiment and marching
loyally whither that should lead them; so that its annals
are great historical lines, inextricably national; part of
the history of political liberty.

—RALPH WALDO EMERSON

Beacon Press   *Boston*

Acknowledgments

Most sincere thanks are due to the staff and supporters of the Boston Athenaeum, the Boston Public Library, the Bostonian Society, the Massachusetts Historical Society, and the Society for the Preservation of New England Antiquities. Books such as this would be impossible without the material and illustrations collected and maintained in these great institutions, and this author owes a particular debt to each of the above-named organizations.

Every effort has been made to trace the ownership of any copyrighted material used in this book. If any infringements have been inadvertently made, apologies are hereby tendered, and the author will be happy upon due notification to correct such omissions in future editions of this work. Sincere thanks are due to the following publishers, agents, or individuals holding copyrights on the selections specified, for permission to use them in this book:

The American Antiquarian Society for the selections from Rev. Ebenezer Parkman's diary, the Autobiography of Rev. Increase Mather, and the manuscript of the Rev. Samuel West.

Atlantic-Little, Brown for the selection from THE LAST HURRAH by Edwin O'Connor, by permission of Atlantic-Little, Brown and Co. Copyright © 1956 by Edwin O'Connor.

The Bostonian Society for the selection from volume 4 of the Society's publications (1907).

The Colonial Society of Massachusetts for the excerpts from volume 31 of their publications.

The co-executors of John Dos Passos for the selection from FORTY-SECOND PARALLEL by John Dos Passos. Copyright by H. Marston Smith and Elizabeth H. Dos Passos, co-executors of the Estate of John R. Dos Passos.

Grove Press for the selection from THE AUTOBIOGRAPHY OF MALCOLM X. Copyright © 1964 by Alex Haley and Malcolm X, copyright © 1965 by Alex Haley and Betty Shabazz.

Harvard University Press for the selections from JACOBIN AND JUNTO by Charles Warren, copyright 1931; from Smith O. Dexter, ed. CONCORD RIVER: SELECTIONS FROM THE JOURNALS OF WILLIAM BREWSTER, copyright 1937; from PRUNES AND PRISM by Charles Hall Grandgent, copyright 1928; and to The Belknap Press of Harvard University Press for the selection from volume four of the JOURNALS AND MISCELLANEOUS NOTEBOOKS OF RALPH WALDO EMERSON.

Hawthorn Books, Inc., for the selection from BEING LITTLE IN CAMBRIDGE by Eleanor Hallowell Abbott.

Houghton Mifflin Company for the selections from Marian Peabody's TO BE YOUNG WAS VERY HEAVEN, © 1967; from Horace W. Wright's BIRDS OF THE BOSTON PUBLIC GARDEN, © 1909; from Mary Antin's THE PROMISED LAND, © 1912; and from James Garrison's BEHOLD ME ONCE MORE, ed. by Walter Merrill, © 1954.

The selection from Dr. Robert Honyman's COLONIAL PANORAMA 1775, edited by Philip Padelford, was reprinted with the permission of the Henry E. Huntington Library and Art Gallery, San Marino, California.

Mrs. Jane B. MacIntire for the selection from WABAN — EARLY DAYS, published in 1944.

The Massachusetts Historical Society for the letters from John (?) Pond, John Winthrop, and Thomas Mayhew in The Winthrop Papers (v. 3); for the selections from its COLLECTIONS, the John Eliot letter (v. 3), Cotton Mather letter (v. 38), Joshua Moodey letter (v. 38), Cotton Mather diary (v. 67), the Samuel Sewall diary, the Ann Griffin piece (v. 38), Jonathan Belcher from the Belcher Papers (v. 56), and James Otis in the Warren-Adams letters; for the selections from its PROCEEDINGS, the Jeremy Belknap journal (v. 4), the Samuel Sewall Jr. diary (v. 28), and the letter of John Torrey Morse Jr. (v. 79); and for the selections from its manuscripts, namely the Aaron White diary, the Mary and Catherine Byles letterbooks, and the P. C. Brooks account books.

William Morrow & Co. for the selection from HOME COUNTRY by Ernie Pyle published by William Sloane Associates in 1947.

The National Geographic Magazine and Frederick Simpich for the selection from "Boston Through Midwest Eyes" (July 1936).

The New England Quarterly for the selections from the article by Mary E. Raymond, "Memories of William James" (vol. 10), from Walt Whitman (vol. 1), from Robert Carter's "Recollections of W. H. Prescott" (vol. 32), from the diary of Julian Ursyn Niemcewicz (vol. 34), and from the letter of Frederick Engels (vol. 22).

G. P. Putnam's Sons for the selection from *Grandmother Tyler's Book* edited by Frederick Tupper and Helen Tyler Brown, © 1925.

The Schlesinger Library, Radcliffe College, for the selections from the Eliza Cabot and Eunice Callendar diaries.

Charles Scribner's Sons for the selections from George Santayana's THE LAST PURITAN, © 1936, and from Rupert Brooke's LETTERS FROM AMERICA, © 1913.

Miss Alice W. Shurcliff for the selection from LIVELY DAYS by Margaret Homer Shurcliff.

University of North Carolina Press for the selections from GENTLEMAN'S PROGRESS by Dr. Alexander Hamilton, edited by Carl Bridenbaugh.

University of Oklahoma Press for the selection from THE NEW DEMOCRACY IN AMERICA: TRAVELS OF FRANCISCO DE MIRANDA IN THE UNITED STATES, 1783–84, Translated by Judson P. Wood. Copyright 1963 by the University of Oklahoma Press.

Yankee, Inc., for the selection by Laura E. Richards from her "My Boston" published in the July 1937 *Yankee*.

Contents

I know histhry isn't thrue, Hinnissy, because it ain't like what I see ivry day in Halsted Shtreet. If any wan comes along with a histhry iv Greece or Rome that'll show me the people fightin', gettin' dhrunk, makin' love, gettin' married, owin' the groceryman an' bein' without hard coal, I'll believe they was a Greece or Rome, but not befure. Historyans is like doctors. They are always lookin' f'r symptoms. Those av thim that writes about their own times examines th' tongue an' feels th' pulse an' makes a wrong diagnosis Th' other kind iv histhry is a post-mortem examination. It tells ye what a country died iv. But I'd like to know what it lived iv.

—Mr. Dooley
(*Finley Peter Dunne*)

Preface

Most of us have but the vaguest notions of history. A few dates, some great names, a battle or two, added to some general impressions (half of which are probably mistaken) make up the sum total of our historical knowledge.

Why should this be surprising? How many of us can remember accurately the important dates and episodes of our own lives? Husbands traditionally are not supposed to remember when they got married. Parents, unless constantly reminded by their offspring, forget their children's birthdays. When was it that Aunt Mary died? What year did I have the measles? Which apartment did we live in when we were young? When did we trade in the Ford for a Chevy?

Family memories can be refreshed by talks with parents and kin, if living and if they remember. Or we can look at old family letters and diaries if they've been saved. It is amazing what facts can be discovered simply from studying cancelled checks.

Perhaps our inability to remember is at its most dismal when it comes to the city we live in. We usually know far more about our country or the world, where we live less, than our hometown where we live more. This book's main function then, is to serve Greater Bostonians somewhat as a family attic. Collected here are the remembrances of our mutual past, of our larger family life as fellow Bostonians.

Certainly in the 350 years of the "current" Boston, most of the story has to be left out. We can only summarize, spotlight, sketch in the main features. The idea is to convey a sense of our "family" past, shared with all who have lived "hereabouts." So we delve in the family trunk, coming up with letters or journals, with pictures or old photographs. Hopefully, when finished, we'll have a better idea of who we Bostonians are and why. It may even be a somewhat different Boston than you thought you were living in.

It should be pointed out at once that this is only half a book. All the Bostons are not here: educational Boston, medical Boston, young Boston, working Boston, sexual Boston, or the various ethnic Bostons. So much had to be included to give proper treatment to the subjects covered that much had to be left for another book.

Meanwhile, here at the northern end of Megalopolis, the top of Bos-Wash, you will discover some of the secrets of an old town and its suburbs. And you will meet many of the people who lived among this furniture of houses and streets and buildings we now use. Welcome them, for they are in many ways — ourselves.

Carl Seaburg

NOTE: All Old Style dates in this book have been silently changed to New Style. All quotations are reprinted exactly as they appear in the original documents except where otherwise indicated.

A panoramic painting of the
Greater Boston area by Austin
Stevens hanging in the Boston
Visitor Information Center on
Lafayette Mallon Boston
Common. (Courtesy of Greater
Boston Chamber of Commerce.)

CHAPTER ONE

The Land, the Sea, and the Air

Fly over Greater Boston in summer and the greenness of the land below you is astonishing. Walking the streets, your landscape is standard "big city"—asphalt, concrete, brick. But soaring clear of the streets, up in the summer blue, Suffolk County and its environs seem like a pleasant park.

Eastward, the sun starts up sudden gleams on the restless sea. The long white breakings of the surf on the shore mark the no-man's-land of those two ancient contenders. The jaunty thrust of craggy headlands, the stretches of curving beaches brightly clustered with sunners and swimmers, the harbor islands and reefs with whitecaps lacing around them, give a clean festive look to the scene.

Glancing inland, the reedy marshes and inlets poke wet sea fingers at the land. That land itself seems defenseless, rising slowly and gently to a fringe of highlands that suddenly interrupt the lowland basin and curve round to hold in the great city and its satellite towns. Much of this basin area is less than fifty feet above sea level. On it, looking like beached whales, are many hills, called drumlins, some rising 150 feet or more above the countryside.

The city proper sits roughly at the center of the semicircle made by the highlands. On the north is the Fells Upland reaching from Swampscott to Waltham. On the south, rising behind the Blue Hills, is the Sharon Upland, stretching from Hingham to Sharon. Linking the two is the Needham Upland, which rises less abruptly from the lowland. Cutting through these three linked uplands are four rivers that drain them. The Saugus and the Mystic from the Fells, the Charles from the Needham, and the Neponset from the Sharon. The Charles and the Mystic meet at Boston, while the other two exit farther above and below the city.

The advantages of Boston's situation for its first settlers are obvious from the air even today: a sheltered harbor deep enough for ocean-going vessels; two navigable rivers permitting easy access to the hinterland; a countryside suitable for grazing and farming; abundant timber for firewood and building; and plenty of fresh water in the ponds and streams. The one advantage apparent in 1630 but not obvious today was its strategic defensive situation. It was then a large peninsula with a long narrow neck of land connecting it to the continent.

1

Boston from Dorchester Heights (South Boston) as seen in 1774 with the drumlins showing prominently.

The need for such protection was clear to people who were wary of the Indians and faced very real threats from French, Dutch, Spanish, and even rival English colonizers. A visitor to Boston in 1663, John Josselyn, noted "two hills of equal height on the frontire part" of the town that were "well fortified on the superfices with some Artillery mounted, commanding any Ship as she sails into the Harbour within the still Bay." Behind these stood "a high mountain that out-tops all, with its three little rising hills on the summit called Tramount, this is furnished with a Beacon and great Guns." It was, stated its first governor in Biblical terms, "a city built upon a hill." But was it also, as in the parable, built upon a rock?

To discover what Boston is fundamentally built upon, one has to come down from the sky and dig. It quickly becomes evident that if the city does not have feet of clay, at least it has foundations of clay. The "modern soil," so called, rests in many places throughout the city upon a thick layer of clays. This modern soil consists of sand, gravel, siltings, peat, and the fill used on the made lands in the Boston neighborhood. In some places the clays are a hundred feet thick; in others they grade down to a few inches. The top-most layer is usually a yellowish clay that is only a weathered form of the "blue" clay underneath.

Boston blue clay is well-known to geologists and contractors. It has been described as "a very tough, plastic clay but containing, as do all glacial clays, a large portion of impalpably fine sand or quartz flour." Sometimes quite hard,

2

this clay is found throughout most of the Boston Basin. It was not left by a single glacier, but deposited by any of a number of retreating glaciers whose melting waters, washing over the sand, gravel, and pebbles accumulated by the glacier, filtered out this residue.

Below the clay is hardpan, which is also a glacial deposit, made up of various rock materials mixed together and known as "till." Till is found in the nearly two hundred drumlins making up the lowland hills and the harbor islands. Buried beneath the clays, the glacial outwash, and the marine silts, this till is rarely exposed except in deep digs. It varies from a few feet thick to more than a hundred—particularly in the drumlins. Till that has not been oxidized by the air has a blue-gray color, while weathered till ranges from buff to rust due to iron oxides in it. It is an extremely compact material, difficult to excavate. Since in most places this till was almost immediately covered by glacial clays, weathered till is ordinarily found only in the drumlins.

Bedrock is under the hardpan. In the Boston region, bedrock is either Cambridge "slate" or Roxbury "Pudding Stone." The slate lies under most of Boston proper and the harbor, Charlestown, Somerville, Malden, Everett, and parts of Cambridge and Waverly. Pudding stone, or Conglomerate, extends under nearly all of Roxbury, and large parts of Dorchester, West Roxbury, Brookline, Brighton, and Newton. Other formations are found in Hyde Park, Milton, Hingham, Quincy, and Hull. Brookline may not think it has anything in common with Roxbury, but deep down it has.

Irregular fault plane in slates of the Mystic quarries in Somerville, 1914. (Gardner Collection, Harvard University.)

An example of Roxbury conglomerate which can be seen on Green Hill in Nantasket. (Dr. James Hume, 1968.)

Pudding stone is aptly named, looking like an old-fashioned plum pudding. The "cake" part of the pudding is a clay into which have been stuck "plums" of sand, gravel, and rounded pebbles, water-worn and from older rocks in the district. Cooked in the oven of time, this has become rock. Its thickness varies but is from fifteen hundred to three thousand feet or more. Locally this stone was often used for building material. It trims to any desired shape, is a pleasing bluish-gray or yellow-drab color, and can be polished—though seldom is. Before concrete took over, it was often used for retaining walls, bridge abutments, and stone arches. Now it is usually crushed for concrete rubble.

Cambridge "slate" is the popular name for the dark, bluish-gray or brownish-gray rock that is a fine lamination of siltstone and mudstone. Its age has not been determined, and no fossils have been found in it. In thickness, it runs from two thousand to thirty-five hundred feet. At one time it was widely used in construction, a number of churches and other large city buildings being built from it. It was also popularly used for house foundations, but now it is rarely used in construction.

How old are these rocks? No one knows for certain, yet the oldest rocks under Boston are said to be over 600 million years old. There's immortality for you! But since the earth itself is estimated to be 4 or 5 billion years old (geologists are quite nonchalant with a billion years), the rocks are actually rather young.

Yet this spot on the globe where Boston is—approximately latitude 71°4′ and longitude 42°22′—has to be as old as the rest of the earth. Any record of the Boston area that goes back to the start of things has to read: "In the beginning was blank." The first 88 percent of Boston's history on the planet is unknown, and a good part of the remainder is studded with careful geological *perhaps*es and *maybes*.

4

The past is buried, but as an acute observer once noted, it is buried alive. Though these rocks and stones, these underpinnings of Boston, are organically dead, they still speak. There are more than sermons in stones. Each sand pebble has its own history. The flowing Charles has a past; hills and valleys have ancestors. Difficult as they are to decipher—hieroglyphics are a snap compared with rock formations—geologists since the early part of the nineteenth century have been scrabbling in the Boston beneath their feet, and the broad outlines of Boston-before-people are coming clear.

Real information begins during the Cambrian geologic period 620 million years ago. The pre-Cambrian history of the area is virtually unknown and can only be vaguely conjectured. Obviously there must have been rocks of pre-Cambrian age. It follows that they would have been deposited on a floor of older rock. Where evidence is available from the geological history of eastern North America, it seems likely that these rocks were ejected by volcanoes. Since little is to be found of these rocks, evidently there was a long period in which they eroded until the land was relatively flat. So much for a few hundred million years!

Workmen digging part of the main drainage tunnel in Boston bedrock, 1956. (Metropolitan District Commission.)

5

Geologists get something solid to work with in Cambrian time: there is a quartzite found chiefly in Westboro; a complex of schists—gray, green, or brown—from Marlboro, and some volcanic rock from the Woburn area. A slaty quartzite mostly from Weymouth is useful in dating since about thirty species of fossils have been found in it, including crustaceans, brachiopods, and gastropods. The rock is dated as Lower Cambrian.

If a camera could have been suspended over Boston and the 120 million years of the Cambrian period recorded by time-lapse photography, each decade one frame on the film, a picture worthy even of the lesser masterpieces of Cecil B. de Mille would have resulted. At that speed it would still take nearly two solid weeks to view it.

It would open showing the worn-down pre-Cambrian land being inundated by a slowly rising sea. Sand and sandy muds would be deposited on the floor of this sea, and generations of mollusks and crustaceans would be born, live, and die in the ooze. By the middle of the picture, the deposits would change from sand to clay—an exciting plot development!—and the cast of characters would now include one- and two-inch trilobites, among the earlier residents of Boston. By the end of the picture, quartz sand would be deposited on the sea bottom, and at least one species of brachiopods would be living in the waters, squatting perhaps over State Street-to-be, their tentacles scooping water past their mouths from which they extract their microscopic food. With their sedentary manner and their capacious appetites, feeding thus on their surroundings, some people might see them as the first bankers and stockbrokers of State Street.

The sequel to the Cambrian movie would be one of the Ordovician and Silurian periods, still in good old Paleozoic time. Unfortunately, a film of this period would have to be largely a blank, for of these 95 million years almost nothing is known. There may have been volcanic outbreaks or other mountain-building activity. Certainly complex events were happening in the bedrock of this time. Some rocks, existing deep in the earth in molten form, were forced up into the faults and crevices of overlying rocks to form dikes and plugs. They, in turn, were later invaded and infused by other flows of fiery rock.

In the face of this activity, the sea had retreated, or the land had risen high enough to be above the waters. By the principle that what thrusts up must erode down, a vast weathering process, forgotten endless centuries of rains and snows, of frosts and ice, of windblows and sunbake, of oxidation and carbonation, wore down this basal matter. When the Devonian period began, the surface of the Boston region was deeply scarred and disintegrated. Whether this surface was fairly flat or had some relief cannot now be determined. In Devonian time, some 400 million years back, the region was warped into troughs and swells which later became the basin and uplands of today. A thick series of glacial sediments were laid down in the basin during the 60 million years when Boston kept its clock by Devonian time.

No sudden changes brought in the Carboniferous period. Heavy layers of sediment continued to be deposited over much of the region. But something

Dike of porphyritic diabase in granite at Nahant, 1914. (Gardner Collection, Harvard University.)

new was added. Temperatures began dropping drastically. Glaciers formed to the northward and slowly, very slowly, edged south. The front of the glacier reached Boston from the east or southeast, not quite covering the southwest basin. Much later, when temperatures rose, this glacier began melting and formed a vast lake from its melting waters. A great thickness of glacial clay settled on the lake bottom and when this mass subsequently underwent great pressure, it hardened into Cambridge slate.

The Carboniferous period ended with a great surge of mountain-building activity that affected much of eastern North America. The rocks of the area were compressed and folded and changed by heat and pressure into other forms. As these layers of rock buckled under the stress, the sides of the basin crowded in toward each other. Further compression caused faulting along the margins of the basin, and rocks on both sides were pushed over upon those of the basin.

A gap of 50 million years now yawns in the Boston story. The Permian period at the end of the Paleozoic era left no records in the rocks to be read. "Presumably," says one authority, "such gaps correspond to long periods of weathering and degradation of the land." Degradation? Quite un-Bostonian!

It is now felt that at the beginning of the Permian period all the continents we know today were one super-continent, which has been given the name "Pangaea." This began to break up some 225 million years ago at the end of the Permian and the beginning of the Triassic period. As they separated, Boston was part of the northern half of this huge continental mass, called "Laurasia," which included North America and Europe-Asia. Because the continental shelf was elevated at this period, Boston was far inland from the new ocean being formed, today's Atlantic. Much geologic activity would have accompanied

Sill and stratified rocks at Nahant, 1914. (Gardner Collection, Harvard University.)

Ripple marks seen in cross section in a sand plain, Auburndale, 1914. (Gardner Collection, Harvard University.)

such a dramatic event: earthquakes, volcanic eruptions, high heat flow, and rock folding and faulting. At its end (though nothing "ends" geologically speaking), Laurasia, too, had separated, becoming the continents we know today, leaving Boston far from Europe with a deep, wide ocean between them.

In Triassic time, all that local rocks reveal is that molten flows erupted into some of the rocks to create underground "dikes." The great Medford dike, beginning in Somerville's Powderhouse Square and running north three miles almost to Spot Pond, is the best known. Some of the dikes run east-west and others north-south. At the end of Triassic time or the beginning of the Jurassic period, the dikes were fractured in numerous places along their fault lines. The fractures (birthmarks of the Atlantic?) were the last important changes in the basic rock formations of the Boston basin. For the last 180 million years they have remained in relatively the same position, sometimes above and sometimes below sea level.

During late Tertiary time, probably in the Pliocene epoch less than 13 million years ago, the land stood higher than now and likely enough the seashore was more than one hundred miles to the east. Perhaps the surface of the land was uplifted several times, and then storms worked it over, reducing it largely to the present shape, except that everything was more accentuated than we find it today. Only the changes made by the glaciers in the last million years have otherwise affected the basic shape of the region.

It is when Boston entered the Pleistocene epoch of the Quarternary period that our imaginary camera hanging over the region would have a significant and fast-moving event to record. Fast-moving, that is, in comparison with what had gone before. The first indications of what was happening far to the north of Boston were the gradual temperature drops and the slow retreat of the sea as its waters were trapped in the ponderous sheet of ice spreading out from the Pole. Taking thousands of years to form, a great mantle of ice began to flow southward over most of North America. It has been given the name of the Wisconsin ice sheet since the best record of it was first noted in that state.

The ice front came from the northwest and moved southeasterly over New England, cutting permanent grooves and channels in ledges and rocks as markers of its passage. Overwhelming everything in its path like some gigantic white bulldozer, it smashed down trees, scraped soil from hills and valleys, tore huge angular blocks loose from ledges dragging them in its path, sometimes cutting long troughs or ravines with them as a tool, then dropping them and surging over and past. Robert Frost speaks of this

> ". . . chisel work of an enormous glacier
> That braced his foot against the Arctic Pole."

But all this violence and upheaval happened in the most frozen of slow motion. The edge of the glacier extended at its farthest one hundred miles below Boston. From the air, our imaginary camera would have filmed for a long number of centuries a white arctic landscape. Even the highest hills were certainly

South side of a hill in Mattapan showing a glacial groove in the rock. (Gardner Collection, Harvard University.)

House rock in Weymouth, left behind by a glacier. (Dr. James Hume, 1960.)

Phaeton rock, a perched glacial boulder, as photographed in 1887 near Lynn. (Gardner Collection, Harvard University.)

South Boston still largely unchanged in the middle of the last century. (First Parish, Unitarian, Dorchester.)

covered by several hundred feet of ice. Think of present-day Boston encased at the bottom of a cake of ice with a hundred feet of ice *above* the Prudential tower.

Summer was in no rush to come back to the region it had abandoned. Eventually, however, the temperatures began to warm and the melting back of the glacier began, only to stop as temperatures dropped for a prolonged period and the glacier might inch forward a bit. About fourteen thousand years ago the ice had fallen back to Lynn. It is estimated that it took four thousand years for the glacier to melt back the two hundred miles from Hartford, Connecticut, to St. Johnsbury, Vermont.

The melting ice left hills first and valleys much later. Ice lakes were formed over these valleys and the debris in the melting glacier—sand, gravel, pebbles, stone, lumped together in the term "outwash"—ringed these valley lakes, forming deltas and sand plains. So clear is the surviving evidence that if it were not for the fact that men settled in the Boston area and destroyed much of the evidence, it would be possible to work out a complete history of these glacial lakes.

Long after the land area of the basin was ice free, Boston Bay was still frozen. Ice walled in the Blue Hills and shut off its drainage into the Bay. At first, the overflow from the glacial lakes on the Charles and the Neponset went south of the Blue Hills. Then as more ice melted, a new outlet opened up to the east, south of Brush Hill. Finally the present course of the Neponset was freed of ice and the lakes drained off that way.

By now, part of Boston Bay had opened up and the drainage patterns of the Charles and the Neponset were fixed about as they are at present. On the northwest side of the basin, lakes that had formed in the Shawsheen River drainage area were blocked by the ice from exiting as they do now into the Merrimac. For a time they emptied into the Charles and the Mystic Rivers, but as temperatures climbed the present outlets opened up.

After the ice had gone, the Boston area had much the contours that the first English settlers were to find: the Uplands surrounding the Lowland with four rivers draining the region. The retreating glacier had dropped huge loads of

outwash and till, creating the many drumlins that give a distinctive look to the vicinity. What would Boston history be without Beacon Hill, Bunker Hill, and the other hills and the harbor islands?

In the last ten thousand years, dubbed by geologists for want of a better name, the "Recent Epoch," there have been no spectacular changes, only what are called "natural" ones. With every rain, loose material washes down steep slopes. Trees are uprooted in storms and help the constant erosion. The shoreline is subtly altered by waves and currents; what the sea takes from one place it puts in another. Sand deposits heaped up by the waves built the chain of islands from Atlantic Hill out to Hull and formed Nantasket Beach.

On the other side of Boston, Winthrop was similarly created out of the "islands" of Beachmont, Grovers Cliff, Great Head, and the hill at Point Shirley.

Sandbar at Hull about 1880. (Gardner Collection, Harvard University.)

Boston as seen from a pastoral Roxbury in the first half of the last century.

Point Shirley and Deer Island as seen at low tide in 1925. (Tufts University.)

Tidal marshes grew behind protecting beaches as at Revere. Some islands were reduced to half-tide shoals or completely disappeared as did Bird Island, seen and named by the first settlers, but now vanished beneath the waves.

Man's hand has been added to Nature's in bringing changes to the surface of the Boston area. Hill after hill has been lowered or leveled. Large acres of marshland have been drained, filled, and built over. Hundreds of new acres were added to the city by filling in tidal flats and wharfing out into the waters of the estuaries. Harbors and channels have been dredged deeper, while some harbor islands have been incorporated into the mainland area. Some ponds have been drained, while numerous artificial ones have been created. Small streams have been buried in conduits. Purists deplore what has been done in Boston, but if man had never altered the area, could we predict the natural changes? In some respects they would be much like what Bostonians have done themselves. The hills would have eroded more slowly, the Back Bay silted up, barrier beaches built across to islands. Man has hastened and accelerated the changes, but largely within the natural framework. It is only our haste that has often made it ugly.

Yet man is introducing changes which are unprecedented. These are the

14

pollutants modern technological society produces as its most lethal by-products. The soil is saturated with deadly pesticides; wastes from domestic and commercial activities are dumped heedlessly into waterways; industry and the internal combustion engine both belch poisonous exhausts into the air that man, animal, and plant must breathe in order to exist.

Until recently, air has been the least regarded of all our natural resources. Suddenly we have been made conscious that even the "inexhaustible" air can be exhausted. The airshed over Boston is not infinite; its capacity to absorb safely the poisons vented into it is determined not only by the fixed topography of the land, but also by the variable layer of warm air which forms a lid over the cooler air underneath. The height of this inversion layer, as it is called, fluctuates, but determines how much air will be available to dilute the wastes. That these are plentiful is indicated by the estimate that Boston ranks seventh among American cities in air pollution. Only the first halting steps have been taken to correct it.

It was not always so. Captain John Smith rhapsodized in 1616 over "the moderate temper of the air." In 1629, Francis Higginson claimed that "a sup of New England air is better than a whole draught of Old England air." Five

Filling in the Back Bay as pictured in a diorama by Mrs. Sarah Annette Rockwell at the New England Mutual Life Insurance Company building. (Courtesy of New England Mutual Life Insurance Company.)

years later William Wood boasted that New England was not often troubled with mists "or unwholesome fogs, or cold weather from the sea," though he did admit to a season of extreme cold weather. He described the settlers in their first winter with "the searching sharpness of that purer climate, creeping in at the crannies of their crazed bodies." It could pass for a description of the frigid pedestrian on the "Windy Corner" of Tremont and Boylston streets whipped by arctic blasts.

Wood pointed out one difficulty then with beards: "some have had their overgrown beards so frozen together, that they could not get their strong water bottles into their mouths." Fortunately, no Bostonian today is so bedeviled. But some things have changed. "In public assemblies," wrote Wood, "it is strange to hear a man sneeze or cough." A visit to any performance of the Boston Symphony Orchestra today would indicate that statement required amending.

Weather was vitally important to these earlier Bostonians. They went to school to it, quickly learning its lessons and peculiarities. By April 1631, Winthrop noted in his journal that "the beginning of this month we had very much rain and warm weather. It is a general rule, that when the wind blows twelve hours in any part of the east, it brings rain or snow in great abundance." And Wood included an observation of the Indians, that "every tenth year there is little or no winter."

They were soon to find that there was more to New England weather than winter. Within five years of their settlement, the greatest meteorological event of the seventeenth century occurred. This was the Great Colonial Hurricane of August 16, 1635. Both Winthrop in Boston and William Bradford in Plymouth recorded it for posterity. It was not to be matched for 180 years until the Great September Gale of 1815, then not again until the September Hurricane of 1938.

Beginning before midnight, says Winthrop, "it blew down many hundreds of trees . . . overthrew some houses, and drove the ships from their anchors." The four-hundred-ton vessel, the *Great Hope,* was twice driven ashore. The tide, which was high, fell three feet in an hour, then an hour later suddenly rose several feet again. Bradford thought that "the signs and marks of it will remain this hundred years."

Three years later the fledgling colony was shaken by an earthquake on June 11. The tremors were generally felt and caused some alarm, with pewter dishes falling off shelves and beds being shifted about. The "providence of God" was thanked for preventing any deaths, but received no blame for sending the earthquake. An earthquake on February 5, 1663, appeared to be even stronger, doing much damage in Boston and in towns along the Bay shore.

The first winters of the new settlement proved mild for New England, fortunately for the colonists, but the third winter of 1632–33 was harsh. The snow was deep and the temperature cold even in January. This winter stood out for several years in the memory of the inhabitants as unusually severe, but the storms of 1641–42 gave them a landmark to measure winters past and future by. Only two were to equal it in that century. Even the Indians said they hadn't seen its equal for forty years. The bay froze over, "so as horses and carts," said Winthrop, "went over in many places where ships have sailed." Deep snows and intense cold made many a colonist yearn for the rain and damp of Old England. John Berryman vividly caught this:

> Outside the New World winters in grand dark
> white air lashing high thro' the virgin stands
> foxes down foxholes sigh,
> surely the English heart quails, stunned.

For five years after Winthrop's death in 1649, Boston weather went unrecorded. Then in 1654, John Hull, silversmith and Keeper of the Mint, began noting the weather in his diary. There were many temperate winters during his period of observations, but he did have a hurricane to note on September 8, 1675. "A very violent storm, that exceedingly blew down the Indian corn and the fruit of trees; did much spoil on the warves and among the ships and vessels in Boston."

Hull's weather-watching had ended before the "terriblest winter" of the century, that of 1697–98. So the selectmen of Sudbury described it and Samuel Sewall agreed with them, remarking in a letter on "the prodigious length and strength of this winter." In Cambridge, snow was reported to have piled up forty-two inches by the end of February, a record for the area if accurate. From the first of December to the middle of March the ground was covered with snow. The Charlestown ferry was frozen up and for six weeks people were able to walk over or ride their horses across. When it finally broke up, guards had to be set at the river to warn people from venturing out on the surface they had grown so used to walking across.

For forty winters this was the one the oldsters talked about as an "old-fashioned winter." It was not equaled even by the winter of 1717–18, when it snowed for four days straight in February and there was no traveling for a week afterward. On the Charlestown road to Medford, a widow and her children were snowed under. Neighbors, seeing smoke come up through the snow, dug them out and found her burning the last of her furniture to keep from freezing.

Indians nearly a hundred years old affirmed to Cotton Mather that their *fathers* had never told them of anything to match the winter of 1717–18. Churches were closed on the Lord's Day which astounded Mather even more. Cattle, eyes glazed by ice, strayed into the sea and drowned. Deer trapped by the deep snows were devoured by wolves. Immediately after one snowfall, "an infinite multitude of Sparrows made their appearance," but finding no hospitable birdfeeders about, soon flew on. "The Ocean was in a prodigious Ferment, and after it was over, vast heaps of little shells were driven ashore, where they were never seen before."

Ten years later, in 1727, another "Act of God" smote the town on November 9. Shortly after half past ten that night there came a flash of light and then a tremendous earthquake. It came from the northwest and went toward the southeast, lasting two minutes. There were repeated shocks through the night. Stone walls were thrown down. People crowded into the churches between shocks, invoking God's protection against this "Act of God." It gave all the ministers good sermon topics for weeks.

In the three and a half centuries since Boston was founded there have been hundreds of tremors. Most are so mild people today dismiss them as the rumble of heavy trucks. Perhaps the most severe came the same year as the Great Lisbon Earthquake of November 1, 1755, which killed sixty thousand people in that unfortunate town. Three thousand miles away and seventeen days later, Boston and New England felt the aftereffects. The shock came suddenly and from the same direction as the 1727 quake, though it lasted a bit longer. Clocks were stopped, stone walls tumbled, and one hundred Boston chimneys were leveled to the rooftops. Another fifteen hundred were partly damaged. Some wooden buildings were knocked flat. Brick buildings were cracked; some having their gable ends toppled. Luckier than Lisbon, nobody was killed, but the shocks continued for several days, and a final jab came on December 19. It was, said one of the local divines, "a Token of Divine Anger."

By the middle of the eighteenth century, weather observations were beginning to be a little more scientific. The first quarter of the century a Boston doctor stated that he knew "of no thermometer or barometer in this place." To make his observations he had "no other instruments than the naked eye, pen, ink, and paper." By 1728, a Londoner had given Harvard College a combined barometer-thermometer, but the first known use of such an instrument for regular observations was not until 1742 when Prof. John Winthrop, a great-grandson of the founder of Boston, began his meteorological records. This

An avalanche of snow from the roof of the Park Street Church catches unwary passers-by in the 1850s; Boston Common in the background.

was too late to furnish accurate data on the long, hard winter of 1740–41. One of the landmark winters of the century in Boston, oldtimers thought it worse than that of 1697. The snow came early and stayed late. Some harbor islands still had drifts in May. When spring finally came, it was "backward" said the farmers and all their chores were delayed. Boston Harbor had frozen solid after Christmas, as had much of the coastal waters down to New York. A gentleman from Barnstable, one of the signers of the Declaration of Independence, took a two-hundred-mile sleigh ride from that Cape Cod town to New York, traveling the entire distance on the shore ice.

Notable as this winter was, historians of the American climate theorize that what they term a "little Ice Age" began later, about 1750, and extended until about 1850. By comparison, the winters of the seventeenth century are judged to be milder than this period of the "cool hundred years."

Probably the most extreme winter of this "cool hundred" came during the middle of the American Revolution, 1779–80. It is the only known time recently when the waters around Manhattan Island were frozen over for several weeks. Early and frequent snows marked the beginning of this winter. Snow lay long and drifted deep. Jeremy Belknap, one of the founders of the Massachusetts Historical Society, did not remember "having ever seen so much snow on the

Keeping the streets open on Boston Neck for the horse railroad, 1854.

ground at once before." Although no registering thermometers were being used at this time, the evidence points to January 1780 as being the coldest month ever in the Northeast.

The deep snows prevented all but the most vital travel and even that was difficult. Deliveries of wood to Boston, so necessary for fuel and cooking, dwindled to near zero. Gangs of men went out and foraged in nearby woodlots to get enough to keep from freezing. A gradual thaw in February continued for a month until a Braintree farmer opined that "the roads in some places was passable with carts." But the winter wasn't over, and a snow-laden northeaster slammed the coast March 31. Even then, spring came late and early June frosts killed beans and corn growing in Waltham.

The century continued its chilly way. People found the winter the war ended, 1783–84, a "long winter" and most "tedious." The century neared an end with another long severe winter in 1798–99. One historian has called January 5, 1799, "one of the coldest days of the century." In Cambridge they reported six below in the morning rising to two above and then dropping back to five below at night. In Charlestown a minus eleven was reported.

The nineteenth century continued the "Little Ice Age," adding its own vagaries. The "Snow Hurricane" of October 9, 1804, was considered a major meteorological event. A late tropical storm, with winds of hurricane force, moved up the coast, passed over southern New England and the center of Boston. It precipitated snow over most of the region, though not in Boston where it did enough damage without adding snow to its indignities. The "celebrated Steeple"—the phrase is Salem diarist Dr. William Bentley's—of the North Church was toppled. The roof of King's Chapel blew off, being carried two hundred feet before the winds dropped it on a shed, where it smashed two carriages to wooden smithereens. Elm trees that had stood for generations were uprooted, fences everywhere were overturned, and at least three people were killed. "A distressing loss," summed up Bentley. He rode out the next day to survey the damage in the shore communities north of Boston and found the destruction widespread. "I cannot refuse to adopt the belief that the late storm was the most severe ever felt in this part of America."

A more famous storm, the Great September Gale of September 23, 1815, did less damage in Boston than the "Snow Hurricane," since the center of the storm passed over central Massachusetts. Chimneys toppled, trees crashed, slate and shingles flew about. Prof. John Farrar at Harvard watched the Charles River rage and foam like a stormstruck sea. "Spray was raised to the height of 60 or 100 feet in the form of thin white clouds." Coming in over the ocean, the gale brought much salt water with it. Housewives complained of windows "frosted over." Leaves looked painted white, then turned black, killed by the salt. Worcester gardeners grumbled at the salt taste of their grapes. So many trees fell that a big building season commenced in 1817 after these had been sawed and seasoned.

1816, the famous "Year Without a Summer," when every month of the year saw a frost, and the farming economy of New England was severely disrupted, had otherwise little meteorological effect in Boston. Snowflakes were reported in Waltham on June 8, and Salem agreed with Waltham. The "inconstant and particoloured month of June," as one suburbanite styled it, produced near-record temperature lows in the Boston area for that month. That, and the high prices of farm products in the fall and winter made the season locally memorable.

During several severe storms, record high tides were measured. A combination of wind, rain, and snow at the end of March 1830 caused a tide one and one-half inches higher, newspapers reported, than the great tide of December 1786 which was ten inches higher than any person then living remembered. The Navy Yard overflowed, and the tide washed into the cofferdam. About three feet of water was in the drydock.

On December 15, 1839, this record was broken with a tide that swept completely across the built-up Boston Neck. Even this was exceeded on April 14, 1851, when a mixture of rain, hail, and snow, added to a very high tide, completely submerged the Charlestown and Chelsea bridges. Water stood three feet or more on Central and Long wharves, and swirled over the floor of the Eastern Railroad station. Deer Island was under water. Rafts appeared on some Boston streets which were otherwise impassable. This was the worst flooding in Boston's history, one "Act of God" from which the town has been largely immune, even though a seaport. The mean tide range at Boston is from 9.0 to 9.6 feet, depending on the harbor location of the measuring station.

An extra high tide created flood conditions around the Custom House in 1851.

Spring tides will surge up to 11.0 feet. Records show that local sea level has varied less than a foot and a half in the last two thousand years.

Tornadoes have also kept their distance. The closest call came in this same year of 1851, on August 22. A small twister cut through Waltham, Arlington, Medford, Malden, Lynn, and blew itself out on the way to Cape Ann. Damage in its path was considerable, but confined to largely rural areas as these towns then were.

The most rigorous winter for forty years came in 1856–57 and the heaviest fall of snow (still a record) landed on the city in 1873–74. Two years later, turning the other cheek as it were, almost the least amount of snow ever measured fell.

Before the first world war, a series of seven warm winters caused much speculation about the apparent warming trend, but the frigid "Influenza winter" of 1917–18 reminded New Englanders that Nature was still mindful of her obligations to provide the region with an "old-fashioned winter."

Several repeats in the twenties, and the setting of a record low temperature in Boston on February 9, 1934, when the thermometer skidded to eighteen

Shoveling out in front of the
State House by the Robert Gould
Shaw Memorial about 1890.

A visualization of the 1851
tornado in the West Medford
area, from *Gleason's Pictorial
Drawing-Room Companion*,
October 18, 1851, p. 244.

Trees uprooted by 1938 hurricane, leaning on Cushing house in Milton, opposite the Public Library. (George M. Cushing, Jr.)

below, showed that it was still too early to change the name of the city to "Miami-North." Nor have recent decades with their alternating mild and harsh winters given any cause to alter that opinion.

It may seem as if we are becoming more susceptible to another Miami perennial, the hurricane. This is more apparent than real; the better reporting of tropical storms and the hourly radio checks on them only make us more conscious of each disturbance in the Caribbean that *might* come our way. Until the hurricane of 1938, the September Gale of September 8, 1869, had been the most destructive in recent memory. The September Gale had flattened the huge Coliseum, uprooted trees in the Public Garden, mowed down steeples, and smashed a Chelsea tenement.

The "New England Hurricane" of September 21, 1938, did all that and more. Three days before, ships in the South Atlantic had radioed warnings of a hurricane moving slowly northwest toward Florida. Then it abruptly veered out to sea, and experts predicted it would dissipate in mid-Atlantic. Instead, it came straight up the coast moving at the incredible speed of six hundred miles in twelve hours. With no ships in its path it was "lost," until it hit the Jersey coast. At 2:30 P.M. on September 21, the Boston Weather Bureau warned it was in the vicinity of New York. Shortly thereafter it was roaring up over Connecticut. Boston was on the periphery of the storm, but the damage was severe in the city. By five o'clock as people were leaving stores and offices to go home, the storm struck the city. At 6:47 P.M. it had reached a peak and unofficial reports were of one-hundred-mile-per-hour winds. Windows were blown out, advertising signs tumbled off roofs, the air was filled with flying gravel, trees crashed on the Common, in the Fenway, on the Fellsway, and on many college campuses. Boats in the Bay and on the Charles were driven

24

Steeple of Old North Church toppled by Hurricane "Carol" in 1954. (Wide World Photos, Inc.)

ashore or smashed against seawalls. Church roofs were blown off, shrines knocked down, and one church in East Cambridge all but blown to the ground.

Beyond the immediate Boston area, the damage was widespread and costly. The hurricane followed much the same path as its famous predecessors of 1635, 1815, and 1869. That the overall disaster was greater is explained by the more built-up nature of the region. Neither the Great Atlantic Hurricane of 1944, nor tropical storms "Carol" of 1954 and "Edna" of 1955 were as destructive, though both memorable in their own inimitable ways.

The Boston Weather Bureau was officially established in 1871 by the federal government. Since 1958, it has been keeping watch on the weather from its new post at the Logan International Airport. Its reports, together with those of qualified observers with reliable instruments, enable us to gain a nearly uninterrupted picture of Boston weather since 1818. Instead of the casual gaps of millions of years in the Boston story, we now have a moment by moment account of the surface changes affecting the Boston region.

To generalize this one hundred and fifty years of accurate knowledge, and the experience of two hundred years before that, what we can expect in any year is—more often than not—that January will have a thaw and be rather pleasant; that February will turn cold and host a good blizzard round about Valentine's Day or Washington's Birthday; that March will be wild and windy and April showery; that May will be charming and June more so; that July and August will be hot; that September will have gales and may manage a hurricane; that October will turn coldish, but give a last respite with a week or so of balmy Indian summer and a gorgeous display of fall leaves; that November will be leafless and cold; and that in December we will be hoping for snow on Christmas and seven times out of ten we'll get it.

But if there is extreme cold in January and thaws in February, if it is mild and dry during March and April, and May and June are cold and rainy, the summer chilly, the fall hot, the foliage drab, and the winter green—well, nobody in Boston or New England will be the least surprised. Excepting, that is, newspaper pundits who will pontificate that "never was the like known before," and then proceed to quote learnedly from Mark Twain.

So here we stand, secure we think, on our asphalt-paved Boston, surrounded by our brick or concrete or glass and steel walls, breathing our air-conditioned air in our fluorescent-lighted buildings. We look at our captive trees and flowers in their permitted parks—ah Nature! Yet under our feet, about our proud artificial town, above our heads in the polluted skies, the natural process continues. We can only record it. It doesn't stop because we have hidden ourselves from it. The changes of the natural order proceed on *their* courses. The winds tear the land. The waves eat the shore. Silt eddies, sinks, settles, stratifies. Rocks weather; the eternal hills flow. Rains beat down; the ice cometh. Deep beneath our feet, rocks boil, strata shift, secret springs infiltrate, chemicals act out their lawful obligations upon each other.

It is a course outside the time span of the human creatures living on this shelf of rock at the edge of this temporary sea, a course that does not comprehend or contain them, but registers only risings, sinkings, gradual or sudden alterations of what is into what is to be. A thousand years in its history are like one heartbeat in a man's passage through his days. As a bystander on that scene, with one eye looking over our shoulder at what we are involved in but cannot lastingly affect, the best we can do in our brief moment is to keep our house in order—and perhaps our mind. A poet in the Boston *Daily Times* for August 8, 1846, put it more practically:

> It's a sorry clime for living in,
> But a first rate one to die in.

Twelve Men, Lashed to a Rope, Start from the Old Colony Depot, Boston, for their Homes in Neponset, Mass.

What Twelve Men did, "who wanted to go home," through the storm.

A party of a dozen men, young and old, who lived at Neponset, congregated at the Old Colony depot on Thursday afternoon, and seeing no other means of getting home, they attempted to go afoot. They started at 3 o'clock, and proceeded as far as South Boston, where it became apparent that there might be some stragglers from the party; and to avoid the loss of any one, the party procured a rope of fifty feet long, to which each individual member lashed himself, and again they faced the elements. They soon picked up a small boy who was near perishing, and after taking him a whole mile they were relieved of his care by a hack which overtook them.

The party reached Glover's corner where they refreshed and warmed themselves. Here it was found that several of them were frost-bitten on toes, noses and fingers; one of the number had lost his hat, and had both ears and both hands badly frozen.

From this point two of the party more muscular than the rest, detached themselves from the remainder and propelled ahead, reaching home in two hours and a half from the time of starting, a distance of six miles. The others were half an hour behind, but they got home safely, although one of them absolutely gave out and sunk helpless in the snow within sight of his house, into which he was carried by his companions. Another of the party attempted to climb a mountain of snow which lay in their track. The mass supported him until he reached near the top, when the foothold gave way and he was instantly plunged out of sight, having sunk in above his head. It was only by the most active exertions of his comrades that he was rescued before he suffocated.

Wood engraving depicting storm of January 17, 1867.

Boston Geological Timetable

Era	Period	Epoch	Time (in millions of years)	Life sequence	Boston events
Archaeozoic	Pre-Cambrian		5000 to 3500	one-celled creatures marine algae	Formation of earth Boston born!
Proterozoic			3500 to 620		
Paleozoic	Cambrian		620 to 500	Trilobites Mosses Invertebrates	Oldest rocks Weymouth formation Braintree slate
	Ordovician		500 to 440	Fishes	Salem gabbrodiorite Dedham granite
	Silurian		440 to 400	Land plants	Erosion
	Devonian		400 to 350	Amphibians Ferns	Blue Hill porphyry Quincy granite Mattapan volcanics
	Mississippian	Carboniferous	350 to 300	Reptiles Insects Forests Spiders	Roxbury conglomerate Brighton volcanics Squantum tillite Cambridge slate Tufts quartzite
	Pennsylvanian		300 to 270		
	Permian		270 to 225		Mountain building Continental separation
Mesozoic	Triassic		225 to 180	Birds	Atlantic Ocean formed Medford Dike
	Jurassic		180 to 135	Dinosaurs Mammals	
	Cretaceous		135 to 63	Grasses Ants	Unknown (erosions, uplifts, erosion, flooding)
Cenozoic	Tertiary	Paleocene	63 to 58	Placental mammals	
		Eocene	58 to 36		
		Oligocene	36 to 25		
		Miocene	25 to 13		
		Pliocene	13 to 1	Dawn of man	Sea 100 m. to east
	Quarternary	Pleistocene	1 to .01	Early man	Glaciers Wisconsin till Glacial outwash Boston blue clay
		Recent	Last 10,000 years	Modern man	"The Proper Bostonian"

Boston Weather Facts

RAIN
The rainiest day—August 19, 1955 (7.06″)
The rainiest twenty-four hours—August 18–19, 1955 (8.40″)
The wettest month—August 1955 (17.09″)
The dryest month—March 1915 (Trace)

SNOW
Average winter snowfall—42.0″
The snowiest winter—1873/74 (96.4″)
The least snowiest winter—1936/37 (9.0″)
The snowiest month—February 1969 (41.3″)
The snowiest storm—February 24–28, 1969 (26.3″)

TEMPERATURE
The hottest day—July 4, 1911 (104°)
The coldest day—February 9, 1934 (−18°)
The hottest month—July 1952 (average 77.5°)
The coldest month—January 1780

WIND
Average wind velocity—12.9 miles per hour (last nine years only)
Windiest five-minute period—September 21, 1938 (73 miles per hour)
Windiest month—January (average 14.9 miles per hour)
Calmest month—August (average 11.0 miles per hour)

SUN
The sunniest month—June 1912 (86% sunny)
The darkest month—October 1913 (26%)
Average 100 clear days per year
        106 partly cloudy days per year
        159 cloudy days per year

BAROMETER
Average sea level pressure at Boston—30.01″
Highest recorded—December 25, 1949 (31.06″)
Lowest recorded—March 7, 1932 (28.45″)

ELECTRICAL STORMS
Average—Twenty days per year (with possibility of more than one storm on a day)

Interlude one: Boston to 1650

Indians walked the streets

Chickatabot came with his sannops and squaws and presented the governour with a hogshead of Indian corn. After they had all dined, and had each a small cup of sack and beer, and the men tobacco, he sent away all his men and women, (though the governour would have stayed them in regard of the rain and thunder.) Himself and one squaw and one sannop stayed all night, and being in English clothes, the governour set him at his own table, where he behaved himself as soberly, &c. as an Englishman. The next day after dinner he returned home, the governour giving him cheese and peas and a mug and some other small things.

> —John Winthrop
> *Journal,* March 23, 1631

Getting by with a little help from father

Loving father, though I be far distant from you, yet I pray you remember me as your child, and we do not know how long we may subsist, for we can not live here without provisions from old England. Therefore, I pray do not put away your shopstuff, for I think that in the end if I live it must be my living. For we do not know how long this plantation will stand for some of the mechants that did uphold it have turned off their men and have given it over. Besides, God hath taken away the chiefest stud in the land, Mr. Johnson, and the Lady Arabella, his wife, which was the chiefest man of estate in the land, and one that would have done most good.

> —John (?) Pond
> from a letter to his father, March 25, 1631
> (modernized)

Lost in the Medford woods

The governour, being at his farm house at Mistick [Medford], walked out after supper, and took a piece [gun] in his hand, supposing he might see a wolf, (for they came daily about the house, and killed swine and calves, &c.;) and, being about half a mile off, it grew suddenly dark, so as, in coming home, he mistook his path, and went till he came to a little house of Sagamore John, which stood empty. There he stayed, and having a piece of match in his pocket, (for he always carried about him match and a compass, and in summer time snake-weed,) he made a good fire near the house, and lay down upon some old mats, which he found there, and so spent the night, sometimes walking by the fire, sometimes singing psalms, and sometimes getting wood, but could not sleep. It was (through God's mercy) a warm night; but a little before day it began to rain, and, having no cloak, he made shift by a long pole to climb up into the house. In the morning there came thither an Indian squaw, but perceiving her before she had opened the door, he barred her out; yet she stayed there a great while essaying to get in, and at last she went away, and he returned safe home, his servants having been much perplexed for him, and having walked about, and shot off pieces, and hallooed in the night, but he heard them not.

—John Winthrop
Journal, October 11, 1631

East of Eden

For Our subsistence heere, the meanes hetherto hath beene the yearly access of new Commers, who have supplied all our wants, for Cattle, and the fruits of our labours, as boarde, pale, smithes work etc: if this should faile, then have we other meanes which may supple vs, as fishe, viz: Codd, basse and herringe, for which no place in the world exceeds vs, if we can compass salt at a reasonable rate: our grounds likewise are apt for hempe and flaxe and rape seeds, and all sorts of rootes pumpins and other fruits, which for tast and wholesomeness far excede those in England: our grapes allso (wherewith the Countrye abonds) afford a good harde wine. Our ploughes goe on with good successe, we are like to have 20 at worke next yeare: our lands are aptest for Rye and oats. Our winters are sharpe and longe, I may reckon 4 monthes for storeing of Cattle, but we find no difference whither they be housed or goe abroad: our summers are somewhat more fervent in heat then in England.

—John Winthrop
from a letter to Sir Nathaniel Rich,
June 15, 1634

Help thy neighbor

And I doe farther Intreate yow to lend mr. Crad-
dock the hellpe of your teeme a day or two to
hellpe Carry the timber for buillding the mill at
watertowne. I haue sent vnto mr. Doomer I hope he
will afford me his hellpe; that with the hellpe of our
owne wee may doe it in two daies; the reason I
desire to haue it donne with such expedition is for
that the Cattell must be watched whillst they are
about it; In regard they will be from home and soe
doubtlesse otherwise woulld stray or at least Runn
home: I will at any time yf your wor[shi]pp haue
occasion in the like kind fullfill your desire: the time
wee intend to goe about it is the second or third day
of the next weeke.

    —Thomas Mayhew
      from a letter to John Winthrop, July 2, 1634

Not everybody went to church on the sabbath

A man's servant in Boston, having stolen from his
master, and being threatened to be brought before
the magistrates, went and hanged himself. Herein
three things were observable: 1. That he was a
very profane fellow, given to cursing, &c. and did
use to [go] out of the assembly, upon the Lord's
day, to rob his master. 2. The manner of his death,
being with a small codline, and his knees touching
the floor of the chamber, and one coming in when
he was scarce dead, (who was a maid, and while she
went to call out, &c. he was past recovery.) 3. His
discontent arising from the long time he was to
serve his master, (though he were well used.) The
same day came a letter from his father, out of the
Bermuda, with money to buy out his time, &c.

    —John Winthrop
      Journal, March 3, 1636

But it was the popular indoor sport

1636—Turning his face to Sun, he [Edward Johnson] steered his course toward the next Town, [Cambridge] and after some small travell hee came to a large plaine. No sooner was hee entred thereon, but hearing the sound of a Drum he was directed toward it by a broade beaten way. Following this rode he demands of the next man he met what the signall of the Drum ment, the reply was made they had as yet no Bell to call men to meeting, and therefore made use of a Drum. Who is it, quoth hee, Lectures at this Towne? The other replies, I see you are a stranger, new come over, seeing you know not the man, it is one Mr. Shepheard. Verily quoth the other, you hit the right, I am new come over indeed, and have been told since I came most of your Ministers are legall Preachers, onely if I mistake not they told me this man Preached a finer covenant of workes then the other, but however, I shall make what hast I can to heare him. Fare you well. Then hasting thither hee croudeth through the thickest, where having stayed while the glasse was turned up twice,* the man was metamorphosed, and was faine to hang down the head often, least his watry eyes should blab abroad the secret conjunction of his affections, his heart crying loud to the Lords echoing answer, to his blessed spirit.

— Edward Johnson
Wonder-working Providence

* [The length of the sermon was measured by an hour-glass. Since this glass was turned twice, the sermon was two hours long.]

Winter was no picnic

About thirty persons of Boston going out in a fair day to Spectacle Island to cut wood, (the town being in great want thereof,) the next night the wind rose so high at N.E. with snow, and after at N.W. for two days, and then it froze so hard, as the bay was all frozen up, save a little channel. In this twelve of them gate to the Governour's Garden, [Governor's Island] and seven more were carried in the ice in a small skiff out at Broad Sound, and kept among Brewster's Rocks, without food or fire, two days, and then, the wind forbearing, they gate to Pullin Point, to a little house there of Mr. Aspenwall's. Three of them gate home the next day over the ice, but their hands and feet frozen. Some lost their fingers and toes, and one died. The rest went from Spectacle Island to the main, but two of them fell into the ice, yet recovered again.

—John Winthrop
Journal, January 13, 1638

The wild life was close at hand

Oct. 9, 1638—I crost the Bay to Charlestown, where at one Longs Ordinary [tavern] I met with Captain Jackson and others, walking on the back side we spied a rattle Snake a yard and a half long, and as thick in the middle as the small of a mans leg, on the belly yellow, her back spotted with black, russet, yellow and green, placed like scales, at her tail she had a rattle which is nothing but a hollw shelly buffiness joynted, look how many years old she is, so many rattles she hath in her tail, her neck seemed to be no bigger than ones Thumb; yet she swallowed a live Chicken, as big as one they give 4 pence for in England, presently as we were looking on.

—John Josselyn
Two Voyages to New-England

Not the best of all possible worlds

Oct. 12, 1638—The Second of October, about 9 of the clock in the morning, Mr. [Samuel] Mavericks Negro woman came to my chamber window, and in her own Countrey language and tune sang very loud and shril, going out to her, she used a great deal of respect towards me, and willingly would have expressed her grief in English; but I apprehended it by her countenance and deportment, whereupon I repaired to my host, to learn of him the cause, and resolved to intreat him in her behalf, for that I understood before, that she had been a Queen in her own Countrey, and observed a very humble and dutiful garb used towards her by another Negro who was her maid. Mr. Maverick was desirous to have a breed of Negroes, and therefore seeing she would not yield by perswasions to company with a Negro young man he had in his house; he commanded him will'd she nill'd she to go to bed to her, which was no sooner done but she kickt him out again, this she took in high disdain beyond her slavery, and this was the cause of her grief. In

the afternoon I walked into the Woods on the back side of the house [East Boston], and happening into a fine broad walk (which was a sledg-way) I wandered till I chanc't to spye a fruit as I thought like a pine Apple plated with scales, it was as big as the crown of a Womans hat; I made bold to step unto it, with an intent to have gathered it, no sooner had I toucht it, but hundreds of Wasps were about me; at last I cleared my self from them, being stung only by one upon the upper lip, glad I was that I scaped so well; But by that time I was come into the house my lip was swell'd so extreamly, that they hardly knew me but by my Garments.

    —John Josselyn
    Two Voyages to New-England

The old Adam—and the young Eve

Lydia Dastin wife of Josiah Dastin of Charlestowne in New England aged about 26 yeares sworne saith upon her oath that about a moneth since this deponent being in the house of Mr. Cradocke at Misticke in a certaine roome there at meate one Robert Panare offered violence to her & would have kissed her & offered to put his hands under her coats & sayd he came of a woman & knew what belonged to a woman & because her husband was not able to give her a great belly he would help him or such most shamefull words & he caused her to cut her hand & her apron in striving with him. And this deponent saith that she refusing to commit this wickednesse he used some threatening words as well I will be meet with you but if you will not do it for love you will not for anything else, and this offence being done late upon a last day of the weeke a little before night this deponent went presently purposing to make it knowne to goodman Knight but he was at top of an house & could not conveniently come downe at that time and her husband coming home late that night she made it knowne to him the next evening after.

    —Thomas Lechford
    Note-Book, September 13, 1639

Better than flying saucers

A light like the moon arose about the N. E. point in Boston, and met [another] at Nottles Island [East Boston], and there they closed in one, and then parted, and closed and parted divers times, and so went over the hill in the island and vanished. Sometimes they shot out flames and sometimes sparkles. This was about eight of the clock in the evening, and was seen by many. About the same time a voice was heard upon the water between Boston and Dorchester, calling out in a most dreadful manner, boy, boy, come away, come away: and it suddenly shifted from one place to another a great distance, about twenty times. It was heard by divers godly persons.

—John Winthrop
Journal, February 4, 1644

A husband's "miscarriage"

Sarah Barnes of Boston the wife of Wm Barnes late of Gloucester in N.E.: being credibly informed of her husbands miscarriage of himselfe with another woman by whom it is reported he hath had a Bastard, but haveing not yet received testimonie under any Magistrats hand & he still deserting her as hath done about 3 yeares without shewing any reasonable cause, hath therefore constituted & ordeined & by these presents doth authorise & constitute mr Wm Tory of Waymouth in N E: her true & lawfull Attorney: giveing him full power & Authority for her & in her name to make diligent inquiry after her said husband, & whether such reports as goe abroad of his unlawfull & adulterous fellowship with another woman be true, & if uppon certaine intelligence he find it so to be then doth she hereby Authorise her said Attorney for her & in her name & behalfe to sue out a Divorce for her there against her husband.

—William Aspinwall
Notarial Records, October 29, 1647

Obey the Sunday laws—or else

Archibald Thomson, of Marblehead, carrying dung to his ground in a canoe upon the Lord's day, in fair weather and still water, it sunk under him in the harbour near the shores and he was never seen after.

—John Winthrop
Journal, September 1641

The Death of Winthrop—The beginning of this year was sad to the people of N.E. by reason of the death of their honoured Governour, John Winthrope Esquire [April 5, 1649], whose indefatigable paines in this Wilderness-work is not to be forgotten, nor indeed can it be; his Funeral was very sadly and solemnly performed, by a very great concourse of the greater part of this Colony, whose mournful looks and watry eyes did plainly demonstrate the tender affection and great esteem he was in with the people.

—Edward Johnson
Wonder-working Providence

After twenty years

Boston in 1650—Invironed it is with the Brinish flouds, saving one small Istmos, which gives free accesse to the Neighbour Townes by Land on the South side; on the North west and North East, two constant Faires [Ferries] are kept for daily traffique thereunto. The forme of this Towne is like a heart, naturally scituated for Fortifications, having two Hills on the frontice part thereof next the Sea, the one well fortificd on the superfices thereof, with store of great Artillery well mounted, the other hath a very strong battery built of whole Timber and filled with Earth. At the descent of the Hill in the extreme poynt thereof, betwixt these two strong armes lies a large Cave [Cove] or Bay, on which the chiefest part of this Town is built, over-topped with a third Hill. . . . The chiefe Edifice of this City-like Towne is crowded on the Sea-bankes, and wharfed out with great industry and cost, the buildings beautifull and large, some fairly set forth with Brick, Tile, Stone and Slate and orderly placed with comply streets, whose continuall inlargement presages some sumptuous City.

—Edward Johnson
Wonder-working Providence

This diorama pictures the way the Back Bay may have looked about 4,000 years ago with Indians repairing a fishweir. Remnants of one were unearthed on the site in 1939. (Courtesy of New England Mutual Life Insurance Company.)

CHAPTER TWO

The Blessings of the Bay

The "Indians" or "First People" saw Boston harbor from the land, perhaps as early as 1500 B.C. They saw it when it was in its prime, unpolluted, teeming with fish and turtles; its flats oozing succulent clams; snails, mussels, quahogs, and whelks plump on the rocks and seaweed; and fat oysters snoozing in their beds. They saw the streams running clean through marsh and meadow, where wonders of shad and alewives could be scooped up in the spring runs. They saw the seals splashing in the waves, and the hake and herring, the sturgeon and cod that could be caught in the bay waters.

The marshes were splendid hunting ground for waterfowl including such now-rare birds as loons and great auks. Beaver, raccoon, and otter were attracted to the brooks. It was like some great supermarket: the harbor area spread out its abundant food supplies and the hungry Indians came and "shopped," canoeing out to establish colonies on many of the islands.

The English and other continental voyagers—fishermen, traders, and explorers sailing up and down the coast from the end of the fifteenth century into the seventeenth century—had to learn the water approaches into the harbor: where dangerous ledges, shoals, and reefs lay hidden; where the safest channel for their ships could be found; where the best anchorage was. Slowly and painfully this knowledge accumulated and was recorded on primitive maps now lost. Existing maps of the harbor in chronological sequence reveal the slow growth of knowledge and the changes that man and nature have made in the area.

The harbor is in the bay, and the great Massachusetts Bay is the forty-mile stretch of sea enclosed by Cape Ann on the north and Cape Cod's tip on the south. Frederick W. A. S. Brown, the Reverend Poet called "the Sweet Singer of the Harbor," rhapsodized about it thus in his 1819 poem:

> Projecting far into the land,
> Toward the setting day;
> Sublimely beautiful and grand,
> Spreads Massachusetts Bay.

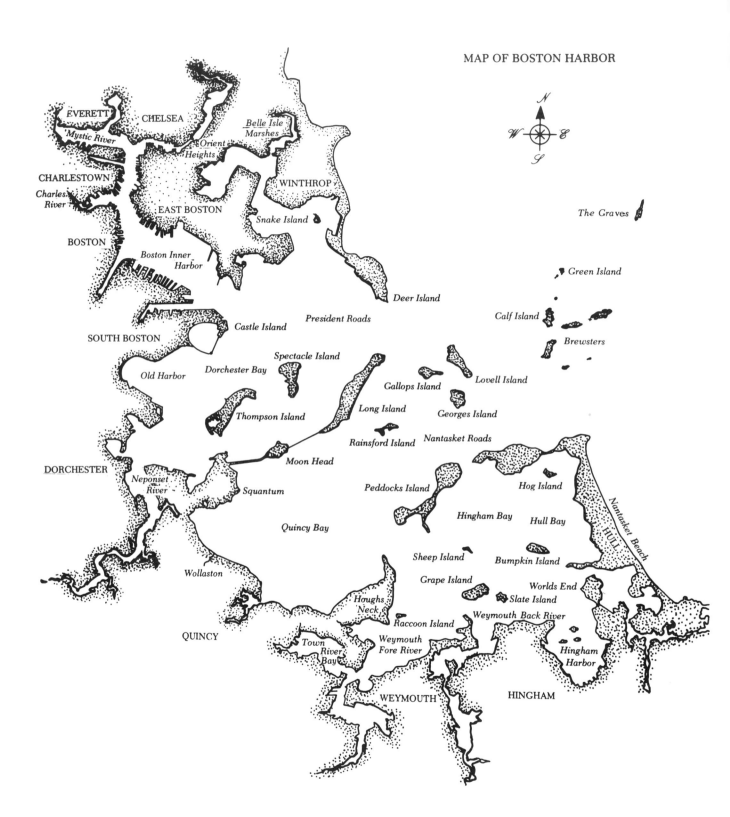

MAP OF BOSTON HARBOR

N
W *E*
S

EVERETT CHELSEA
Mystic River
Belle Isle Marshes
Orient Heights
CHARLESTOWN
WINTHROP
Charles River
EAST BOSTON
The Graves
Snake Island
BOSTON
Boston Inner Harbor
Green Island
Deer Island
Calf Island
SOUTH BOSTON *Castle Island*
President Roads
Brewsters
Spectacle Island
Old Harbor *Dorchester Bay*
Lovell Island
Gallops Island
Thompson Island *Long Island*
Georges Island
Rainsford Island *Nantasket Roads*
DORCHESTER
Moon Head
Neponset River
Hog Island
Squantum
Peddocks Island
Hingham Bay *Hull Bay*
Quincy Bay
Wollaston
Sheep Island
Bumpkin Island
Grape Island
Houghs Neck
Worlds End
Slate Island
Raccoon Island *Weymouth Back River*
QUINCY
Town River Bay *Weymouth Fore River*
Hingham Harbor
WEYMOUTH HINGHAM
Nantasket Beach
HULL

40

Boston Harbor, or Bay, is all that area between Point Shirley in Winthrop and Point Allerton in Hull. The area beyond Castle Island is called the Outer Harbor, while the area from Castle Island to the city is the Inner Harbor.

William Wood described Boston Bay in 1633 as "both safe, spacious and deep, free from cockling seas as run upon the coast of Ireland and in the channels of England. There be no stiff running currents, or rocks, shelves, bars, quicksands." Wood had not had time to discover the very evident "rocks, shelves, bars, quicksands" that awaited the unwary sailor in the harbor. "The surrounding shore being high, and showing many white cliffs," he thought was "a most pleasant prospect, with divers places of low land, out of which divers rivers vent themselves into the ocean." What "vents" itself into the harbor today is much less of a "pleasant prospect." Daily, 400 million gallons of treated sewage empty into the harbor from sewage plants on Nut, Moon, and Deer Islands. An unknown quantity of raw, untreated sewage still flows in via rivers from upstream communities and from many unconnected private drains flushing directly into the harbor waters. A steady oil pollution of the harbor, by accidents or leaks or deliberate discharges, damages animal, bird, marine, and plant life; and this contamination is long lasting. Over fifty derelict ships and barges, beached or submerged, clutter the harbor. There is enough floating debris and shore trash in the harbor, according to the Army Corps of Engineers, to fill a railroad train nineteen miles long.

(Top) Approaching Boston Bay. (Bottom) The entrance to the harbor, both as drawn by Joseph F. W. Des Barres for the guidance of navigators, reproduced from his *Atlantic Neptune,* ca. 1774.

Nearly two hundred years after William Wood's visit, when the tiny settlement had become a large city, a gentleman from Philadelphia with almost the same name, William Wood Thackera, found equal pleasure in sailing into the bay.

> The great number of Islands, rocks and Beacons; The Castle, Fort, and vessels of every size and description, in motion, or at anchor, and in every variety of position; the faint outline of the distant town, the dome of whose State-house towers above every other object; and occasionally, a view of Charlestown, the Navy-yard, and Ships of War, with turrets and spires of both towns, and constantly before the eye, afford a rich, lively and animated view.

It was, he thought, better than anything Philadelphia could offer.

By Thackera's time, Bostonians knew their harbor intimately. Schooners coming home from China sailed up the coast past Minot's Ledge, until they caught sight of the "cheering" white shaft or beam of Boston Light, at the Brewsters. They turned left toward George's Island, then right to shoot through the "Narrows" between Gallop's and Lovell's islands, then left once more when past Nix's Mate, which brought them safely into the ample anchorage of President Roads. From here it was a short sail between the Castle on port and Governor's Island on starboard into berth at one of the many city wharves. This was the northern route of the main ship channel.

There was a southern route, sometimes used. Instead of going right at George's Island, the ship sailed left into Nantasket Roads, then toward the middle of Long Island, around its southern end, then northwest between Thompson and Spectacle and into President Roads. Using either entrance in the old days, the ship's captain would find himself in a harbor where "500 ships may anchor."

When the Puritans first sailed into the bay, there were thirty-eight islands; now only twenty-eight survive the erosion of the waves or attachment to the mainland, a loss of one-fourth in 350 years. Still, the remaining islands contain more acreage (over nine hundred) than did the original Boston peninsula (estimated at about seven hundred). Much of the fun of the islands has been lost too, now that they serve more utilitarian purposes: prisons, sewage plants, school, pumping station, hospital, and the remnants of old forts. As a different awareness of the harbor develops, however, it is bound to become a playground for the new leisure at the end of the twentieth century. Now that the islands are state owned, these recreational possibilities can be realized.

Almost the first business of the English settlers was to avail themselves of the splendid harbor. They had not been on the Shawmut peninsula a year before Winthrop mentioned in his journal the construction of a thirty-ton bark at Medford, christened *Blessing of the Bay*. These English, who had a pretty good acquaintance with the seas at home, were prompt to discover the blessings that this new bay could bring them. They had little else going for them. In the same journal, Winthrop remarked on the boys bringing in eels and lobsters from the bay. One of the local ministers, the Reverend Hugh Peters, preached, publicly and privately, on the necessity of pooling their funds to buy proper fishing equipment at reasonable prices.

In six years, Bostonians could look out at their harbor and see fifteen great ships riding at anchor. During that year Winthrop recorded that at least one ship, aided by favoring winds, made the trip to England in a remarkable eighteen days. Many that same year, he added, took only five weeks for the voyage that had taken his fleet nine weeks.

By the fall of 1641, Winthrop proudly reported that Bostonians had sent 300,000 dried fish to market. Already theirs was a busy harbor, with the necessary commercial facilities. Three men whose enterprise had put up wharves and warehouses for both the coastal and overseas trade petitioned the General Court in October that rates to compensate them fairly be set for "wharfage, porterage & housing of goods." One of these three was the ingenious Edward Bendall. He had purchased a ship that had accidentally blown up in the harbor and then invented a diving bell to salvage its equipment and cannon. The bell consisted of

> . . . two great tubs, very tight, and open at one end, upon which were hanged so many weights as would sink it to the ground (600 wt.). It was let down, the diver sitting in it a cord in his hand to give notice when they should draw him up, and another cord to show when they should remove it from place to place, so he could continue in his tub half an hour and fasten ropes to the ordnance, and put the lead, etc. into a tub or net. And when the tub was drawn up one knocked on the head of it, and thrust a long pole under the water which the diver laid hold of and so was drawn up by it.

These were not the only men developing the waterfront. The merchant Valentine Hill, with one group, improved the Town Cove area, while Governor Winthrop and another were interested in doing the same for Shelter Cove on the other side of State Street from Town Cove. It was the beginning of a never-ending process, the wharves pushing farther and farther out onto the flats and gradually enclosing and including them, causing the original shoreline to disappear, long since.

While there was a community wharf since at least 1634, it was not until 1710 that the great Long Wharf was begun. This began at the foot of King Street and stretched far out into Town Cove. Its beginning can be seen on State Street today where that street suddenly narrows at the corner of Chatham Row. Debris from the great fire of 1711 was carted down and used as filling between the piles and cob-work of the new wharf. Crossing the remnants of the old "Barricado" of 1673, it made a spur on one side, which in time became the well-known T-Wharf.

Atlantic Avenue about 1865 with shipping clustered about Commercial and T Wharves.

When Long Wharf was finished in 1715, it was 1,586 feet long and 54 feet wide, of which 30 feet were for a roadway. The rest was used for store lots on the north side of the wharf. The end of the wharf was wider, and about the 1740s it was fortified with what was called the "Shirley Battery" after the then governor. Subsequently the wharf was to be widened and extended.

The Proprietors of Boston Pier (its official name) were incorporated in 1772, and the same corporation exists today with forty-eight hundred shares outstanding. In 1797, they tried to get a pipe laid out on the pier to bring fresh spring water to the ships, but the town set so many conditions that the proprietors decided to dig their own well at the end of the wharf. This remarkable engineering project for the times necessitated drilling a 10½-inch hole down through 16 feet of wharf filling, 14 feet of clay, 6 feet of old marsh, and 4½ feet of pure clay. Next they drove a log with a 5-inch hole in it, 13 feet beyond this using a large iron weight. Then with a long auger, they bored 35 feet further through clay, 23 feet through sand, and 7 feet through more clay to a slate ledge. Drilling 3 feet through the ledge, they tapped an abundant supply of water. A wooden pipe was driven down through the 121½-foot hole, and three months after the project began, the proprietors were selling fresh water to the ships. When the East Boston subway tunnel was under construction in 1903, they ran into the old shaft and suddenly lost the pressure in their tube.

Central Wharf was built in 1817, and was for its time an equally remarkable piece of construction. The engineering challenge here was to provide waterproof basements in the four-story brick buildings that were to be constructed on the wharf for merchants. Two long granite bulkheads were built out into the harbor, and the mud flats between them filled in. Outside them, the harbor bottom was dredged to provide adequate depth for vessels alongside the wharf.

Granite building foundations were laid on timber piles driven sixteen feet into the harbor clay and cut off a foot below low tide. Always fully immersed, they were protected from rotting, and 150 years later, when the Aquarium was built on this site, a force of forty tons exerted to pull up these old piles failed to dislodge them. A double-planked floor system, keyed into the granite walls, with air pockets between them, provided the pressure to make the basements waterproof. Any water seeping into the lower section could be quickly pumped out before it reached the goods stored in the second deck.

When Atlantic Avenue was built in 1868, it cut right through Central Wharf. The Fitzgerald Expressway destroyed more buildings in 1939 when it crossed above the old Central Wharf. In 1958 the wharf was sold, and four years later all the old buildings were torn down. The new Aquarium obtained the site in 1964 and opened its new building in 1969. Atlantic Avenue here has since been relocated and space provided for new structures facing the waterfront.

Boston's decline as a port, symbolized by the razing of Central Wharf, was a long way in the future when Bostonians were building their first quays. To stay alive, the new community had to trade. Their first and most natural market was back home in England. Furs and lumber were the major products they had to ship, and iron, cloth goods, and luxury items were the merchandise they principally wanted. Later, when New Englanders had developed trade with West Indian ports, there was much transshipment of island products to England via Boston.

Very quickly Boston merchants discovered the potential wealth of the West Indian Islands. Boston ships carried down dried fish, lumber and lumber products, flour, hats, and rum, importing to Boston the sugar, cotton, dyewoods, oils, wines, and molasses that could not be grown or produced in the temperate zone. A third trade area was opened with Newfoundland and Nova Scotia to whom Bostonians sold beer, butter, candles, dried meats, livestock, and even soap and vegetables.

Later, trade expanded to include many European ports and Boston ships made voyages to the Canary Islands, Spain, and Mediterranean ports. Early in the eighteenth century, most of Boston's European trade was still with England, but just before the Revolution, English goods accounted for only 40 percent of Boston's European trade. That factor, too, played its small part in making rebellion possible. The restrictive British trade policies, of course, were a much more important cause.

Donald McKay (1810–1880).

Independence brought many changes to Boston's commercial patterns. Shut off from preferred treatment in British markets, new trade areas had to be opened, and Bostonians took the lead in exploring such ventures. The most important new trade was with China and India. A by-product of the Chinese trade was that which developed with the northwest coast of America. This coast trade gradually became concentrated in the hands of Boston merchants. Barter with the coastal Indians gave them furs that could be sold or traded with the Chinese in Canton for teas, silks, and chinaware.

Baltic trade expanded, and Bostonians quickly took advantage of the business opportunities afforded them as neutrals in the Napoleonic Wars, although these same conflicts caused many difficulties which resulted in embargoes, Non-Intercourse Acts, and finally the war of 1812. After this war, Boston's sea trade began an amazing upward spiral. One of the odd items Bostonians sold during this period was ice from their ponds. Principally initiated by Frederick Tudor, this trade with tropical countries peaked just before the Civil War, then slowly declined during the rest of the century.

In spite of depressions, commercial panics, discriminatory tariffs, and similar commercial headaches, Boston business flourished in the first fifty years of the nineteenth century. When capital went into textile mills, the merchants imported wool from the Mediterranean and cotton from Southern states to keep the mills busy. As the steam engine became the wonder machine of the century, merchants brought in coal from Pennsylvania to keep it going. Coastal traffic boomed. During the 1830s in Boston, there were almost two ships in domestic trade for every one in foreign commerce. The Middlesex Canal, fully operative after 1803, brought barges and boats into the harbor from a new direction—inland from Concord—drawing on central New Hampshire.

Not least, passenger transportation became profitable—another of the "blessings" of being a town on the bay. Steamboats appeared in the harbor in 1817, and a regular service in summer commenced to such "distant" places as Salem, Nahant, and Quincy. A "Packet" line of ships, sailing when "wind and weather" permitted, was operating from about the same year to ports north and south of Boston. From 1821, the "Dispatch" line sailed every Saturday for New York. An overseas packet line to Liverpool began the next year, but ended in 1826. The Cunard Company commenced its service to Boston in 1840 and continued until 1967.

By 1850, ship design had changed radically, and ships were becoming much larger. The first Boston-built ship, the *Trial* of 1641, was 160 tons. Bostonians favored small ships for commercial voyages well into the nineteenth century. The fiasco of the eight-hundred-ton *Massachusetts*, built in Quincy in 1789, unreasonably prejudiced Bostonians against big vessels. It took the success of the large Baltimore clippers—and the higher freight rates they could charge—to convert Bostonians. Of the 433 listed clippers, 159 were built in or near Boston.

Clippers were used by Bostonians principally in China trade and in carrying passengers and freight to the gold fields of California. The best of these clip-

A view of the activity in an East Boston shipyard during the era of building the great clippers.

pers, the *Sea Witch,* the *Flying Cloud,* or the *Andrew Jackson,* could cut the trip from the East Coast around Cape Horn to California—a 17,000-mile voyage—down to about three months in contrast to the previous five or six months. At their best, they could sail two hundred miles a day.

The first and one of the most successful clipper ships built in Boston was the *Surprise,* a 1,261-ton vessel designed by Samuel Hartt Pook and built by Samuel Hall. It was launched on October 5, 1850. Donald McKay, a transplanted Nova Scotian, who had been building sailing ships since 1845 in East Boston, quickly became the master builder of clippers. His longest clipper, the *Great Republic,* was launched before thirty thousand cheering spectators in East Boston on October 4, 1853. A third longer than his *Flying Cloud,* she measured 335 feet in length, and was registered at 4,555 tons. The *Great Republic* was destined for the Australian trade, but before she could leave New York on her maiden voyage, sparks set her rigging afire and she burned to the water's edge. Rebuilt and cut down to 3,357 tons, she was still the largest vessel on the ocean and a fast sailer, though not breaking any records as she usually ran out of the winds.

McKay's shipyard built twenty-one clippers, as well as two dozen other types of vessels. His *Lightning* covered 436 miles on March 1, 1854, logging a record speed of 18.2 knots for a consecutive twenty-four-hour period. His *James Baines,* thought by Liverpool experts to be his finest ship, crossed the Atlantic on her maiden voyage in twelve days and six hours. Her best speed was 21 knots on a voyage to Australia. His ships were romantically named— *Sovereign of the Seas, Westward Ho!, Stag-hound,* and the famous *Flying Cloud.* There were other noted clipper ship builders in East Boston, South Boston, Chelsea, Medford, and Quincy.

47

An atmospheric etching of Foster's Wharf by Darius Cobb. (Courtesy of Massachusetts Historical Society.)

The Boston clippers were among the handsomest ships ever built. Only the best materials went into them—solid oak beams and southern pine planks. They were sheathed on the outside with the best copper, and their inside fittings made abundant use of rosewood, teak, mahogany, and brass. Queen Victoria, inspecting the *James Baines,* was astonished at such lavish appointments for a commercial vessel.

These ships were possible only because of the experience and skills acquired over generations by local shipbuilders and their allied tradesmen: riggers, sailmakers, boatbuilders, shipchandlers, painters, carvers, gilders, mast and spar makers, and such. Of all these maritime artisans, a word must be said about the shipcarvers, the men who carved figureheads, quarter galleries, badges, and stern decorations. One of the most noted families in this business was the Skillin family. Before 1737, the two brothers John and Simeon had been active in the field. Three of Simeon's sons continued the trade, and Simeon, Jr. (1757–1806) practically monopolized the business during the Revolutionary period, so handsome was his work. Another son, Samuel, was active until his death in 1830. Isaac Fowle, probably a Skillin apprentice, continued the fine tradition through the clipper ship period, as did the firm of S. W. Gleason & Sons and John W. Mason.

But such beautiful handiwork was doomed, as were the clippers themselves, with the advent of steam-powered iron vessels. Wooden ships had depended upon an abundant supply of local timber, but there were no local iron mines. Boston began to decline as a shipbuilding center, and this decline was reflected even before the Civil War, in its commerce, too.

In the China trade Boston had been eclipsed before the Civil War by New York. New wool markets in South America and Australia expanded, partly

From sea to consumer, selling fish from the pushcarts, May 4, 1895.

compensating for this loss in trade. The Calcutta trade held up, as did the Mediterranean markets, both wanting the products of Massachusetts factories and mills. But the Civil War hastened the decline of the American merchant marine since both foreign and domestic merchants preferred ships that would not be attacked by Confederate raiders. The war hiked insurance rates; it ended Boston's carrying trade to Southern ports, and diverted the country's production to war, reducing the supply of exports.

After the war, Boston merchants concentrated on rebuilding their commercial markets. There were enough successes to disguise the downward trend. The largest merchant fleet in the nation belonged to the William F. Weld Company, whose fifty sailing vessels flew the company's famous "Black Horse" house flag. When Capt. Lorenzo Baker made money on a cargo of bananas, a trade in this item began, forming the Boston Fruit Company, and then by mergers establishing the United Fruit Company in 1899 with headquarters in Boston. Converting to refrigerated steamships, painted white, their "Great White Fleet" became a distinctive sight in the harbor for many decades.

By the 1880s there were over two hundred wharves in Boston. Commercial Wharf with its fifty-four granite stores had been built and was the center of the grain trade. The railroads were developing large areas in East Boston, South Boston, and Charlestown with well-equipped piers, warehouses, and grain elevators. Foreign traders and the big shippers flocked to use these new facilities, while the coastal trade, the fishing vessels, and excursion boats gravitated to the old waterfront.

Technical improvements helped the Boston fishing fleet to grow rapidly after the Civil War. Using ice to pack fresh fish greatly expanded the market. Previously the market for fresh fish had necessarily been local, though dried fish had

The "new" Fish pier.

been a staple export item since 1635. Fish dealers moved the center of their operations to T Wharf in 1884, putting up new buildings to fit their needs. So rapid was the expansion of their industry that by the turn of the century they were looking for more space. Old T Wharf was a romantic place to people who didn't have to work there. Artists painted it, and landlubbers stopped to watch the colorful activities.

Cod and haddock were brought in from the Newfoundland Banks, halibut from Greenland and Iceland, salmon and mackerel were caught in both Maine and Canadian waters. Herring ran locally in October and November. Lobstermen dropped their traps off the nearby coast, and even more lobsters were brought down from Maine.

Once the catch was landed, it was "either dried, pickled, frozen, or canned" for delivery to the ultimate consumer. Naturally with so much fresh fish available, Boston restaurants made it a specialty, and gourmets did their bit for the traditional Boston–New York rivalry by turning up their noses at the peculiar way Manhattanites prepared their chowders—with tomatoes yet!

Boston merchants trailed doggedly in New York's wake, but at the turn of the century Boston was still second to that city in shipping volume. New Yorkers carried a billion dollars worth of goods in 1900, while Boston vessels shipped almost $200 million. Things still looked good on the surface for Boston. In 1914, it was the world's leading wool market, the leading exporter of boots and shoes, the largest importer of hides and skins. It could point to its wooden schooners—called New England's "one great maritime invention"—which made it the largest coal port in the world up to World War I. It could point with pride

50

A flooded T-wharf, about 1930.

at the new concrete drydock built at the Navy Yard in 1905; at the largest pier in the world built in South Boston in 1914 (Commonwealth Pier No. 5) and the well-equipped Fish Pier built the next year; at the many 10,000-ton ocean-going steamers belching their smoky way into the harbor. With its 141 miles of waterfront and forty miles of berthing space, it looked prosperous.

But it was deceptive. The bulk of commerce was shifting to New York; even Canadian business seldom passed through Boston as before. The wooden schooners ultimately could not compete with the steamships. By 1929 Boston owned no ships in foreign trade. High freight rates drove away commerce. Immigration steadily dropped off. Shipbuilding continued to diminish. Even Quincy's Fore River Yard was mainly busy with repair work after World War I. Only in coastal trade and fishing did Boston hold its own.

Even the establishment of the Boston Port Authority in 1929, with its vigorous rehabilitation and expansion programs could not ward off the inevitable decline, only partly accelerated by the depression years. The artificial stimulation of World War II was only temporary and the port continued to lose ground. The shift of much cargo to speedier airlines, and the vested opposition to changes that would improve the port (now ameliorated), have meant the end of Boston as an important sea terminal. However, a seaport receiving over twelve hundred cargo vessels each year and handling more than $700 million annually in foreign commerce is not to be written off completely. Use of container terminals may help the port too.

One of the strengths of the port of Boston has been the quality of men who have devoted their talents to its improvement and progress men like the

The decaying condition of the Boston waterfront in the 1960s. (Copyright © 1971, Mark Silber, Dimension.)

founders of the Boston Marine Society. Organized in 1742 as "The Fellowship Club" by a group of sea captains, they incorporated in 1754 as "The Marine Society at Boston" and acquired their present name in 1809. It is the oldest marine society in America and still numbers more than 250 members. For many years it supplied and supervised pilots for the harbor and until 1948 it arranged for Port Wardens to report damage to ships and goods during voyages. In its early years it was a relief organization for its members. But its most important work has been to promote safe navigation in the harbor and to collect marine information to develop safer and more accurate sailing charts.

Another group of men who have kept the port functioning is the pilots, who guide expensive ships and cargoes safely in and out of the harbor. Both lives and dollars depend on their knowledge of the harbor's tides, dangerous shoals, reefs, ledges, shifting sandbars, and channel depths. Today five pilot boats and twenty-four pilots are subject to call from their office on Long Wharf.

The sea enterprise of Bostonians has shown itself in other ways. One of these was the development of visual telegraph systems. In 1799, the commander at Fort Independence in the harbor, began flying flags to identify the type of ship entering the harbor. For twenty years, newspapers would report an item such as "Brig below the Fort at sunset." No further attempt was made to identify the vessel or owner. In 1801, Jonathan Groat, Jr., began operation of a line of visual semaphore signals from Martha's Vineyard to Telegraph Hill in Dorchester. Sixteen stations were built to pass along the signals, and news could be sped from the Vineyard to Boston, not in the two days it formerly had taken, but in nine minutes.

52

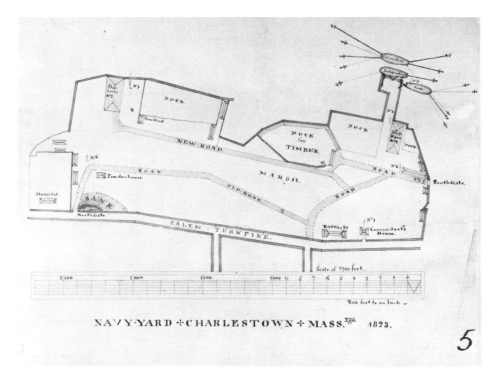

The Navy Yard in Charlestown as it looked in 1823. The Navy Yard was established in 1800.

The ferry boat *Winthrop* in 1895.

This system ended in 1807, but another was ready to take its place. Samuel Topliff, who in 1814 took over the operation of Samuel Gilbert's newsroom in the Exchange Coffee House, made it a center of commercial information. In 1820 he extended the marine telegraph at Fort Independence a long distance out by erecting a station on Long Island head. By a system of balls and flags, more information could be transmitted to Boston and the patrons of his Reading Room. John Rowe Parker refined and improved Topliff's system beginning in 1828. With stations on Point Allerton, Nantasket Heights, and several harbor islands, he developed a telegraphic dictionary enabling elaborate and precise information to be speedily transmitted to the city. A merchant could then make necessary arrangements for the reception and disposal of his cargo long before the vessel docked. Parker's system lasted until the invention of Morse's electric telegraph.

But the cleverest inventions could not cope with the freaks of nature. Often Boston harbor has frozen out to various distances. The most noteworthy was in February 1844 when a prolonged cold spell froze the harbor at least ten miles out from the wharf in East Boston where the Cunard Royal Mail steamer *Britannia* was preparing to sail for England. Icemen who cut the fresh water ponds in winter were hired for $1,500 to make a 200-foot-wide passage for the ship out to open sea, plus a second channel from the ferry to India Wharf. Two large gangs were put to work, for the ice was at least six to twelve inches thick, and they had only two days to accomplish the task.

Men, horses, and apparatus covered the harbor, working diligently. Tents for food and rest were put up on the ice. Thousands of other men, boys on

Boston harbor partly frozen over in 1835 as painted by John S. Blunt. At far right a group of men appear to be hauling in a vessel. (M. & M. Karolik Collection, The Museum of Fine Arts, Boston.)

skates, ladies in sleighs pulled by horses, boats on runners came to watch the spectacle. Enterprising chaps at Long Wharf charged people one cent to use ladders to get down to the ice. There was even a horse race out on the ice: "a Yankee horse attached to wheels and a Canadian pony to runners. The horse conquered after a short but spirited contest." Then about eleven o'clock on February 3, the *Britannia* majestically moved down the channel toward the open sea on schedule.

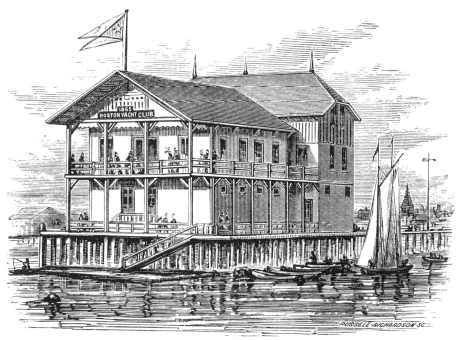

Boston Yacht-Club House, City Point.

Harbors are for more than business, no matter how vital that is to a community. The seaside is also for fun. This can be one of the most pleasant blessings of the bay. Col. Samuel Pierce in his diary for July 24, 1765, described what many a Bostonian before and since has done: "I went a frolicking on the water." Long before the days of yacht clubs and marinas, Bostonians boarded boats of some kind or other and went "frolicking" out to the islands or along the shores of the bay, perhaps just for a sail, a fishing expedition, or a moonlight excursion. Such events became so common, that the editor of "The Symbol" in 1846 satirized one such water frolic. The day was "hot enough to boil the bay," he wrote. They sailed on the *Foam Flake* a little steamboat "of one horse-team power," with its pitch "frying out of the seams." It finally had to be towed out of the dock "by a fast mud-scow from Chelsea flats." They had a "band"—a violinist, a hurdy-gurdy man, and a boy who played the bones. They knew only one whole tune among them. A "pickerel-faced girl in brown boots and a green mantila" thought the band was "divine." The only food available on the boat was some cheese and doughnuts, exorbitantly priced. A "withered beau" of forty-five but "with the heart of a zephyr" tried to persuade the editor to join a quadrille. The dancing finished with a "waltzing speculation" in which a "thick-headed young gentleman" plunged over the netting into a "quarter-boat." The *Foam Flake* grounded in an easterly fog and it was seven hours before she returned her merry-makers to Boston. So much, sighed the would-be imitator of Dickens, for "Water Parties."

But such water parties are the exception. Doubtless the members of the twenty-five or so Yacht Clubs on Boston Bay would have livelier tales to tell—perhaps of the memorable races held in the harbor or Massachusetts Bay, such

A series of 6 drawings by "Chinks" (Dr. Charles E. Stedman) excerpted from his *Mr. Hardy Lee, His Yacht,* illustrate the attractions and perils of the sea. First, he kibitzes the building of his vessel.

Second, it is christened by the girlfriend.

Third, the girlfriend is taken out for a sail.

Fourth, it proves a rough voyage.

Fifth, but the girlfriend consents to be married.

Sixth, and finally our sailor is berthed in a safe harbor.

as the Quincy Bay Race, or Marblehead's famous Race Week, or the annual race between the fishermen of Boston and Gloucester. Some older members may reminisce of the days of prohibition and rum-running in the harbor. Other citizens of Boston, yachtless, enjoy the swimming or what is left of it in the polluted harbor waters. In 1913, Samuel Richards became the first man to swim from Charlestown out to Boston Light and back. Some tottering ancients can recall "Nickle Day" at Revere Beach, when you could get proper seasick on land rides. The redoubtable L Street "Brownies" who do their swimming in the winter when they have to chop through the ice to get at the water, scorn the summer swimmer. Each to his own "blessing of the bay."

There are tragedies of the bay, too—shipboard accidents when a sailor falls from the rigging to smash onto the deck or tumble into the waves, deaths at sea, partings on docks, letters written and never received, letters never written and ardently awaited. There are ships that sail and never return, drunks who fall off wharves and perish, and uncounted men, women, and children who have drowned in this bay over 350 years. This is a melancholy chronicle and the stuff of a hundred melodramas, but an actual part of human lives, and one of the many truths about Boston Bay.

Water gathers a whole way of life around itself, including sailors and their fish stories, their decorated trunks, the scrimshaw they brought back from long voyages, and their pursuit of female companionship after weeks, months, or

Ship-to-shore dealing on South Boston bridge in the mid-nineteenth century.

CODFISH?

Panel 1: A BOSTONIAN INFORMS US THAT HE BOUGHT A COD FISH THE OTHER DAY AND THAT EVERYWHERE HE WENT ABOUT BOSTON PEOPLE ASKED WHAT THE "PECULIAR" ODOR WAS. — THE HUB, THE ATHENS — WHAT HAS HAPPENED TO IT?

Panel 2: OUR CHUM SAYS THAT EVEN THE CATS FAILED TO RECOGNIZE THE PERFUME OF COD. — IT DIDN'T USE TO BE THAT WAY.

Panel 3: HERE'S TO DEAR OLD BOSTON, THE HOME OF THE BEAN AND THE COD — BOSH! — TODAY THE CABOTS AND LOWELLS NOT ONLY SPEAK TO ANYONE BUT THEY ASK HIM WHAT THAT "PECULIAR" ODOR IS.

Panel 4: COD FISH NEVER USED TO BE DISGUISED AS SOMETHING ELSE AND COD CHEEKS AND TONGUES WERE A DELICACY. — BOSTONIANS ATE COD FISH AS SUCH AND ESCHEWED RED CORNED BEEF AND CLAM CHOWDER WITH TOMATOES IN IT.

Panel 5: THEY TOOK COD LIVER OIL TOO. — NONE OF THESE VITAMIN PILLS.

Panel 6: IN OUR STATE HOUSE HANGS THE SACRED COD! MUST WE HAUL IT DOWN? — PLEASE GO BUY - AND EAT - A COD FISH.

DAHL

F. W. Dahl comments on the decline of the codfish for readers of the *Boston Herald.* (Courtesy of F. W. Dahl.)

years of only men—in one century in the brothels on Ann Street, in another in the "playground" that was Scollay Square, and for the current Jack Tar in the "Combat Zone" of Washington Street. For every Richard Henry Dana, Jr., who returns to write of his *Two Years Before the Mast,* there are thousands with no tale to tell. Dana arrived back in Boston after two years on September 20, 1836. The *Alert* that night anchored in President Roads. Leaning over the rail they watched

> the dome of the State House fading in the western sky; the lights of the city starting into sight, as the darkness came on; and at nine o'clock the clangor of the bells, ringing their accustomed peals; among which the Boston boys tried to distinguish the well-known tone of the Old South.

The next morning they brought the ship into dock, furled the sails,

> took the warp ashore, manned the capstan, and with a chorus which waked up half the North End, and rang among the buildings in the dock, we hauled her into the wharf. The city bells were just ringing one when the last turn was made fast and the crew dismissed; and in five minutes more not a soul was left on board the good ship Alert but the old ship-keeper, who had come down from the counting-house to take charge of her.

60

The Islands in Boston Harbor

(NOTE: Extinct islands are enclosed in parentheses.)

(APPLE ISLAND)   The 8 acres that made up Apple Island are now part of the extension of Logan International Airport. It was a roundish island, rising gently from the waterline to its center. It was first granted to Boston and used for pasturing sheep and cattle, and later privately owned. The two most notable owners were the father of Gov. Thomas Hutchinson and the mysterious Englishman, William Marsh, who lived there from 1814 to 1833. He prompted a poem, "An Island Ruin," by Oliver Wendell Holmes. The city bought the island back in 1867. For many years, a tall elm tree in the center of the island was a familiar harbor landmark until felled by vandals in 1938.

(BIRD ISLAND)   The wind and waves have gradually eroded away this small island, and what remained was incorporated into Logan airport. Supposedly named for a Mr. Bird, this island was rented out by Boston in the seventeenth century to various farmers for its salt marsh hay. On several occasions in the eighteenth century, the bodies of pirates hanged in Boston were afterward brought here to hang in chains as a warning to other sailors. Some pirates were also buried here.

Boston, seen from South Boston, about 1873, with the sloop *Matilda* in the right foreground.

A "Boat Race, Boston Harbor" painted by A. A. Lawrence in 1852. The island is probably Thompson Island with the mainland of Dorchester in the background. (M. & M. Karolik Collection, Museum of Fine Arts, Boston.)

THE BREWSTERS   Seven islands in the outer harbor named in honor of the Elder William Brewster family of Plymouth. They include Great, Outer, and Middle Brewsters, and Calf, Little Calf, Green, and Lighthouse islands. (See individual entries.)

BUMPKIN ISLAND   This island has had various names—Bomkin, Ward's, Pumpkin, and Round. Its 27 acres lie off Sunset Point in Nantasket. Since 1682, it has belonged to Harvard College, the bequest of Samuel Ward. In the early years, Harvard rented it out to farmers or fishermen. Much later Burrage Children's Hospital was located on the island. During World War I more than a thousand sailors were housed there. For years Capt. John Glawson was caretaker on the island and rescued many people from drowning.

BUTTON ISLAND   Toward the head of Hingham Harbor, barely a mile south of Sarah's Island, is the little heap of rock (felsite diorite) and gravel with very little verdure, appropriately named Button Island. It is mostly used by boaters as a picnic spot.

CALF ISLAND   The 17½ acres of Calf Island lie north of Great Brewster. Sometimes called Great Calf to further distinguish it from its northerly neighbor, Little Calf Island, it has also been known as Apthorp's Island. A number of private owners have lived on the island over the years, and there are still houses to be seen. The federal government took possession of it during the first world war. There are some pleasant beaches, notable rock formations (particularly Pope's Rocks and North Rocks on the Eastern point), and a small graveyard.

(CASTLE ISLAND)   The 18 plus acres that made up Castle Island have now been included in South Boston proper. A long plank bridge from Marine Park first linked it to the mainland in 1891, and later a roadway on made land in 1932 completed the process. From earliest times, this island, two and one-half miles from Long Wharf by sea, was seen as an ideal site for a fort protecting the town of Boston. In 1634 a mud-wall "Castle" was built, though it did not last long. Successive forts took its place; one in 1689 was known as Fort William and Mary, the building erected in 1701–03 was called Castle William, and in 1797 christened Fort Independence. The present building dates from 1801 and its five bastions are named: Winthrop (on the East), Shirley (South), Dearborn (North), Adams (Northwest), and Hancock (West). This fort was decommissioned in 1879, though temporarily used by the government in 1898 as a mine and torpedo station.

The only major engagement of the fort was in March 1776, when the British bombarded Dorchester Heights. Thus its principal use was in attacking the town, not protecting it. Many disasters mark the history of the island: guns exploding, killing and maiming their crews, fatal duels and suicides, the capsizing of a floating wharf in 1896 drowning four boys, and a harbor mine explosion in 1898 killing four men. The fort has often been used as a civil prison. Indian hostages were kept here in 1721, Governor Andros in 1689, and from 1785 to 1805 the Commonwealth used it as its first state prison.

The town lent the fort an alarm bell in 1656 which was used until 1831 and is now preserved at the Old State House. In 1933, a fifty-two-foot white Maine granite shaft was put up on Castle Island in memory of Donald McKay and his clipper ships.

(CAT ISLAND)   This small bit of land, located in Town River Bay of Quincy, was undistinguished in its history, and eventually mined for filling material and so disappeared.

(DEER ISLAND)   When the English first arrived, this island—joined to Winthrop since 1937—was well-wooded and inhabited by many deer who had escaped the mainland wolves by swimming across Pudding (later Shirley) Gut. Both woods and deer were quickly eliminated by the English. The island is four and one-half miles by sea from Long Wharf and 197 acres in area. There were two ponds on the island once, Ice Pond and Cow Pond. Boston has owned it since 1634, leasing it to private tenants until 1847. During the hysteria of King Philip's War, five hundred Indians were confined on Deer Island, prophetic of its future use as a penal colony. Island residents watched the Battle of Shirley Gut on May 19, 1775, won by the rebelling Americans. During the next war with Britain, the *Constitution* sailed through Shirley Gut to escape British cruisers blockading the harbor. As late as the 1920s, the Nahant boats could sail through the gut, but since then it has filled in and become part of the mainland.

Throughout the first half of the nineteenth century, the island was a popular place for water parties. William Tewksbury was the most famous resident, and by 1825 was credited with saving thirty-one people from drowning. In 1847, Boston took over the island, moving its almshouse there the next year, its paupers in 1854, and its convicts in 1858. The area is presently shared by Boston with its Suffolk County House of Correction on the Winthrop end, the Commonwealth with its pumping station for the North Metropolitan District in the center, and on the south end (used for Fort William Dawes during the second world war) there is a huge sewage treatment plant built by the Metropolitan District Commission. On Fawn Bar, five hundred yards off Deer Island, is the Deer Island Light, established in 1890 and now automatically operated. Since the island is subject to drastic erosion by waves, a seawall has been protecting its edge since the Civil War era.

GALLOP'S ISLAND   This 16.2-acre island was owned by John Gallop until his death in 1649. It was one of the most fertile islands for farming in the harbor. A high bluff on the north was fortified during the Revolution. Through the middle of the last century, the island was a popular resort for fishing and chowder parties, and temporarily known by the names of some of the resort owners: Newcomb's and Snow's island. Boston bought it from its private owners in 1860. During the Civil War it was used by the federal government. From 1866 to 1937 it was a quarantine station. German sailors were interned here during the first world war. During World War II, the United States Maritime Service ran a radio school here. The government, which bought the island in 1916, misspelled its name as Gallup's Island, and once it was Frenchified as Galloupe's Island.

GEORGE'S ISLAND   This 28-acre island, seven miles from Long Wharf by ship, belonged to James Pemberton in 1628 and was then known as Pemberton's Island. Privately owned for two centuries, it took its present name from a tenant, John George, in the early 1700s. The federal government acquired it in 1825, and began construction of a great five-sided granite fort in 1833, completed in 1850. Taking the name Fort Warren, it became headquarters for harbor defense. During the Civil War, many regiments trained at the fort and over a thousand Confederate prisoners were imprisoned there. Manned in both the Spanish-American and the first world war, harbor defenses were shifted to Fort Banks in 1922, and the fort decommissioned in 1928, only to be reactivated during World War II. Once more it has been returned to caretaker status. Under Metropolitan District Commission care, thousands of people visit this easily accessible island each year.

(GOVERNOR'S ISLAND)   The 70 acres of Governor's Island have become, since 1941, part of the enlargement of Logan International Airport, and the island where apples are said to have first grown in America is no more. Roger Conant was the first owner of the island, before the Puritans arrived, and then it was called Conant's Island. In 1632 Boston leased, and later sold, it to Gov. John Winthrop calling it "Governor's Garden." It was later known as Winthrop's Island, but the name which lasted was "Governor's Island." In 1808, the federal government took over six acres for fortifications, first called Fort Warren, then after 1833 renamed Fort Winthrop. The fort was unimportant and abandoned after 1905, but not before a tremendous explosion of eighteen thousand pounds of gunpowder on September 7, 1902, in a powder magazine had killed two men, amazingly sparing hundreds of Sunday sightseers. Edward Rowe Snow, the harbor historian, was the last man to sail around the island just before it became part of the airport.

GRAPE ISLAND   Off Eastern Neck in Weymouth is Grape Island with its two hills and 50 acres. It had its moment in history on May 21, 1775, when the British sent some soldiers after its hay. The local minutemen turned out and a sharp skirmish sent the British hayless back to Boston. Succulent clams once were dug from the flats around Grape Island until twentieth-century contamination made them unsafe.

A fishing party landed for a cook-out on one of the harbor islands, as depicted for the October 2, 1852, issue of *Ballou's Pictorial Drawing-Room Companion.*

THE GRAVES A dangerous rocky ledge of 10 acres—not really an island—The Graves stands at the entrance to Boston Harbor. A lighthouse was built on it in 1903 when Broad Sound was deepened. Its double white flash is familiar to many shore residents.

GREAT BREWSTER Largest of the Brewsters, this island has 23 acres. On the north end, a hundred-foot high cliff is protected by a seawall, but the southern bluff, half as high, is much eroded. From its westerly point extends a mile and a half of rocky debris, visible at low tide, at the end of which Bug Light or Spit Light shone from 1856 to 1929. It has since been replaced with an automatic beacon. (See also entry for Lighthouse Island.)

GREEN ISLAND This island of nearly 2 acres was known as North Brewster at the time of the Revolution. Its most famous resident was the hermit Samuel Choate who lived here for twenty years from 1845. During the high tides of the 1851 storm that destroyed Minot's Ledge lighthouse, he was rescued by a pilot boat. From time to time, a few other people have lived on the island, but the last house burned in 1932 and now it is visited only by picnickers and harbor explorers. Rum-runners were said to have used the island during prohibition days.

(HALF MOON ISLAND) This semicircular island was appropriately named. Formerly on the Quincy Flats, Colonel John Quincy once gave celebrated "strawberry parties" on this island. Some of it was later used for earthfill, and the rest eroded by the tides.

HANGMAN'S ISLAND This rocky area in Quincy Bay, from which slate was cut in Colonial times, is also called Hangman's Ledge. It is owned by the Commonwealth, which has leased it to various people. It is also frequented by fishermen.

(HOG ISLAND) This island is now the Orient Heights section of East Boston. When it was an island, it contained about 450 acres and flats. Samuel Sewall owned it for many years after 1687. John Breed lived here in a monumental stone house for several decades in the last century. It was bridged to Chelsea in 1816, and to Winthrop in 1839. The Eastern Railroad went through in 1838. A number of attempts have been made to refine its name, and it has been called variously Susanna Island, Breed's Island, Belle Isle, and, after 1877 when the railroad to Winthrop was built, Winthrop Junction.

LANGLEE'S ISLAND This largest island (4 acres) in Hingham Harbor was once called Ibrook's Island after the presumed early owner, Richard Ibrook, who came to Massachusetts in 1635. Steep ledges surround it, except where a few gravelly beaches exist. Its shrubby uplands, and trees planted by a turn-of-the-century owner, make it a beautiful spot, now owned by Hingham.

LIGHTHOUSE ISLAND   Boston Light was erected on Lighthouse Island and lit for the first time on September 14, 1716. It was the first proper lighthouse in America. This island is, in effect, a separate island, although a long bar of land, exposed at low tide, connects it with Great Brewster Island. Before the establishment of the lighthouse it was sometimes called Little Brewster, although that name has also been applied to Outer Brewster. After the lighthouse was operating, it was also called Beacon Island. Destroyed during the Revolution, the lighthouse was reconstructed in 1783. The island and the lighthouse became the property of the federal government in 1790.

LITTLE CALF ISLAND   This ledgy mass, about an acre in area, is inhabited only by sea gulls, and probably rats.

LITTLE HOG ISLAND   Inside the bend that Hull makes of Nantasket, behind Stony Beach, is Little Hog Island, a small oblong area of 8.5 acres. Formerly a place to break up old ships, during World War II it was the site of Fort Duvall. The federal government still owns it.

LONG ISLAND   Five miles by water from Long Wharf are the 213.1 acres of the largest and longest island now in the harbor, appropriately called Long Island, though for thirty years after 1690 it was known as Nelson's Island, after John Nelson who owned most of it. It was largely farmed or used as pastureland by a number of private dwellers, until the Long Island Company bought it all in 1849, intending to develop the area with a hotel and summer residences. However, during the Civil War, Camp Wrightman was established there as a soldiers' training center, and after the war in 1867, Fort Strong was relocated there. Since then it has been manned in the Spanish-American war and both world wars. Boston took over part of the island unused by the federal government in 1887, and built its almshouse there, and later a hospital for the chronically ill. A beacon was put up on the island in 1819, has been moved several times since, and was made automatic in 1929. Sunday prize fights, illegal in Boston, were held here after the Civil War until a police raid in 1873 ended them. A bridge now connects Long Island to Moon Island and thence to Squantum, but access is restricted.

Boston Light.

67

LOVELL'S ISLAND   Oldtimers thought the 57.3 acres of Lovell's Island, three quarters of a mile long and a third of a mile wide, was shaped like a dried fish. It was probably named after Capt. William Lovell, a Dorchester resident in 1630. Granted to Charlestown in 1636 for the use of its fishermen, it came into private hands in 1767, then was sold to the federal government in 1825. A lighthouse buoy station was run here from 1874 until the government decided to build Fort Standish here early in this century. The fort, manned in both world wars, is now only a crumbling ruin. In 1951 the island was deeded to the Metropolitan District Commission. Once heavily wooded, the trees were soon cut down. In the nineteenth century, horses were pastured here, and it was later used to raise rabbits both as pets and food for the Boston market. The wreck of a French warship off the island in 1782 was still yielding relics as late as 1929 and helped alter the shape of the island when a sandbar developed around the remains of the ship. Whiting Ledge is on the south and Rams Head on the north, with marshes and several small salt-water ponds in between.

MIDDLE BREWSTER ISLAND   This rocky island of 12 acres for years had a few fishermen's shacks on it, propped up against the fierce winds that blow at the harbor's mouth. For twenty years, Augustus Russ, known as "the King of Middle Brewster" lived here. Later, the island was owned by Melvin O. Adams, and until recently was in private hands. A small channel, called Flying Place, separates this island from Outer Brewster Island.

MOON ISLAND   Now often called Moon Head, these 44.6 acres were off Squantum and early used for pasturage. Some references give the name as Mennen's or Manning's Moon. A high bluff on the north made a harbor landmark. One of the Revolutionary war skirmishes took place here. In 1878, the sewer from Boston was built to Moon Island, where it still discharges waste into the harbor. It is bridged to the mainland and Long Island.

(NIX'S MATE)   The 12 acres of island granted to John Gallop in 1636 have now dwindled to a tidal ledge through erosion and pilferage. Gallop used it for pasturing sheep. Later the bodies of executed pirates were sometimes hung here as a warning to passing sailors. It then returned to its pastoral purpose until it nearly washed away. The Boston Marine Society took the lead in 1805 to preserve its remains, and it is now marked by a black and white cement pyramid on a high stone base.

(NODDLE'S ISLAND)   Noddle's Island has had several names: Brereton's Island, after an owner whose claim was denied; and William's Island, after a family that lived there many years. Occasionally the name is spelled Nottell's in old accounts. William Noddle was a tenant on the island for a few years, drowning in 1632, but his name has stayed with the island. The 663 acres that made up the original island, have since been considerably extended by building out on the extensive flats, and by including Hog, Bird, Governor, and Apple islands, to make the present East Boston. During its first two centuries, the island was a wildfowl paradise, and its meadows supported a few farmers including the noted Samuel Maverick. Fishing parties and clambakers from Boston often camped on the island. Fort Strong was built on Jeffries Point in 1814 to protect Boston from the British during that war, but never saw combat. In 1833, the East Boston Company was formed to develop the island, and settlement of the area began that year. A bridge to Hog Island in 1838, already bridged to Chelsea, made the area more accessible, although a ferry had been running from Boston since the seventeenth century.

(NUT ISLAND) The less than 6 acres of Nut Island was once called Hoff's Thumb, since it was just off Hoff's Neck (now Hough's Neck). Another variant of the name was Hoff's Tombs. By the end of the eighteenth century a cattle driftway, built on its bar, connected it to the Neck; this has since been expanded, so that it is no longer an island. After the Civil War, ordnance was tested here. Now it is the site of the Nut Island Pumping Station for the South Metropolitan District, pouring treated sewage into the harbor.

OUTER BREWSTER This island of 17.5 acres has been described as one of the most romantic places near Boston with its "wild rocks, chasms, caves, and overhanging cliffs." It is the furthest out of the Boston Harbor group. Within its huge rocky mass is an "oasis" of about five acres of good land with a natural pond and spring. For the first half of the nineteenth century the island was owned by the Austin family who cut a channel into the island, nearly dividing it in two, to provide safe anchorage in stormy weather. Boston took stone from the island for building. Various families lived on the island until it became government property, since visited only by venturesome boating parties. Other names for this island have been Outward Island and, on a few charts, Little Brewster.

PEDDOCK'S ISLAND One quarter mile off Windmill Point in Hull lies this 130-acre island which in the past has also been called Pettick's or Pethick's island. It is said to have the longest shoreline of all the harbor islands. Originally granted to Charlestown, then Nantasket, it has been divided, since 1642, among private owners. The Americans stole British cattle off the island during the Revolution. Eighty-eight acres on the East Head were sold to the government, and Fort Andrews built there. It was used in both world wars, then abandoned in 1958. A small summer colony will soon disappear as the new owner of the island, the Metropolitan District Commission, develops it for recreation.

RACCOON ISLAND Off Hough's Neck in Weymouth Fore River are the 3 acres of Raccoon Island. It has always been privately owned and made no history.

Rainsford's Island, Boston Harbor, probably painted by Robert Salmon in 1840. The building in the foreground was called the "Grecian Temple" and was used at that period as a smallpox hospital. (Courtesy of The Museum of Fine Arts, Boston.)

RAGGED ISLAND   In Hingham harbor, this picturesquely indented island of 2 acres with its rocks and sumacs, and rockweed revealed at half tide, makes a spot of color in the water. A bridge to Downer's Landing at one time connected Ragged Island to the shore.

RAINSFORD ISLAND   Named for Elder Edward Raynsford, the first proprietor, who kept cattle on it, this 11.4-acre island lies along the Nantasket Roads and is seven miles from Boston by sea. Bluffs on either end are joined by a low narrow beach, protected from erosion by a seawall. From 1737 to 1852 Boston used the island as the site of a hospital for infectious diseases and as a quarantine station, hence its other names of Hospital Island and Quarantine Island. When no infectious diseases prevailed, the island was a favorite summer resort for many people. After 1852, the Commonwealth established a State Almshouse on the island. In 1872, Boston bought the property back from the state and for years sent city paupers there. From 1895 to 1920, the House of Reformation for boys was located on the island. The buildings have since decayed or burned, and the island is not presently in use. On its West Head is an old graveyard with quaint inscriptions.

SAILOR ISLAND Old names for this island of 3.9 acres in Hingham harbor included Sarah's or Sayles's island. Owned by Hingham, it is the summit of a great rocky ledge rising from the water, and covered with shrubby growth.

SHEEP ISLAND South of Peddock's Island and near the entrance to Hingham harbor are the 2 acres of Sheep Island, supposedly used for keeping sheep in early times. Lately it has been a private summer residence and hunting lodge. For such a small island, this one has had many names: Sun, Ship, Sheen, Shean, and Sheaf.

SLATE ISLAND Just southeast of Grape Island are the 12.4 acres that make up Slate Island. Hundreds of tons of slate have been quarried from this island since earliest times, though the quarry is no longer used. A hermit lived on the island in the middle of the nineteenth century. In recent years it has been used by a Scout group and as a duck preserve.

SNAKE ISLAND Two acres of marshy land about half a mile from Winthrop make up the irregularly shaped Snake Island. In the last century a few people lived on the island in shacks until the Winthrop Board of Health declared it a health hazard. Today it attracts adventuresome youngsters.

SPECTACLE ISLAND Named because its shape resembled a pair of spectacles, this 73.9-acre island consists of two peninsulas (North Head and South Head) connected by a short bar of land. Abundantly wooded when granted to Boston in 1635, it was denuded by early settlers. Later it was sold to private owners and the Samuel Bill family owned most of it from 1684 to 1742. For twenty years from 1717, the Quarantine Hospital was on this island. In the nineteenth century, there were two summer hotels, until their gambling games were raided by police in 1857. A factory rendering dead horses and cattle was on the island many years after that, to be succeeded by a garbage dump. There has been no dumping since 1959. Gulls and rats are the only residents.

THOMPSON'S ISLAND About three miles from Long Wharf and half a mile north of Squantum in Quincy lies the 157 acres of Thompson's Island. It is about a mile in length and a third of a mile wide. The Indians frequented the island, especially for excellent clams once bedded there. Under the name Island of Trevor, it was claimed in 1621 for David Thomson, a Scotchman, whose name is variously spelled, but has remained with the island. He apparently lived there from 1626 to 1628 running a trading post. Some of the foundation of his brick house was found in 1889. This was probably the first English building in Boston harbor and was burned by American rebels during the Revolution. For two hundred years the island was farmed by its many private owners. In 1832 it came into the possession of the Boston Farm School Society, which has until the present run what is now called the Boston Farm and Trades School. Perhaps its most famous graduate was Clarence De Mar, the marathon runner. The original woods have been replaced with many fine trees. It is possible that in the near future, Thompson's Island will be joined to the nearby mainland, and become a new residential area of the city.

Alternate Names

(At various periods, the harbor islands have had other names, and for ready reference they are listed below.)

Apthorp's—*see* Calf
Beacon—*see* Lighthouse
Belle Isle—*see* Hog
Bomkin—*see* Bumkin
Breed's—*see* Hog
Brereton's—*see* Noddle's
Conant's—*see* Governor's
Gallup—*see* Gallop
Galloupe—*see* Gallop
Governor's Garden—*see* Governor's
Great Calf—*see* Calf
Hoff's Thumb—*see* Nut
Hospital—*see* Rainsford
Ibrook's—*see* Langlee
Little Brewster—*see* Outer Brewster, also Lighthouse
Manning's Moon—*see* Moon
Mennen's Moon—*see* Moon
Moon Head—*see* Moon
Nelson's—*see* Long
Newcomb's—*see* Gallop's

North Brewster—*see* Green
Nottell's—*see* Noddle's
Outward—*see* Outer Brewster
Pemberton's—*see* George's
Pettick's—*see* Peddock's
Pumpkin—*see* Bumpkin
Quarantine—*see* Rainsford
Round—*see* Bumpkin
Sarah's—*see* Sailor
Sayles's—*see* Sailor
Sheaf—*see* Sheep
Sheen—*see* Sheep
Ship—*see* Sheep
Snow's—*see* Gallop's
Sun—*see* Sheep
Susanna—*see* Hog
Ward's—*see* Bumpkin
William's—*see* Noddle's
Winthrop Junction—*see* Hog
Winthrop's—*see* Governor's

The Boston Farm School on
Thompson's Island as it appeared
in 1852. The boys on the lower
right are busy haying.

Interlude two: Boston to 1700

Boston litterbugs

At a meeting of all the Seleckt men, it is ordered that noe person inhabiting within this Town shall throw forth or lay any intralls of beast or fowles or garbidg or Carion or dead dogs or Catts or any other dead beast or stinkeing thing, in any hie way or dich or Common within this neck of land of Boston, but ar injoynened to bury all such things that soe they may prevent all anoyanc unto any. Further it is ordered that noe person shall throw forth dust or dung or shreds of Cloth or lether or any tobacco stalks or any such thing into the streats.

—Boston Selectmen's Minutes
May 31, 1652

Light my fire

Whereas many careless persons carry fire from one house unto another in open fire pans or brand ends, by reason of which greatt damage may accrew to the towne; It is therefore ordered that no person shall have liberty to carry fire from one house to another, without a safe vessell to secure itt from the wind, upon the poenalty of ten shillings to bee paid by every party so fetching, and halfe so much by those that permitt them so to take fire.

—Boston Selectmen's Minutes
June 29, 1658

Violence in the streets, circa 1661

Upon a Lecture-day at *Boston* in *New England*, I was much pressed in Spirit to go into their Worshiphouse among them, where I stood silent until the Man had done Preaching, then my mouth was opened to the People with a word of Exhortation, but through the violence of some of the People was haled to Prison, from whence, about three hours after, they fetched me out to the Court, where I was examined, and so returned to Prison again until the Morning: and into the Court I was brought again, where they had drawn up a Paper against me, as they thought, of what I had said the day before; and they said, *Come thou Vagabond, and hear this Paper read with two Witnesses, their Hands to it, for we will handle thee:* and I said, *Read on;* Where I stood until they had done: And they asked me, *Whether I owned it, or no:* And I said, *Yea, every Word and would make it good by sound Proof if I might have Liberty to speak.* But they cried, *Away with him;* and some took me by the Throat, and would not suffer me to answer to it, but hurried me down Stairs, to the Carriage of a great Gun, which stood in the Market-Place, where I was stripped, and tied to the Wheel and whipped with Ten Stripes, and then loosed, and tied to a Cart's-tail; and whipped with Ten more to the Town's End; and at *Roxbury*, at a Cart's-tail, with other Ten; and at *Dedham*, at a Cart's-tail, with Ten more, and then sent into the Woods.
—Thomas Newhouse
    from *An Addition to the Book . . .* by Ellis Hookes

Elevens

For the more convenient and exspeditious dispatch of Marchants affayres or any other, or any other relatcing to strangers and our Inhabitants.

Itt is ordered that the Bell should be runge att a 11 of ye Clocke every workeing day to give notis thereof to all persons concernned and that the ringer shall be allowed 12 d. p yeare by every parson that commonly resort there unto and that that they may assemble in the Rome under the Towne house, for the space of one hower for the ends above expressed.
—Boston Selectmen's Minutes
July 25, 1664

The Reverend Mr. Eliot
tells a fish story

There hath been a rare work of God this summer in a great pond at Watertown, where all the fish died, and were not willing to die in the waters, but as many as could thrust themselves on shore, and there died; not less than twenty cart load, by estimation, lying dead, all at once, round about the pond. An eel was found alive in the sandy border of the pond, and being cast into the water, she wriggled out again, as fast as she could, and died on the shore. An inhabitant of the town, living by the pond, his cattle use daily to drink there; but then, for three days together, they refused there to drink, but after three days, they drank of the pond, as they were wont to do. When the fish began to come ashore, before they died, many were taken and eaten, both by English and Indians, without any hurt; and the fish were very good.

—John Eliot
from a letter to Robert Boyle
September 30, 1670

Re-iterated whoredoms

This County Court, three or four young men were convicted of several burglaries in breaking open warehouses, ketches, and cellars; Mary Moor and several, of fornication; some suspected for re-iterated whoredom; and also one Alice Thomas, of great suspicion to keep a brothelhouse. The good Lord give check to such wickedness, and grant it be not a punishment judicial! (Hos. iv. 13, 14).

—John Hull
Public Diary, January 30, 1672

Nothing love can't cure

Saturday Even. Aug 12, 1676, just as prayer ended Tim. Dwight sank down in a Swoun, and for a good space was as if he perceived not what was done to him: after, kicked and sprawled, knocking his hands and feet upon the floor like a distracted man. Was carried pickpack to bed by John Alcock, there his cloaths pulled off. In the night it seems he talked of ships, his master, father, and unckle Eliot. The Sabbath following Father went to him, spake to him to know what ailed him, askcd if he would be prayed for, and for what he would desire his friends to pray. He answered, for more sight of sin, and God's healing grace. I asked him, being alone with him, whether his troubles were from some outward cause or spiritual. He answered, spiritual. I asked him why then he could not tell it his master, as well as any other, since it is the honour of any man to see sin and be sorry for it. He gave no answer, as I remember. Asked him if he would goe to meeting. He said, 'twas in vain for him; his day was out. I asked, what day: he answered, of Grace. I told him 'twas sin for any one to conclude themselves Reprobate, that this was all one. He said he would speak more, but could not, &c. Notwithstanding all this semblance (and much more than is written) of compunction for Sin, 'tis to be feared that his trouble arose from a maid whom he passionately loved: for that when Mr. Dwight and his master had agreed to let him goe to her, he eftsoons grew well.

—Samuel Sewall
Diary

A criss-cross of coffins, 1678

Never was it such a time in Boston. Boston burying-places never filled so fast. It is easy to tell the time wherein we did not use to have the bells tolling for burials on a sabbath day morning by sunrise; to have 7 buried on a sabbath day night, after Meeting. To have coffins crossing each other as they have been carried in the street;—To have, I know not how many corpses following each other close at their heels,—To have 38 dye in one week,—6, 7, 8, or 9 in a day. Yet thus hath it lately been; and thus it is at this day. Above 340 have died of the Small Pox in Boston since it first assaulted the place. To attempt a Bill of Mortality, and number the very spires of grass in a Burying Place seem to have a parity of difficulty and in accomplishment.

—Cotton Mather
from a letter to John Cotton, circa November 1678

Bedbugs in Boston

June 23, 1680—We permitted those most in haste to go ashore before us, and then went ourselves. The skipper received us politely at his house, and so did his wife; but as it was Sunday, which it seems is somewhat strictly observed by these people, there was not much for us to do to-day. Our captain, however, took us to his sister's where we were welcome, and from there to his father's, an old corpulent man, where there was a repetition of the worship, which took place in the kitchen while they were turning the spit, and busy preparing a good supper. We arrived while they were engaged in the service, but he did not once look up. When he had finished, they turned round their backs, and kneeled on chairs or benches. The prayer was said loud enough to be heard three houses off, and also long enough, if that made it good. This done, he wished us and his son welcome, and insisted on our supping with him, which we did. There were nine or ten persons at the table. It being in the evening, and we strangers, Mr. Padechal requested us to lodge with him this night, as we did, intending in the morning to look out for accommodations. We were taken to a fine large chamber, but we were hardly in bed before we were shockingly bitten. I did not know the cause, but not being able to sleep, I became aware it was bed bugs, in such great numbers as was inconceivable. My comrade who was very sleepy, fell asleep at first. He tumbled about very much; but I did not sleep any the whole night. In the morning we saw how it was, and were astonished we should find such a room with such a lady.

—Jasper Danckaerts
A Voyage to New York etc.

When fig leaves were roses

A Vintner in Boston put up a new Sign called *The Rose and Crown,* with two Naked Boys being Supporters, and their Nudities Pendent: the sight disturbed one Justice S——r, who commanded it down; and away were the Boys sent to the Carvers to be dismembered: but the unlucky Dog of a Carver sent them back again two chopping Girles with Merkins exposed. This enraged the Justice more, and the sign was summoned before the wise Court, where they gravely determined (to keep the Girles from blushing) they should have Roses clapt upon their Merkins; which is the original of our new Proverb, *Under the Rose a Merkin.*

—J. W.
Letter from New-England, 1682

The Twenty-third Psalm in Algonquian

Jehovah, nussahkommoonukoowaenum; wanne teagwohnukquenuahikoo.

2. Nusseepsumwahik ashkolkohkontu nutussoowunuk ahtotapagodtut.

3. Wonkomohkinau nukketeahogkounoh nutussoowunuk wunnomwausseongane mayut newutche oowesoonk;

4. Nux, pomushaon wutonkauhtemut oonaunkoae nuppooonk; matta woh nukquehtamoo woskehittuonk: newutche kooweetomeh, kuppogkomunk, kah kutanwohhou noonenehukquog.

5. Kooncchoohkah ut anaquabeh, anaquabhettit nummatwomog; kussissequnum nuppuhkuh nashpe pummee, nootattamwaitch poomponeetupohshau.

6. Wunnamuhkut oonayeuonk kah monaneteaoak pishnutasukkonkqunath tohsohkcpomantam: kah pish nuttaih wekit Jehovah micheme.

—John Eliot
Up-Biblum God
1685 version

Boston had witches too—1688

Wee have a very strange thing among us, which we know not what to make of, except it bee Witchcraft, as we think it must needs bee. 3 or 4 children of one Goodwin, a Mason, that have been for some weeks grievously tormented, crying out of head, eies, tongue, teeth; breaking theyr neck, back, thighs, knees, leggs, feet, toes, &c. & then they roar out, Oh my head, Oh my neck, & from one part to another the pain runs almost as fast as I write it. The pain is (doubtles) very exquisite, & the cries most dolorous & affecting, & this is noteable, that two or more of them cry out of the same pain in the same part, at the same time, & as the pain shifts to another place in one, so in the other, & thus it holds them for an hour together & more; & when the pain is over they eat, drink, walk, play, laugh, as at other times. They are generally well a nights. A great many good Christians spent a day of prayer there. Mr. Morton came over, & wee each spent an hour in prayer, since which the parents suspecting an old woman & her daughter living hard by, complaint was made to the Justices, & compassion had so far, that the women were committed to prison & are there now. Yesterday I called in at the House, I was informed by the parent that since the women were confined the children have been well while out of the House, but as soon as any of them come into the House, then taken as formerly; so that now all theyr children keep at their neighbors houses. . . . Wee cannot but think the devill has an hand in it by some instrument.

—Rev. Joshua Moodey
from a letter to Increase Mather
October 14, 1688

Death at an early age

I took my little Daughter, *Katy*, [9 years old] into my Study; and there I told my Child, that I am to *dy* shortly, and shee must, when I am *Dead*, Remember every Thing, that I said unto her.

I sett before her, the sinful and woful Condition of her *Nature*, and I charg'd her, *to pray in secret Places*, every Day, without ceasing, that God for the Sake of Jesus Christ would give her a *New Heart*, and *pardon* Her Sins, and make her a *Servant* of His.

I gave her to understand, that when I am taken from her, shee must look to meet with more humbling *Afflictions* than shee does, now shee has a careful and a tender *Father* to provide for her; but, if shee would *pray* constantly, God in the Lord Jesus Christ, would bee a *Father* to her, and make all *Afflictions* work together for her Good.

I signified unto her, That the People of God, would much observe how shee carried herself, and that I had written a Book, about, *Ungodly Children*, in the Conclusion whereof I say, that this Book will bee a terrible Witness against my own Children, if any of them should not bee *Godly*.

At length, with many Tears, both on my Part, and hers, I told my Child, that God had from Heaven assured mee, and the good Angels of God had satisfied mee, *that shee shall bee brought Home unto the Lord Jesus Christ, and bee one of His forever.* I bid her use this, as an Encouragement unto her Supplications unto the Lord, for His Grace. But I therewithal told her, that if shee did not now, in her Childhood seek the Lord, and give herself up unto Him, some dreadful Afflictions must befal her, that so her Father's Faith, may come at its Accomplishments.

I thereupon made the Child kneel down by mee; and I poured out my Cries unto the Lord, that Hee would lay His Hands upon her, and bless her and save her, and make her a *Temple* of His Glory. It will bee so; It will be so!

—Rev. Cotton Mather
Diary, January 17, 1698

Of Boston, and the inhabitants

On the *South-west* side of *Massachusetts-Bay*, is *Boston;* whose Name is taken from a Town in *Lincoln-shire:* And is the Metropolis of all *New-England*. The Houses in some parts joyn as in *London*. The *Buildings*, like their *Women*, being *Neat* and *Handsome*. And their *Streets*, like the *Hearts* of the *Male Inhabitants*, are Paved with *Pebble*.

. . .

The Inhabitants seem very Religious, showing many outward and visible Signs of an inward and Spiritual Grace: But tho' they wear in their Faces the *Innocence* of *Doves*, you will find them in their Dealings, as *Subtile* as *Serpents*. *Interest* is their *Faith, Money* their *God*, and *Large Possessions* the only *Heaven* they covet.

Election, Commencement, and *Training-days*, are their only *Holy-days;* they keep no *Saints-Days*, nor will they allow the *Apostles* to be *Saints*, yet they assume that Sacred Dignity to themselves; and say, in the Title Page of their Psalm-Book, *Printed for the Edification of the Saints in* Old *and* New-England.

They have been very severe against *Adultery*, which they Punish'd with Death; yet, notwithstanding the Harshness of their Law, the Women are of such noble Souls, and undaunted Resolutions, that they will run the hazard of being Hang'd, rather than not be reveng'd on Matrimony, or forbear to discover the Corruption of their own Natures.

. . .

A couple of *Deacons* Marching along the Street, espied a Woman in a corner relieving Nature from the uneasiness of a Burthen she could keep no longer, one of them cryed out to tother, pointing to the Stooping object, *Brother, Brother, what a Shameful thing, what a Beastly thing is this? I Vow, Brother, this is a thing that ought to be Peep'd into.* The other being a more sensible Man, *Prithee Brother* (said he) *do thou Peep into't then, for I care not to run such a hazard of my Eye-sight. Besides* (said he) *the thing's to Deep for our inspection; and therefore we shall only be laugh'd at for meddling with the matter.*

. . .

I was mightily pleas'd one Morning with a Contention between two Boys at a Pump in *Boston*, about who should draw their Water first. One Jostled the other from the Handle, and he would fill his Bucket first, because his Master said *Prayers* and sung *Psalms* twice a Day in his family, and the others Master did not. To which the Witty Knave made this reply, *Our House stands backward in a Court; if my Master had a Room next the Street, as your Master has, he'd* Pray *twice to your Masters once, that he wou'd; and therefore I'll fill my Pail first, Marry will I;* and did accordingly.

—Edward Ward
A Trip to New-England (1699)

Piety in the privy

I was once emptying the *Cistern of Nature,* and making *Water* at the Wall. At the same Time there came a *Dog,* who did so too, before me. Thought I; "What mean, and vile Things are the Children of Men, in this mortal State! How much do our *natural Necessities* abase us, and place us in some regard, on the same Level with the very *Dogs!*"

My Thought proceeded. "Yett I will be a more noble Creature; and at the very Time, when my *natural Necessities* debase me into the Condition of the *Beast,* my *Spirit* shall (I say, *at that very Time!*) rise and soar, and fly up, towards the Employment of the *Angel.*"

Accordingly, I resolved, that it should be my ordinary Practice, whenever I step to answer the one or other *Necessity of Nature,* to make it an Opportunity of shaping in my Mind, some holy, noble, divine *Thought;* usually, by way of *occasional Reflection* on some sensible Object which I either then have before me, or have lately had so: a *Thought* that may leave upon my Spirit, some further *Tincture of Piety!*

And I have done according to this Resolution!

—Rev. Cotton Mather
Diary, June 1700

83

CHAPTER THREE

Kilroy Was Here

A Boston Light Infantryman of 1798, sketched by E. G. Austin. These men were members of a volunteer local military corps chartered by the Commonwealth. (Massachusetts Historical Society.)

The first military conflict in New England which concerned Bostonians took place some years before the town was founded. A frigate sent from the Jamestown Colony made two raids in Maine and the Bay of Fundy to eliminate some French outposts. Discouraging such rivals cleared the way for peaceful settlement of Massachusetts.

Any immediate threat to the Bay Colony would now come from its Indian neighbors. The settlers were careful to maintain correct relations with them, but in 1637 they got into a conflict with one tribe, the Pequots. Twenty Bay Colony men, led by Capt. John Underhill, joined with ninety Connecticut soldiers and five hundred Narragansett warriors to crush the Pequots. By September they had slain nearly nine hundred of them; the tribe was effectively destroyed, and Pequot lands were now available for English settlement.

Perhaps as a result of the military spirit roused by the Pequot war, the oldest military company in America was founded the next year. First named The Military Company of the Massachusetts, since 1738 it has been known as The Ancient and Honorable Artillery Company of Massachusetts. Gov. John Winthrop signed their charter in 1638, writing, however, a warning in his journal against the dangers of establishing "a standing authority of military men." Temporary levies to meet emergencies were better, these colonists felt, than any permanent military force.

The company was patterned on the Honorable Artillery Company of London dating from 1537. The merchant Robert Keayne was elected their first commander, and their first regular headquarters was in the town house erected by a bequest in his will on the present site of the Old State House. In 1746, they moved their headquarters to Faneuil Hall, where it still remains. The first Monday of June each year, they remember their founding almost in the same way as in 1638: a street parade, joined by the governor, a religious service, a drum-head election on the Common, and finally a dinner at Faneuil Hall.

A general militia was organized in 1644; all men except the "timerous" had to attend eight training days a year. After the Common had been purchased from William Blackstone, it was "laid out a place for a trayning field" for the militia. The hills behind it had military use, too. From them, said Edward Johnson in 1654, they keep "a constant watch to fore-see the approach of foreing dangers, being furnished with a Beacon and lowd babling Guns, to give notice by their redoubled eecho to all Sister-townes."

Indian trouble broke out again in 1675. Bitter toward Plymouth Colony for the murder of his brother, resentful over land encroachments, and generally distrustful of English expansion, the sachem of the Wampanoags, Metacomet (called "King Philip" by the English), plotted with the Nipmucks, the Pocumtucks, and the Narragansetts to destroy the English settlements. About six to eight thousand Indians supported him. At least five thousand Indians clearly favored the English, while the rest stayed neutral. It was a savage conflict on both sides. Raiding Indian bands came as close to Boston as Weymouth, Scituate, Sudbury, and Braintree.

A hysterical public grew distrustful even of the loyal Christian, or "praying" Indians in their midst. Many grave injustices blemished the record of relations between the two groups in these war years. Some of the English, notably John Eliot, Daniel Gookin, and Daniel Henchman, fought valiantly but vainly for their Indian friends. The General Court ordered the praying Indians into what today would be called a concentration camp on Deer Island in Boston Harbor. Here, more than five hundred men, women, and children endured a severe winter and over a year of hunger and disease before being released at the end of the war. This came in August 1676 when Capt. Benjamin Church of Plymouth and his Indian auxiliaries trapped Metacomet at Mount Hope and brought his bloody head in triumph into Plymouth for a special religious service of Thanksgiving. Some five thousand Indians and many more than a thousand English died in this war. It is estimated that a greater percentage of the population were casualties in this conflict than in any subsequent American war.

The threat of Dutch or French invasions from the sea had prompted the building from 1673 to 1681 of a defensive wall across the town cove from Copp's Hill on the north to Fort Hill on the south. Large trees and stones were used to make a suitable foundation for this seawall. Some 2,200 feet long, this "Barricado" as it was generally called, was to be manned with guns to defend the town. It was built across two little islands, and had a passageway

The monument on the Common commemorating the "Boston Massacre." Photo by H. G. Peabody (The Society for the Preservation of New England Antiquities).

Castle William on the left (now Castle Island) protected Boston from attack by the sea. Pictured just before the Revolution by Joseph F. W. Des Barres in *The Atlantic Neptune*.

either side of Long Wharf so ships could enter the protected area. Since the wall was built by private subscription, investors had the right to build wharves and warehouses on the Barricado. Nobody ever attacked the town by sea, and it gradually fell into disuse. Bits of it survived for at least a century, and parts of it were incorporated into T Wharf and Central Wharf. Atlantic Avenue today, partly follows the old Barricado line.

As the threat from the Indians declined, that of the French rose. America was naturally dragged into the European conflicts of Great Britain and France. In King William's War (1689–97), Boston merchants financed an expedition of five armed sloops against Port Royal in Nova Scotia, under the command of Sir William Phips. The success of this expedition paid off handsomely in booty for its investors. In Queen Anne's War (1702–13), Boston troops joined Col. Benjamin Church's expedition of 1704 to punish the French for an Indian raid on Deerfield. That same year, Sarah Kemble Knight watched one of the Boston training days, always a great social occasion. "The Youth divert themselves by Shooting at the Target." There were prizes for the winner: "hee that hitts neerest the white has some yards of Red Ribbin presented him, which being tied to his hatt band, the two ends streeming down his back, he is Led away in Triumph with great applause, as the winners of the Olympiack Games."

King George's War (1739–48) saw Boston participate in the attack on Cape Breton's great Louisbourg fortress which commanded the entrance of the St. Lawrence River. Massachusetts sent three thousand men on this expedition, including twenty Ancient and Honorables. Joined by a small British squadron, the fort was captured by daring and audacious enterprise, only to see the peace treaty restore it to the French to the complete disgust of the Americans.

The French and Indian War (1754–63) that gave Col. George Washington his baptism by fire, saw two thousand New Englanders joining a campaign against Nova Scotia. The forcible relocation of the Acadians, prompting Longfellow's poem "Evangeline," occurred on this expedition. In 1757 Louisbourg was attacked unsuccessfully, only to be captured and destroyed the following year after a costly battle. The treaty ending this war gave Canada to the British.

With little to fear from the French or Indians, problems arose between England and America. After this succession of wars, the British faced a large

debt, principally from defending the colonies. The London government felt they should bear some of the expense, yet the colonists were accustomed to a liberty which the home Englishmen did not know. The "Stamp Act," only a minor tax such as any twentieth-century government could easily levy, was fiercely opposed. Bostonians showed their resentment by burning the house of the Chief Justice, Thomas Hutchinson, destroying unique historical documents in the blaze. Life was made so miserable for tax collectors that the act became unenforceable, and Parliament eventually repealed it.

But with a change of ministries, new duties were laid on certain imports. Patriotic merchants retaliated with nonimportation agreements, and imports from England dropped significantly. Troops were sent to Boston to cow the rebellious subjects. Their presence was skillfully exploited by such discontented citizens as Samuel Adams. After a winter of scuffles and incidents between soldiers and certain inhabitants, Monday night, March 5, 1770, there was a street encounter between a snow-balling mob and a squad of soldiers protecting the King's Custom House. Unduly harassed, a soldier fired, followed by the others. The crowd scattered, leaving five dead or dying, and more wounded. The Adams group quickly and expertly exploited the incident, calling it the "Boston Massacre." Military units had to be withdrawn from Boston. A legal trial of the involved soldiers brought "not guilty" verdicts for all but two, who were granted legal exemption called "benefit of clergy," and burnt on the thumb. One of them was a tough private named Matthew Kilroy. "Kilroy was here!" Not, of course, the Kilroy made famous in the second world war, but nevertheless a genuine Kilroy who for the rest of his anonymous life bore Boston's brand on his thumb.

Much to Samuel Adams' displeasure, English–American relations seemed to improve after the "Massacre." Although Adams arranged yearly "Orations"

The blockade of Boston in 1768 as depicted by Christopher Remick. (Massachusetts Historical Society.)

The old powderhouse at North Somerville, pictured in 1900 by H. G. Peabody. This was raided by Gage's troops some little time before his fateful expedition to Concord. (The Society for the Preservation of New England Antiquities.)

in memory of the Massacre dead, touching on Governor Winthrop's ancient theme of the dangers of standing armies, he could stir up few real grievances until London did it for him. A tax on tea, laid and paid in England, but passed on to drinkers in Boston brought new agitation. Failing to bar the taxed tea from Boston, a group of activists, disguised as Indians, went down to the vessels, and made salt-water tea. London reacted by closing the port of Boston, and to enforce this, sent over troops under Gen. Thomas Gage. A prudent, patient man, Gage, to nobody's satisfaction, generally kept the potentially explosive situation damped down. Then he made one mistake—and it only took one to turn the world upside down. He sent out an expedition of seven hundred soldiers on the night of April 18, 1775, to destroy military stores illegally accumulated in the town of Concord.

Incredible delays permitted two messengers from Boston to warn Adams and John Hancock, then in Lexington, of the danger, while a third rider took the alarm to Concord, all before the British troops had even left Boston. When the Redcoats reached Lexington Common in the morning chill, forty minutemen, in a straggling line confronted them, with perhaps thirty more milling nearby. It was a foolish confrontation, probably engineered by Samuel Adams who would have welcomed any "incident" to further his plans. Ordered to disarm and disperse, the minutemen did only the latter. Somebody fired, nobody knows who, and immediately, the British began "a scattered fire" as their officers tried to restrain them. Some of the colonials fired back. Shortly, eight Lexington men lay dead, with more wounded, and Adams had his "incident."

When the British had restored order, they marched to Concord, five miles beyond. There more than two hundred and fifty militia had assembled, with more constantly arriving. While the British destroyed the few supplies they could find, the militia kept out of their way, across North Bridge. A small British unit of about thirty-five men was sent to guard the bridge. Smoke from the burning supplies in town led the minutemen to assume mistakenly their homes were burning. They attacked and easily drove off the unit at the bridge, then withdrew realizing the town was not on fire. For two more hours, the British lingered aimlessly in Concord, then started the long nineteen-mile hike back to safety. Before they reached Lexington, minutemen were engaged in hot skirmishing with the British on the road, while the locals took every advantage of trees, stone walls, fences, houses, and barns. If the guns of the day hadn't been so inefficient, it would have been a slaughter. Near Lexington, the British panicked, running into the arms of reinforcements under Earl Percy sent out by Gage. After resting and regrouping, Percy conducted them back to Charlestown under continual harassment. Flanking troops Percy put out helped keep the British deaths down. Still, seventy-three British and forty-nine Americans died as a result of that day's action.

This day's event triggered a war. It unified Massachusetts and the other colonies in resistance to the King and it shut the British up in Boston. Some twenty thousand men converged on Boston from all over New England. The rebels rushed their account of the battle to England where it arrived two weeks before Gage's official report. Standard propaganda, it was replete with imaginary murders, plunderings, burnings, and atrocities—all committed by the dastardly British army upon helpless Americans. Inside Boston, all was confusion. Arrangements were made to let rebel sympathizers depart once they had given up their firearms and left most of their goods behind. The besiegers, too, permitted Tory refugees to enter the town. Eventually the British retained people when they realized their value as hostages.

Food prices soared. It became a major problem to feed horses and cattle. Soldiers were sent to harvest hay on the harbor islands. Outside Boston, the food situation wasn't much better, with such a sudden influx of hungry males. It became more of a problem than Gage. Eight soldiers stationed in Roxbury petitioned their representatives about bad food. "We many times have drawn

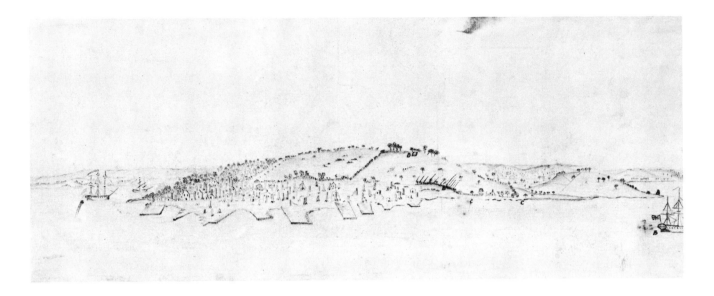

Charlestown, shortly after the battle of Bunker Hill had left it a ruin. The view is from Boston's North End, by a British artist, with notations apparently in Lord Howe's hand. The letter *C* indicates where his troops landed, and the redoubt of the rebels on the hill is marked *D*. (Unpublished drawing in the Gage papers at the William Clements Library, University of Michigan.)

Such Roten Stinkin meat that the Smell is Sufficient to make us lothe the Same." If things didn't get better, they threatened to "Swing their packs Emediately and go home boldly throu all the Guards."

Soon such complaints faded in a dangerous threat by Gage to occupy the deserted Charlestown peninsula. To prevent this, the rebels moved a thousand men into the area the night of June 16, and fortified Breed's Hill, the lower eminence nearer Boston. It was a tactical blunder. The British only needed to send ships and troops around the peninsula, land them on Charlestown Neck, and bottle up the lot of them. Instead, British generals decided on a standard frontal assault. Although they had known of the rebels on the hill since at least 4:00 A.M., that morning's only activity was cannonading of the position by the ships. Not until 2:00 P.M. did British troops under Gen. William Howe arrive by barge on Charlestown, unloading some 1,500 infantry on Morton's Point.

Spectators jammed the hills and housetops of Boston and outside the town, watching the meadows and hills of Charlestown as if it were a gigantic coliseum. Howe's first action was to set fire to Charlestown to deny snipers sanctuary on his flank. Shortly the old town was blazing fiercely, as spectators watched with mixed horror and fascination.

About three o'clock, Howe attacked. His left was to swing around Breed's and come in on the redoubt from behind; his right was to strike the rebel line that ran down to the Mystic River; his center was to march up the meadows and storm the redoubt. Nothing went right. With little ammunition, the rebels were ordered not to fire until the enemy was very close, and to aim particularly at the officers. Howe's right got to the rebel barricade first. A deadly blast tore apart both their first and second line, and broke up their attack, the soldiers fleeing in panic. Howe's center was blasted in the same fashion moments later, and they too reeled back. Howe's left never got to carry out their part, since

they shifted to aid the center. Howe now collected all units and mounted a second straight attack on the redoubt. This, too, was driven back by deadly fire of the protected rebels.

After a longer breathing pause, the British gamely returned. The rebels were nearly out of gunpowder ,and only halted them briefly. Then the British went in with bayonets, while the rebels retreated in great clouds of dust, protected by their own undefeated left flank. Most escaped across the Neck, in the face of deadly cannon fire from the ships. By 5:30 the British held the field with at least 226 (more likely 250) dead out of the 2,300 involved. (Their total casualties were 1,150 or 50 percent.) The rebels perhaps had 3,500 engaged in the battle at various times, and suffered casualties of 13 percent (about 138 killed).

British casualties were brought by barges to Long Wharf, where various vehicles including wheelbarrows took them to shelter. Doctors and surgeons gave what little help they could. Said an eyewitness, it was "the most melancholy scene ever beheld in this part of the world." Outside Boston, the rebels were desperately short of powder, and uncertain when or where the British might hit them next. So they dug in. Said a Boston observer five days after the battle for Bunker Hill, the rebels were "fortifying at Chelsea, Malden, Winter-hill, the hills in Roxbury, Dorchester, and *where* not? Every inch of ground will be

Monument on Breed's Hill to the battle of Bunker Hill, begun in 1825, completed in 1843. The Mallory view, now at the Massachusetts Historical Society.

disputed." But this was the last big battle around Boston. Skirmishes occurred, a house would be burned, a horse "knocked in the Head," a man or two would be killed, "or lose a Leg or an Arm," said an onlooker, as if in jest. Generals changed. Gage went home. Washington was appointed by the Continental Congress to take charge of the American "Continental Army."

During the brisk winter of 1775–76, Henry Knox brought the heavy guns captured at Fort Ticonderoga the previous May down to Boston across New York and Massachusetts, fortunately crusted with snow and ice. This gave Washington needed artillery power, and on the night of March 4, he had them carted to fortifications on Dorchester Heights overlooking Boston. This put the British in an impossible situation. Howe planned a counterattack, but "about midnight the wind blew almost a hurricane," and it was impossible for boats to cross the channel. March 17, the British sailed away from Boston, never to rule there again.

The Declaration of Independence text reached Boston in mid-July, and was read to the townspeople from the balcony on the Old State House on King Street. That evening, any signboard which bore symbols of the British rule, or had belonged to Tories, was yanked down, lugged to King Street, and consumed in a huge bonfire. With the field of battle now far south of Boston, the townfolk turned to such more profitable endeavors as sending out privateers to raid ships supplying the British army. Many brought rich prizes into port and made much money for their owners and crews.

Early in November 1781, the victory over Cornwallis at Yorktown several weeks before was celebrated on the Common with bonfires and happy crowds. The end was approaching, and news of the signing of the peace treaty early in 1784 was almost an anticlimax, though celebrated with the jubilation it deserved. From now on Americans were their own masters—and Boston was where it all began!

After little more than twenty-five years the country was again fighting the British. In late June of 1812, Boston heard the news of President Madison's declaration of this second war with England. Of all the wars fought by the United States, this was the most unpopular one in New England. Federalists from the first excoriated "this most vile war." But they were willing to honor and parade for the early victories of the American navy, while "detesting the Authors of such unnecessary Carnage, our war-making Administration." The local chapter of the Washington Benevolent Society became one of the foci of the protest of the town's prominent and well-to-do citizens. Then the navy suffered a defeat just beyond Boston harbor when the British *Shannon* on June 1, 1813, forced the U.S. *Chesapeake* to lower its flag, after killing the captain and many of its crew. When the Democrats brought back the captain's body for burial, the funeral turned into a political football, with Federalists refusing to take part, asserting it honored "an unlawful & wicked war."

The boys of Boston were not worrying about such matters. On the backside of Beacon Hill, where the leveling off had exposed many huge boulders, their vivid imaginations made privateers out of the rocks. Chalking names of their

Broadside issued in Boston celebrating Perry's victory over the British on Lake Erie in the War of 1812. (Courtesy of Massachusetts Historical Society.)

BRILLIANT NAVAL VICTORY.

YANKEE PERRY, BETTER THAN OLD ENGLISH CIDER.

"TUNE---THREE YANKEE PIGEONS."

HUZZA ! for the brave Yankee boys,
　Who touch'd up John Bull on lake Erie,
Who gave 'em a taste of our toys,
　From the fleet of brave Commodore *Perry*.

They were not made of 'lasses but lead,
　And good solid lumps of cold iron,
When they hit JOHNNY BULL in the head,
　They gave him a pain that he'll die on.

Now the *Niagara* bore down,
　To give 'em a bit of a whacking,
The *Lawrence* came up and wore round,
　And set her nine pounders a cracking.

They soon felt the *Scorpion's* sting,
　And likewise the *Æriel's* thunder,
The *Porcupine* give 'em a quill,
　And made the Queen Charlotte knock under.

The *Somers* now gave 'em a touch,
　And the *Tygress* she gave him a shock sir,
Which did not divert Johnny much,
　For it put him in mind of the BOXER.

The *Trip* she was hammering away,
　The *Oris* soon made 'em smell powder,
The brave *Caledonia* that day
　Made her thunder grow louder and louder.

We gave 'em such tough yankee blows,
　That soon they thought fit to surrender ;
That day made 'em feel that their foes,
　Were made in the masculine gender.

Poor Johnny was sick of the gripes,
　From the pills that we gave them at Erie,
And for fear of the stars and the stripes,
　He struck to brave Commodore PERRY.

Now as for poor old Johnny Bull,
　If we meet him on land or on Sea sir,
We'll give him a good belly full,
　Of excellent gun powder tea sir.

Old England is fam'd for her perry and beer,
　Which quickly bewilders the brain,
But such PERRY as she's taken here,
　She never will wish for again.

Huzza ! for our brave Yankee Tars,
　Who pepper'd the British so merry,
Who fought for the stripes and the stars,
　Under brave Commodore PERRY.

☞ Printed by N. COVERLY, Milk-Street.

favorites on the sides of the rocks—"The Saucy Jack" or "The True Blue Yankee"—they climbed up and refought their battles using the abundant crop of local stones for ammunition.

The British fleet gradually tightened the blockade around Boston, and the war which was being fought elsewhere in the west and south, began to look as if it might touch home. By summer 1814 Bostonians began to worry in earnest. The British fleet was chasing ships ashore and burning them at Beverly, Manchester, and Gloucester on the north and at Scituate and Cohasset on the south. They were even sailing boldly into the harbor. After the burning of Washington, Boston took hasty defense measures. Forts were put up. Adults and children alike (even eleven-year-old Ralph Waldo Emerson) worked to construct Fort Strong on Noddle's Island.

September and October were the months of most danger. By November the threat had passed, but politically the situation became critical. Extreme Federalists, frustrated by their impotence in persuading the government to change or moderate its war policy, were ready to remove New England from the Union. A convention at Hartford that December run by moderates didn't recommend secession. Three Boston men were sent by the state to consult with the government about war problems. News of the victory at New Orleans, then of the peace treaty, ended their mission. On February 13, 1815, when the peace news reached Boston, it was something both Democrats and Federalists could cheer. The town was in an uproar of clanging bells, firing guns, and shouting people. The popular quip with some was: "Peace ratified; Federalists gratified; Democrats mortified."

Three decades passed and in May 1846 President Polk took the country into a war with Mexico. A few romantic spirits saw this war as "the eagle of liberty" spreading "his broad pinions over the plains of the west." More, like Charles Sumner, not yet a senator, saw it adding new lands to the Union that could be exploited by slave-owning cottonmen. Many Northern textile manufacturers supported the war, but Sumner denounced this union between "the lords of the lash and the lords of the loom." Charles Francis Adams, descendant of two Presidents, excoriated Massachusetts Sen. Robert C. Winthrop for his "grievously wrong" support for "the atrocity of this war." Wendell Phillips went him one better, passionately proposing to a public meeting that they nail Winthrop "right to the floor of Faneuil Hall, and leave him there." Theodore Parker preached vigorously against the war, calling it "treason against man" and advising his congregation to refuse "to take any part in it; we can encourage others to do the same; we can aid men, if need be, who suffer because they refuse."

So opposed were the Massachusetts "Conscience Whigs" to this war that they obstructed efforts of the government to raise a volunteer regiment to take part in it. Col. Caleb Cushing headed the regiment, but when he made a dramatic plea in the General Court for funds to support it, they turned him down by a whopping majority. He outfitted his unit largely from his own funds, though he was later reimbursed by Congress.

Capt. G. T. Bigelow of the New England Guards (a corps whose initials were humorously said to stand for "Not Enough Grog") pictured in an 1840 lithograph by P. S. Duval for a piece of music.

Banner of the National Lancers.

View of the training encampment of the New England Guards at Savin Hill, Dorcester, in 1819. Painted by Benjamin B. Curtis. (Courtesy of The Bostonian Society, Old State House.)

Raising recruits on Washington Street for the war with Mexico (Old South Church in the background). Drawn by Howard Pyle (1853–1911), a sort of Norman Rockwell of the late nineteenth century. (Courtesy of The Bostonian Society, Old State House.)

There were many inaudible people who either approved of the war, or who went along with it. It was hard not to celebrate American victories, and private subscriptions paid for a one hundred-gun salute on the Common the end of May 1846 to mark these. That Fourth of July, a fireworks display on the Common included an elaborate representation of the bombardment of Vera Cruz. An enterprising lad the next day scavenging on the Common, recovered three ladies' bustles somehow lost as Vera Cruz had surrendered in fire and flame.

Two Greater Bostonians made literary history because of the Mexican War. Thoreau, clapped into jail in July of 1846 for not paying taxes to support that war, developed his "Essay on Civil Disobedience" which is still influencing the world. James Russell Lowell wrote his first series of Bigelow Papers, in amusing rural dialect, against the war. They were immediately popular and reflected the deep misgivings of many New Englanders about the war.

(Top) Entrance to the Navy Yard at Charlestown in the mid-nineteenth century. (Middle) Cannon balls stacked neatly inside the Navy Yard, photograph by Josiah J. Hawes. (Bottom) Parade ground and barracks in the Navy Yard, 1852.

Seeking enlistments for the Civil War, 1862, in front of the Old South Church on Washington Street.

When peace came in early 1848, it brought joy only that the killing had stopped. The annexing of foreign territory was not popular with all. Daniel Webster voted to reject the peace treaty for this reason, and the antagonisms revealed under the surface of American life between the North and South, now spluttered in the open until they exploded, nearly tearing the Union apart.

After the firing on Fort Sumter, President Lincoln proclaimed war between the United States and the seceding States on April 15, 1861. Despite their diverse feelings about slavery and abolition, most Bostonians rallied behind Lincoln and the Union. Boston streets soon had hundreds of flags draped across them flapping in the brisk spring breezes. Both ladies and horses proudly wore the national colors, the horses having theirs in the form of small flags fastened to their harnesses. Military processions, parades, reviews, and receptions jammed the streets. The militia were heroes of the hour as they reported for duty, many thinking of themselves as the "Minutemen of '61."

Not all were so bellicose. Henry James, Sr., felt that "no existing government . . . is worth an honest human life." He wanted neither of his sons, William or Henry, Jr., to enlist, nor did they. "No young American," he maintained, "should put himself in the way of death until he has realized something of the good of life." There was no mass enlistment of college students during the war, though many served, and quite a few died. Nor was there any great public propaganda to get them to enlist. Lincoln kept his own son at Harvard until his graduation in 1864, and then got him a safe staff job. The two sons of Edward Everett, former governor and senator, paid their fee and escaped the draft. College life went on pretty much undisturbed, although Harvard's Boat Club gave up races for three of the war years.

The great carnage of this uncivil war finally proved the volunteer system inadequate to supply the manpower needed. A year after the South adopted conscription, the North did too. The response to this in July of 1863, just after the battle of Gettysburg, was a great draft riot in New York City, closely followed by a minor one in Boston on Tuesday, July 14. It began about 1:00 P.M. when two marshals distributing draft notices in the North End were attacked by a woman who thought they had come for her husband. Her screeching attracted a crowd that beat up the marshals. Police sent to disperse the crowd were mauled. A mob of nearly two thousand gathered at the Hanover Street police station but eventually dispersed without incident.

This gave the city administration time to prepare for the evening. Soldiers were ordered into the city to supplement the police. By 7:00 P.M., the mob had returned for an assault on the Cooper Street Armory, where both police and soldiers were stationed. Stones and bricks were thrown, windows broken, and the main door forced. Inside, a gun loaded with cannister shot was fired at the mob. At least six were killed, others wounded. A bayonet charge discouraged even the most combative. A group of rioters ran off to Dock Square to break into a gun shop shouting, "We'll give 'em New York." But the police successfully prevented this. The arrest of several of the apparent ringleaders helped to dampen enthusiasm. Patrolling soldiers also calmed things down,

Ribs of the *Sparrowhawk,* a
Confederate vessel, exhibited on
Boston Common about 1865,
photographed by Josiah J. Hawes.

"Warriors Against Slavery" as
seen by Dr. William Rimmer in a
watercolor of 1863 which he contributed to raise money for the
Union cause. (Courtesy of
Museum of Fine Arts, Boston.)

though toward 1:00 A.M. an attempt was made to burn the Cooper Street
Armory. This was quelled with only minor injuries to a few firemen attacked
by the hostile crowd. Five men were eventually tried for "causing" the riot and
convicted. At least twenty lives were lost in the affray, and for some weeks
afterward, Boston was never so quiet.

More than a year of bloody fighting lay ahead of the Union troops, but the
end was no longer in doubt. Boston seemed much nearer the battlefield than
it was, with regiments constantly passing through its streets and railway
stations, on their way home to friends and furlough, or back to join the Army
of the Potomac in the deadly woods of The Wilderness. Mayor F. W. Lincoln
could report as 1864 began that more than twelve thousand Bostonians were
serving on land and sea, while over $300,000 had been spent in the past year
on relief for their families.

Finally the long agony ended. When news reached Boston on April 10, 1865,
that Lee had surrendered, Boston burst with delight. "Cannon are roaring on
the Common," reported one observer, "flags are thrown out from almost every
building, bells are pealing, twenty steam-engines are rushing, screaming
through the streets, and people are running crazy with joy." The joy lasted only
five days, turning to deepest sorrow on the fifteenth with news of the President's

assassination. Shops immediately shut their doors, and in a few hours black buntings draped buildings and homes and tried to say what people couldn't.

Another President who was going to be assassinated, William McKinley, took the country into war with Spain in April 1898. One wag called it the Yanko-Spanko war. New England's immediate concern—after "beautiful, bleeding Cuba"—was for its own coastline. Suppose the Spanish navy should seize the Portsmouth, New Hampshire, navy yard? It would serve as a useful base for an attack on Boston or New York. So mines were laid in the harbor and no vessels permitted to enter or leave from 8:00 P.M. to 4:00 A.M. The First Corps of Cadets was sent to Nahant and Hull to man coast defenses, while the Second Corps went to Naugus Head. Even Grover's Cliff in Winthrop was fortified against possible Spanish assault.

Merchants felt it their patriotic duty to secure a government supply depot for Boston. Society girls volunteered for the Red Cross. Harvard alumni collected money to outfit an auxiliary cruiser bearing the name *Harvard*. Local militia companies were mustered into governmental service at Camp Dalton in South Framingham. The end of May, fifteen hundred people crowded onto a special train to visit the camp and bid good-by to their relatives in the Ninth Regiment before it sailed for Cuba.

The Frigate *Constitution* ("Old Ironsides") returns to Boston on the 100th anniversary of her launching, 1897. She is being saluted by the ships of "The Great White Fleet." (Courtesy of Massachusetts Historical Society.)

Massachusetts Volunteers passing in review before Governor Wolcott on Beacon Street, on their way to the Spanish-American war, 1898.

Patriotism ran high. The Chelsea Congregational Church hung a huge American flag above the pulpit and lustily sang "The Star-Spangled Banner" one Sunday. Victory followed victory. The Boston *Journal* reported every skirmish at great length, with maps and pictures of local men in Cuba. Enthusiasm for the war collapsed, as quickly as it soared. The distinguished Col. Henry Lee was but one of many Greater Bostonians in "extreme distress" because of "our precipitation into an inexcusable war." He called for a "most solemn" protest against it as "contrary to justice, contrary to our best traditions and directly opposed to the fervent wishes of a majority of our people." Gamaliel Bradford strongly opposed any "territorial expansion," and felt the country had gone into the war just to keep the Republican party in power.

The most determined of these vocal opponents of the war undoubtedly was Prof. Charles Eliot Norton of Harvard. Soon after Congress declared war, he told his students that it could have been avoided, was being conducted in a barbarous manner, and consequently was "criminal." He urged them to consider if the best use an American could make of his life was to "enlist in such a war." For this stand he was abused by popular papers and the super-patriots. One illiterate Massachusetts soldier denounced him as "a unamircan ass." William James seconded Norton, though, advising the students not to "yelp with the pack."

ARMORY OF THE FIRST CORPS OF CADETS MASSACHUSETTS VOLUNTEER MILITIA · BOSTON Wm GIBBONS PRESTON ARCHITECT ·

Armory in the style of a castle of the First Corps of Cadets on the corner of Arlington Street and Columbus Avenue, now temporarily in use as a library for the University of Massachusetts, Boston.

Few were displeased in August with the armistice that stopped the short war while a treaty was hammered out. Fierce were the arguments, however, about the morality of annexing the Philippines. Most Bostonians contentedly returned to smoking their Lillian Russell five-cent cigars, drinking their Paine's Celery Compound, and watching the Odd Fellows parade through town. Some few of these smokers, drinkers, and watchers were also busy postdating their pension vouchers and violating the internal revenue laws passed to pay for the war. Norton was not, apparently, the only "unamircan ass" in Boston.

America's entry into World War I surprised few; for more than two years they had seen themselves gradually being sucked into the European whirlpool. Sen. Henry Cabot Lodge was one of the first to advocate—in a vulgar phrase— "putting the fist in pacifist." In April 1917 he got his wish. Soon men in khaki were seen everywhere. Brookline plowed up town lands for food gardens. The Museum of Fine Arts thought of moving their rarer objects to safety in case the Germans should bomb Boston. The Houghton and Dutton store on Tremont Street flew the flags of the allies. Recruiting tents blossomed on Lafayette Mall. "Liberty Bond" drives were started with posters promoting them in "every car, every office window." "Those who did not wear a button to prove that a bond had been purchased felt very uncomfortable." Camp Devens

ENSE PETIT PLACIDAM
SVB LIBERTATE QVIETEM

© R·RUZICKA·1917·

View of Camp Devens, near Ayer, Mass. Colored engraving on wood made by Rudolph Ruzicka in 1917. (Courtesy of Rudolph Ruzicka.)

at Ayer opened to train thousands of draftees. Bishop Lawrence worried about the preservation of "sound morals" at the camp, fearing that "the brewer and the prostitute" would become the "chauffeur, comrade and friend" of "our 'Sammies'."

A distressing intolerance of any antiwar opinion gripped the country and Boston. Pacifist Prof. Clarence Skinner at Tufts College was shunned by colleagues, while Prof. Emily Greene Balch at Wellesley College was dropped because of her staunch peace opinions. Rev. A. J. Muste had to resign his pastorate at Newton Center because of his pacifist convictions. Even Mrs. Jack Gardner got called "that hateful pro-German." When Karl Muck, the conductor of the Boston Symphony Orchestra, was arrested in March 1918 as an enemy alien, Major Higginson, founder of the orchestra, took to his bed, and Bostonians enjoyed the ridiculous rumor that Muck had been reporting troop movements to the Germans through his contacts in the "white slave" business.

When Hugo Munsterberg, psychology professor at Harvard, defended the German cause, an English alumnus offered the university $10 million if President Lowell would fire him. Munsterberg promised to resign if the man would send over half the sum. There was no reply from the Englishman, nor was Lowell even tempted. Instead Lowell vigorously defended academic freedom and somehow, Harvard limped on without the Englishman's millions.

The war lifted Boston out of an economic slump. A big Army Supply Base was built in South Boston at a cost of $75 million. The city became the military and naval headquarters of New England, and a principal war shipping port to Europe. The harbor was mined, and a wire net stretched across the channels to keep out German submarines. The war completed the federalization of the former Massachusetts Volunteer Militia, now part of the National Guard. When taken into federal service, it became the Twenty-sixth Division, the famed "Yankee Division," under Maj. Gen. Clarence R. Edwards. Norman Prince, a Boston aviator, organized and led the celebrated Lafayette Escadrille.

Bostonians who stayed behind were busy in the Red Cross, the YMCA, YWCA, the National Catholic War Council, the Jewish Welfare Board, the Salvation Army, and dozens of other agencies that sprang up to meet war needs. Colleges became veritable armed camps. Uniformed Tufts students marched and countermarched over their hill-top campus. Harvard students dug trenches around Fresh Pond and fought mimic battles. Through its aeronautical school, M.I.T. aided in training American aviators.

Food and fuel shortages brought the war into everybody's home with wheatless, meatless, fat-saving, and sugar-saving days. Five small Conservation Cottages were put up on the Common to promote these special days. Coal was severely rationed and Bostonians shivered through the frigid winter of 1917–18.

For some, the "cruelest month" was April 1918 when the state joined the rest of the nation in voting for prohibition. Overjoyed, the bells at Park Street Congregational Church rang and rang to welcome the era of national dryness. Fortunately, the ban didn't include the soldiers in France, or the war might have been lost.

The final blow of the war was the influenza epidemic in the fall of 1918. Boston had ten times as many cases as New York, and "whole families die two days after being taken sick." All theaters and movie houses were closed, and the telephone company asked subscribers not to phone if possible since many of their staff were either sick or dead.

After a false armistice report November 7, the real thing came at last with the shriek of a whistle at 3:15 A.M. on November 11. Church bells began

Emily **Greene Balch,** who shared the Nobel **Peace Prize** in 1946.

When the "boys" came back from "over there." Huge victory parade of the Twenty-sixth Division down Commonwealth Avenue between Charlesgate East and Massachusetts Avenue on April 25, 1919.

ringing in half an hour, and Boston streets were crowded with joyful people, one girl striking a tin plate with a curry comb, a fellow banging away on a metal typewriter cover. The whole performance was duplicated on April 25, 1919, when troops returned and Boston held a mammoth welcome-home parade for its "doughboys."

The coming of World War II, particularly after the Munich Pact of 1938, did not surprise many Bostonians. The city's sympathies were largely with the Allies, and against the Axis even before American involvement. The Japanese attack on Pearl Harbor united most Americans after December 7, 1941. Poet Robert Frost noted that it was the first radio war, with the radios burbling out "gay songs, big talk about our celebrating Xmas in Berlin and next Fourth of July in Tokyo." The "home front" learned to press tin cans, use war ration books, fit on air raid warden helmets, practice first aid, and "knit for Britain."

The war was not all fun and games with German submarines sinking ships off the Atlantic coast. Merchant ships had to move in and out of Boston harbor in convoy. War industries worked round the clock, and with men drafted, women swelled the factory ranks. After a test blackout in February 1942, Bostonians became familiar with living in dim-outs and blackouts. Dahl cartoons in the Boston *Herald* pictured the amusing results.

106

Not only Boston men and women went to war, Boston's iron fences were conscripted too. In December 1942, Mayor Tobin took an acetylene torch to make the first cut in the fence around the Common. The State House fence went too. Newspapers carried lists of private contributors of fences, too few of which were replaced after the war. The mayor's wife christened the sixth navy vessel bearing the name *Boston*, while the mayor himself dug the first of more than ten thousand Victory Gardens, some of which still are planted several wars later.

Over the winter months of 1943–44, while the gas ovens at Auschwitz were operating full blast, an ugly series of antisemitic incidents plagued Dorchester's Fourteenth Ward. This ward was then a 98 percent Jewish-American island in an Irish-American ocean. When New York newspapers broke the story (Boston papers hadn't reported it), Gov. Leverett Saltonstall indignantly denied it, only to admit his error later, and take what few steps can be taken to ease such stupid situations.

The war years created many pressing moral problems for thoughtful Bostonians: the firebombing of enemy cities, the inflexible demand for "unconditional surrender," the problems of a postwar world, and then the consequences of dropping the world's first atom bomb, *twice*. On August 14, 1945, while the

Crowd of 100,000 (including author) protesting the Vietnam War on Boston Common on October 15, 1969, as photographed by *Boston Globe* photographer Jack O'Connell.

107

city celebrated the new peace, and while North End youngsters whooped it up with whistles and kettles and their own lung power, such people, glad that slaughter was stopped, wondered what lay ahead now that imperfect man knew the secrets of the atom.

During the second world war, Emily Greene Balch, still living in Wellesley, shifted her pacifist position somewhat, for she regarded the conflict with Nazism as an inevitable tragedy. Yet she still worked, in her words, "Towards a Planetary Civilization." She continued to lead the Women's International League for Peace and Freedom. In late 1946, the news came that she was to share the Nobel Peace Prize for that year with Dr. John Mott. It recognized what the private citizen, who held no political office or public position, could contribute to conditions for international peace.

When President Truman took the United States into the Korean conflict in June 1950, it was officially termed not a war but a "police action." So few Bostonians were involved that the affairs of everyday life went merrily on. Local murders and muggings shared the headlines with suspect gifts of mink coats and deep freezes to certain officials in Washington. The fact that men's haircuts jumped to a new high of $1.15 was more important than seesaw battles to control hills bearing numbers rather than names many thousands of miles away.

When Congress reinstituted the draft, it began to affect local young men. The last Sunday in May 1951 saw six thousand area college students taking a "snap" draft classification test that would exempt most of them. Some unknown person or persons helped the men unprotected by college by breaking into a Dorchester Selective Service office that same May and destroying more than five hundred registrants' records.

Preparing even for the possible bombing of Boston by the North Koreans, civil defense air-raid sirens were installed on top of the new Courthouse. When they screamed in a surprise test, alarmed Bostonians jammed newspaper and police station switchboards with anxious calls. The war reached into local families when the Hingham national guard unit was called into service, and a symbol of this involvement was a ceremony by Mayor Hynes in City Hall to present scrolls to the next of kin of thirty local men who had died in Korea.

For those less closely touched, the war was almost a diversion. Wage and price freezes were only invoked briefly. People smiled at the news from Washington that under the rubber conservation rules, "falsies" would no longer contain natural rubber. Would morale sag under such restrictions? Few showed the concern of the Boston University faculty group denouncing Americans who boasted of mass killings of Chinese in Korea. For them it was "too reminiscent of Hitler's program for exterminating Poles and Jews." But this was a war soon stalemated, and written off.

Perhaps, however, it set the pattern for the future. President Johnson's escalation of the Vietnam civil war into a full-scale conflict deeply distressed the thinking people of Greater Boston and the country. At first, these protests largely fell on deaf ears. Local newspapers, almost hysterically at times, to judge by headlines and cartoons in the Boston *Traveler,* backed the President. An early demonstration against the draft in South Boston saw protestors attacked by high school students while police stood by and watched. But the opponents of violence in Asia were not deterred by violence in South Boston.

Boston became one of the active antiwar centers. Professors held "teach-ins" on the background of the conflict. Protest marches paraded downtown streets and rallies against the war flooded the Common with resisters. Defense Secretary McNamara came to Harvard on November 7, 1966, and refused to debate the war, so eight hundred frustrated students hemmed him in, in his Cadillac. More than one Boston campus was the scene of "sit-ins" against on-campus recruiting for Dow Chemical, the CIA, or Armed Services. Eloquent voices such as John Kenneth Galbraith and David Riesman of Harvard, Noam Chomsky of M.I.T., and Howard Zinn of Boston University led an almost unanimous chorus of intellectual dissent. Bishop Henry Sherrill and Dr. Dana Greeley spoke out for many in the local religious community.

A draft resistance group was organized in Boston and draft cards were burned on the Common and in the Arlington Street Church and Old West Church. The concept of "sanctuary" was revived and several area churches opened their doors to draft resisters. Sanctuary spread to the universities—Harvard, B.U., M.I.T., and Brandeis all took part, with often as many as twenty-five hundred students and faculty participating. One couple, more frustrated than most, went to the Customs House and poured black paint over the files of Selective Service's Local Board No. 30.

Although few of these protesters of the Vietnam War were aware of the fact, they were acting in a centuries-old Boston tradition, one that traces its roots back to John Winthrop's caution against "a standing authority of military men," one reinforced both actively and passively during every war Bostonians have taken part in. For three hundred and fifty years Bostonians have gone to war, though only once was on their doorstep. Many Boston men and women fought in those wars, and some died in them. Others thought about them, with that characteristic Boston independence which, at its best, refuses to let somebody else do its thinking for them, not even a President.

Sanctuary broken as FBI agents haul Army Private Raymond Kroll, 18, out of Marsh Chapel at Boston University. Kroll had claimed "sanctuary" in the Chapel until he was seized on October 6, 1967. Agents roughed through a crowd of more than 700 college students and war protesters to arrest him. (Photograph by Manuel Russell.)

Interlude three: Boston to 1750

Welcoming in the new century

Just about Break-a-day Jacob Amsden and three other Trumpeters gave a Blast with the Trumpets on the common near Mr. Alford's. Then went to the Green Chambers, and sounded there till about sunrise. Bell-man said these verses, a little before Break-a-day, which I printed and gave them.

—Samuel Sewall
Diary, January 2, 1701

WEDNESDAY, January 1. 1701.
A little before Break-a-Day, at *Boston* of the *Massachusetts*.

ONCE more! Our GOD, vouchsafe to Shine:
Tame Thou the Rigour of our Clime.
Make haste with thy Impartial Light,
And terminate this long dark Night.

Let the transplanted ENGLISH Vine
Spread further still: still Call it Thine.
Prune it with Skill: for yield it can
More Fruit to Thee the Husbandman.

Give the poor INDIANS Eyes to see
The Light of Life: and set them free;
That they Religion may profess,
Denying all Ungodliness.

From hard'ned JEWS the Vail remove,
Let them their Martyr'd JESUS love;
And Homage unto Him afford,
Because He is their Rightful LORD.

So false Religions shall decay,
And Darkness fly before bright Day:
So Men shall GOD in CHRIST adore;
And worship Idols vain, no more.

So ASIA, and AFRICA,
EUROPA, with AMERICA;
All Four, in Consort join'd, shall Sing
New Songs of Praise to CHRIST our KING.

—Samuel Sewall
Broadside (Boston Public Library)

Blackbird killers

Voated that Each house holder in the town shall some time before the 30th Day of May Next Kill or Cause to be Kild six blackbirds & bring the heads of the same on or before ye Day above sd to Ebenezer Stocker Samll Collins Thomas Burrage or John Gowing or Either of them whoe are apointed to Receive the same & take account their of & to prosecute any person for the breach of this order and if any house holder shall Neglect or Refuse to bring six black birds heads as afore sd Every such person shall pay three pence p head for Each head so wanting as a fine to ye town or poore their of to be recovered as the Law Directs

—Lynn town records
March 20, 1701

Good confessions make good neighbors

Upon the Reading of mrs Margaret Lanyons Confesstion of her abuseing her neighbour mrs Williams; in speakeing ill of her and spreading ill Reports abought her acknowledging her sin in so doing; she was Restored to communion with the Church by a Vote of the Church.

—*Records* of the First Church in Boston
May 11, 1707

Stone cold Bacon

Ephraim Bacon of Roxbury Next to Dedham was a coming to Boston with wood and milk. The storm growing bad left his wood by the way. When come to Smith Woods he would have perswaided him to have gone home because the storm was so fierce. When come to Meers's he would have perswaided him proffred him money for his milk and so would have him return home when came to Boston Mr Wardwel would have took care of his Horses and Lodgd him but he said he promised his wife to come home, went out of Town about 7 o Clock wandred to the left hand and in the morning was found Dead by a stack bottom upon his Knees with his Hatt upon his [head.?]

—Samuel Sewall, Jr.
Diary, January 29, 1714

Death of a wife and mother

On April 4. 1714, the Lord saw meet to take from me my wife, who had bin the dear companion of my pilgrimage for more than 52 years. God made her a great blessing to me. By her hee gave me ten children, 3 sons and Seven daughters. My sons have all of them, bin an honor to their Fathers name, and which is a thousand times better an honor to Religion. I have also had Comfort in my daughters, who have bin dutifull to me and I hope they fear God. Their dear mother was of a very loving tender disposition. I kept close to my Study, and committed the management of the affairs of the Family to her. When I have bin absent from my Family, I was easy in my spirit, because my heart did Safely trust in her, who did me good and not evill all the dayes of her life. She was always very carefull not to do any thing which she thought would trouble me. Her honor for me was too great. For She has sayd to many, that She thought I was the best Husband, and the best man in the whole world. I often prayed that She might outlive me. But in mercy to her God ordered it to be otherwise.

—Rev. Increase Mather
Autobiography

Things that go bump in the night, 1715

Some time about the latter End of the Last Year, one whose Name is *Ruth Weeden*, lodging in the House and Bed with *Mrs.* [Ann] *Griffin*, about break of Day, being awake, while Mrs. *Griffin* was asleep in the bed by her side, plainly saw the Apparition of the Deceased Mrs. *Crawford*, (who had been dead above five years before,) first at the foot of the Bed, from whence it came up to the left side thereof, where now she lay. She had on her a suit of striped Calaminco; a White Apron; a White Neckcloth; a Laced pinner on her head; and a fresh Countenance. But all over so luminous, that tho' the Room were darkened with window-shutters, as well as the Remainders of the Night, the whole Room was enlightened. She said unto Mrs. *Weeden*, to this Effect, *I gave* Ann *that money!*—and without any more Words disappeared.

Mrs. *Weeden* took the first opportunity to ask her awakened Friend, whether Mrs. *Crawford* had ever given her any money. Whereupon Mrs. *Griffin* told her *That she had*; That is, that a little before she dyed, Mrs. *Crawford* had expressly bid her Keep for her own, a Little Summ of Money, that she had in her hands. And then also gave her a Ring, that she wears ever since.

> —Edward Hutchinson, J.P.
> Deposition of Ann Griffin and Ruth Weeden
> November 24, 1716

Things that go bump in the day

The last time I saw your father was in the beginning of 1724, when I visited him after my first trip to Pennsylvania. He received me in his library, and on my taking leave showed me a shorter way out of the house through a narrow passage, which was crossed by a beam overhead. We were still talking as I withdrew, he accompanying me behind, and I turning partly towards him, when he said hastily, "Stoop, stoop!" I did not understand him till I felt my head hit against the beam. He was a man that never missed any occasion of giving instruction, and upon this he said to me, "You are young and have the world before you. *Stoop* as you go through it, and you will miss many hard thumps." This advice, thus beat into my head, has frequently been of use to me, and I often think of it when I see pride mortified and misfortunes brought upon people by their carrying their heads too high.

> —Benjamin Franklin
> from a letter to Rev. Samuel Mather,
> May 12, 1784

A *captain boards his son*

20. Mr. Gee preach'd the publick Lecture on Psalm 122. I went in the Afternoon to Mr. Lewis's to see Mrs. Edwards, but she herself was so ill with a broken Breast, and her son was apprehended to be dying, that therefore I could not see her. Captain Storey convers'd with me about his Sons living with me. His words were these about the Conditions of our Discourse. 'Take the Lad, Sir, Till about May, when I expect to return from Sea, but if it please God to prevent me, if you like the Boy keep him till he is 15 or 16 years old, when I would have him put to apprentice. All I Desire is that you keep him warm, and feed him Suitably. Instruct him Christianity. My main Expectation and hope is that you'll give him Education proper to such an One. Let him Serve you as he is able, impose not on him those heavy burthens that will either Cripple him or Spoil his Growth. But in all regards I am willing he should Serve you to his Utmost. Upon my Consenting to this he said he has no Hatt. Let him have one of yours, and if it should so happen that he doth not remain with you I'll pay for it.' Upon all which I got him a Hatt at my Brothers and took him with Me at the Entrance of the Evening. It was very Cold and for the Sake of the Boy I was forc'd to call in twice by the way to Cambridge. We got up to Father Champney's in good Season, but very Cold.

21. It was near Eleven before I could Mount for home. [Westborough, Mass.] I Stopp'd and Din'd at Captain Brintnalls, and got home before Day Light in. Engag'd in My Preparations for the Sabbath, which were now to Begin.

—Rev. Ebenezer Parkman
Diary, January 20–21, 1726

The high price of a college graduation

Saltonstal & Church, as sent by their Class ye Senior Sophisters, who speedily expected their first Degree, came to debate about their paying 20 shillings a piece for ye Commencement Dinner, reckoning it would be more than ye Dinner would cost; I shew'd them ye Law requir'd it, yt ye cost of ye Dinner could not be known before hand, nor in some considerable time after when many of ye Commencers would be gone from College; I think they went away pretty easy.

—President Benjamin Wadsworth
Diary, June 20, 1727

"From the thick smokes, and noisy town, o come"

. . . tho' rich Dainties never spread my Board,
Nor my cool Vaults Calabrian Wines afford;
Yet what is neat and wholsome I can spread,
My good fat Bacon, and our homely Bread,
With which my healthful Family is fed.
Milk from the Cow, and Butter newly churn'd,
And new fresh Cheese, with Curds and Cream just
    turn'd.
For a Desert upon my Table's seen
The Golden Apple, and the Melon green;
The blushing Peech and glossy Plumb there lies,
And with the Mandrake tempt your Hands and
    Eyes.

This I can give, and if you'l here repair,
To slake your Thirst a Cask of Autumn Beer,
Reserv'd on purpose for your drinking here.

Under the Spreading Elms our Limbs we'll lay,
While fragrant Zephires round our Temples play.
Retir'd from Courts and Crouds, secure we'll set,
And freely feed upon our Country Treat. . . .

—Mrs. Jane Turell (1708–35) of Medford
"An Invitation into the Country"

College customs anno 1734–35
(a selection)

1   No freshman shall ware his hat in the College yeard except it rains, snows, or hails, or he be on horse back or haith both hands full.

6   No freshman shall talk saucily to his senior or speak to him with his hat on.

9   Freshman are to find [furnish] the rest of the scholars with bats, balls, and footballs.

14   When a freshman knockes at his seniors door he shall tell [his] name if asked who.

15   When any body knockes at a freshmans door he shall not aske who is there, but shall immediately open the door.

16   No freshman shall lean at prayers but shall stand upright.

20   No Freshman shall mingo [urinate] against the College wall or go into the fellows cuzjohn [Cousin John, i.e., a privy].

—Harvard College records

A fierce February freeze

. . . The weather has been so severe for 8 or 9 weeks past as has hardly been known in the memory of man, and a land of ice for near 10 miles from this town into the ocean has in a manner stopt all vessels from coming in or going out, and the excessive snows have render'd the roads unpassable for horses for about a month past. . . .

—Gov. Jonathan Belcher
February 21, 1741

Keeping commencement

Honoured Sir,—I wrote to you the 11th Currant, but omitted Some Things which I Shall now enumerate viz. 15 Shillings for Printing Theses, for three Quarters shoing 24 shillings, for a Sett of Buckles 15 shillings, and if I make any manner of Entertainment there will be a great many things to buy, tho I shall not put you to much Charge for that, not intending to keep much of a commencement and what I do will be with [Lothrop] Russel. Pray Sir send me money Enough for I believe I Shall not write again before commencement.

Your most Obedient Son,
James Otis
—James Otis, Jr.
Letter to father, June 17, 1743

Get out of town!

Essex ss To Joshua Collins Constable in Lynn—Greeting—Whereas the selectmen of Lynn are Informed that John Giles Junr & Mary his wife & five children Viz Marcy Sarah John Lidia & Ann Came into this toown ye first of Aprill Last 1744 & Came from ye Town of Salem where they properly belong and had their Last Resadence—Therefore In His Majesties Name you are Required to warn the sd John Giles & wife and Children to depart out of this Town of Lynn or they shall be procceded with as the Law Directs—you are alick Required to Inquire of ye above sd persons when they came into this Town & from whence they came & where they had their Last Resadence—fail not & make Retorn with your Doings hereon—Dated at Lynn July ye 18th 1744—

By order of ye selectmen Richard Johnson Town Clerk

Lynn the 30th of July 1744 pursuant to this warrant I have warned the above persons John Giles with his wife with their children to Depart out of This Town—I also Inquired from whence they came they answered from ye Town of Salem where they had dwelt almost all their time heretofore as to the time when they came into this Town & their surKamstances they would give me no answer
Joshua Collins
Constable

—Town Records of Lynn

Hauling the fox, 1744

I had occasion to see a particular diversion this day which they call *hawling the fox*. It is practised upon simple clowns. Near the town there is a pond of about half a quarter of a mile broad. Across this they lay a rope, and two or three strong fellows, concealed in the bushes, hold one end of it. To a stump in view, there is tied a large fox. When they can lay hold of an ignorant clown on the opposite side of the pond, they inveigle him by degrees into the scrape—two people pretending to wager, one upon the fox's head and the other upon the clown's, twenty shillings or some such matter that the fox shall not or shall pull him thro' the water in spight of his teeth. The clown easily imagines himself stronger than the fox and, for a small reward, allows the rope to be put around his waste. Which done, the sturdy fellows on the other side behind the bush pull lustily for their friend the fox who sits tied to his stump all the time of the operation, being only a mere spectator, and haul poor pill-garlick with great rapidity thro' the pond, while the water hisses and foams on each side of him as he ploughs the surface, and his coat is well wet. I saw a poor country fellow treated in this manner. He run thro the water upon his back like a log of wood, making a frothy line across the pond, and when he came out he shook himself and swore he could not have believed the fox had so much strength. They gave him 20 shillings to help to dry his coat. He was pleased with the reward and said that for so much a time he would allow the fox to drag him thro' the pond as often as he pleased.

—Dr. Alexander Hamilton
Itinerarium

A widow's keep

Item. I give and Bequeath unto Rebecca my Dearly beloved wife the improvement of my East Lower Room of my Dwelling house and Chamber over the same and one third part of the cellar during her natural life, with free Liberty of coming at the same as occasion shal call for: I do give her the improvement of one third part of my household goods within doors: and the Improvement of two of my best Cows to be kept for her Winters and Summers yearly and every year by my Executors during her natural Life. I also give her two bushels of Malt two barrels cyder three bushels of Rye nine bushels Indian Corn ground and brought into her house the cyder and grain to be provided yearly and every year seasonably during her natural Life by my Executors. I also give to her six cords of good wood to be cut and split and brought Seasonably to her door fit for her fire. I also give her five bushels of Apples two bushels Turnips half bushel carrots and half bushel of white beans fourscore pounds Pork and seventy pounds Beef four pounds hackled flax and four pounds Sheeps Wool all to be provided yearly and every year by my Executors during her natural Life. Also Ten pounds Money per year during her Life. Likewise that she shall be carried to meeting when she is able and desirous to attend the same all above mentioned to be performed eaqualy between my two Executors.

—Will of Jonathan Barrett of Malden
August 26, 1749

The lady and the monkey, Boston 1744

Monday, August 13. I made a tour thro the town in the forenoon with Mr. Hughes and, att a certain lady's house, saw a white monkey. It was one of those that are brought from the Muscetto shore and seemed a very strange creature. It was about a foot long in its body and, in visage, exceeding like an old man, there being no hair upon its face except a little white, downy beard. It laugh'd and grinned like any Christian (as people say), and was exceeding fond of his mistress, bussing her and handling her bubbies just like an old rake. One might well envy the brute, for the lady was very handsome; so that it would have been no dissagreeable thing for a man to have been in this monkey's place. It is strange to see how fond these brutes are of women, and, on the other hand, how much the female monkeys affect men. The progress of nature is surprizing in many such instances. She seems by one connected gradation to pass from one species of creatures to another without any visible gap, intervall, or *discontinuum* in her works; but an infinity of her operations are yet unknown to us.

—Dr. Alexander Hamilton
Itinerarium

William Barnicoat (?), Chief Engineer of the Boston Fire Department, 1836–1854, dressed in his parade uniform and carrying a silver presentation speaking trumpet, which contains flowers for ceremonial occasion. Oil on tin, artist unknown. (Courtesy of The Bostonian Society, Old State House.)

120

CHAPTER FOUR

The Dreadful Cry of Fire

From the beginning, Boston response to fire has been pragmatic. Shortly after Thomas Sharp's thatched house burned down on March 26, 1631, from a defective wooden chimney, the town passed a law prohibiting wooden chimneys in thatched houses. With each successive major disaster, steps have been taken to prevent *that* disaster (if possible) from happening again.

Fire was probably more of a danger than local Algonquians to the success of the Boston settlement. The Puritans' first houses were temporary shelters: tents, huts, lean-tos, even bark wigwams. A few rich people had the money and the servants to have suitable homes built. Others, not so rich, had smokey cottages. The remainder huddled in their primitive shelters constantly endangered by household fires, usually burning just outside. These open fires were essential for cooking. For heating, the settlers relied on chimneys, but without bricks and limestone they could not make safe ones. The first chimneys were laid up of "splinters" of wood in log-cabin style. Gaps were filled with mud and the inside smeared with clay. If patches of clay dropped off later, the chimneys turned into torches, shooting sparks onto the thatch roofs and quickly consuming both house and contents. Few as these household goods were, they were all a family had. Since the nearest stores were three thousand miles away in England, they were not easily replaced. Insurance being unthought of, the burned-out family, looking at the ruins of its hut, could only rely on the charity of their neighbors.

Although there were numerous fires after Mr. Sharp's, the first one to be called a "Great Fire" came on April 14, 1653. It destroyed eight houses in the State and Washington street area and killed three children, the first recorded deaths by fire. Governor Winthrop's son thought it "the most dreadfull fire that I ever saw, by reason of the barrells of gunpowder which they had in their howses, which made men fearfull to come neere them." Immediately after the fire, a town meeting ordered inhabitants to provide themselves with long ladders "that shall reach to the ridg of the house." Also they were to have a twelve-foot pole "with a good large swab at the end of it," to damp out sparks that might land on roofs. The town itself purchased six long ladders to be hung "at the outsyde of the metting house" and to be "branded with the town marke." Capt. Robert Keayne, beginning his long will that August, included a gift to the town of money to construct a conduit or reservoir for water to be used "in danger of fyre." And the General Court passed the first law against arson.

By March of the next year they were discussing with Joseph Jenks a possible engine "to convey water in case of fire." Jenks was an ingenious fellow brought over from England to help produce iron, but he could turn his hand to many things. He had designed the dies for the pine-tree shillings, invented a new kind of sawmill, a better method of wiredrawing, and even improved the farmer's scythe. Now he devised the first fire engine for Boston—seventy-seven years before New York provided itself with one. It was manned by anyone handy when a fire was discovered.

Anne Bradstreet, whose home in Andover burned on July 20, 1666, copied out on a loose sheet of paper some fifty-eight lines of a Puritan's response to being awakened "in silent night" with "thund'ring noise / And piteous shrieks" of "Fire!" Her heart, she exclaims, immediately cried to God

> To strengthen me in my distress
> And not to leave me succorless.
> Then, coming out, beheld a space
> The flame consume my dwelling place.
> And when I could no longer look,
> I blest His name that gave and took.

It was not for Mistress Bradstreet to "repine." Was not all God's? Still she could not repress a womanly sigh when, walking by the ruins, she observed (in jogging iambic tetrameter)

> My pleasant things in ashes lie,
> And them behold no more shall I.

But "all's vanity." And when she bethought herself of her home in heaven, it was "farewell" pelf, "farewell" store—"There's wealth enough. I need no more."

About five o'clock on the morning of December 7, 1676, the dreadful cry of fire was heard in the north end of town. A young boy, a tailor's apprentice, roused before daylight, fell asleep at his work and his candle set fire to the house. A strong southeast wind whipped up the flames and within four hours, nearly fifty houses were in ashes. A sudden downpour of rain, said Samuel Sewall, checked "the (otherwise) masterless flames." Increase Mather was burned out in this fire, but not until he had time to save most of the thousand books in his "beloved library." The town took advantage of this fire to straighten out some of the streets in the burned district. They also ordered a fire engine from England, and when it arrived "Thomas Atkins, carpenter" was asked to take care of "the manageinge of the sd. engine." He was to choose his own assistants, whom the town promised to pay "for their pains about the worke."

That work was cut out for them, for a rash of fires plagued the town in 1679, most of them suspected of being set. The worst came at midnight of

August 18, when a tavern near the dock, The Sign of the Three Mariners, was discovered on fire. Flames quickly spread from building to building and the little engine and its crew were helpless before its fury. Twelve hours later, seventy warehouses and eight dwellings were in ruins. A Frenchman working at another tavern, because of his "rash and insulting speeches" during the fire, was thought to be the incendiary. He was tried for arson, but could only be found guilty of having counterfeiting tools in his possession. He stood two hours in the pillory and had both ears cut off. Ten other persons, suspected of arson, were banished from Boston, but repeated fires of suspect origin proved that not all had been caught.

For several years the town was threatened by incendiary fires, which fortunately did no serious general damage. When Joshua Lamb's house in Roxbury burned down on July 22, 1681, and a neighbor's house with it, it was discovered that Maria, his Afro-American servant, indignant at some wrong done her, had started the fire. Arson of a dwellinghouse had been made a capital crime in 1652. Maria was tried, found guilty, and condemned to death. Aggravating her crime was the fact that a young child had perished in the blaze. She was executed on the Common on October second, but there is a confusion in the records as to whether she was burned at the stake, or hanged first and then "burnt to Ashes in the fier."

A representation of how William Blaxton's cottage on the southwestern slope of Beacon Hill might have looked. It was typical of many of the first fire-prone houses in Boston. (Diorama, courtesy of New England Mutual Life Insurance Company.)

123

After the 1679 fire, the town ruled that only stone or brick buildings could be constructed in Boston. Later, certain necessary small buildings were exempted. Thus a man was not compelled by law to build a brick privy. Looking back in 1698 over the first seven decades of the settlement, Cotton Mather could say that "ten times has the fire made notable ruins among us." But they had suffered no such general devastation as the settlers of Sagadohoc, Maine, had in 1614, which compelled them to give up their plantation. Serious as Boston's fires had been, worse were yet to come.

On the evening of October 13, 1711, a Scottish woman picking oakum while drunk, was too slow to smother sparks falling on the stuff from a nearby fire. Soon her tenement was burning rapidly out of control, and flames raced from building to building on Cornhill (now Washington Street). Next morning, about one hundred houses in this wealthiest and most thickly settled part of town were only heaps of smoldering ashes. Both the First Church and the Town House had been destroyed. Most of the library in the latter was saved, somewhat singed, although valuable records were lost. Queen Anne's portrait, however, was triumphantly carried out unharmed.

The town's three water engines couldn't cope with the inferno and houses were blown up to make a barrier to the flames. In so doing, several young men were killed. Sailors who had climbed into the belfry of the meetinghouse to rescue the bell, were trapped there when the stairs below them burned. The roof fell in, and they perished before the eyes of the horrified spectators.

Increase Mather, in a sermon, ascribed the cause of the town's disaster to the fact that Boston had "profaned" the Lord's Day. "Have not Bakers, Carpenters, and other tradesmen been employed in servile work on the Sabbath day?" he asked his mute contrite congregation. "Have not burdens been carried through the streets on the Sabbath day?" Thus the burden Bostonians were now carrying through the streets was rubble from burned areas used to fill up Long Wharf, then being built. But what had been carried through the streets on the night of the fire too often was loot which "evilminded and wicked persons, on pretence of charitable offering their help," had stolen from their distressed neighbors.

As a result of this fire, the town was divided into fire districts and a board of firewards created, "prudent persons of known fidelity," responsible for direct-

ing the fight against each conflagration. Also established on October 11, 1718, was the Fire Society, the first of many such private organizations. Most were patterned after this pioneer group, with a limited membership, meeting quarterly for a meal and a social occasion. Their main purpose was to protect the property of members from fire and looting. Each member was required to have two water buckets, properly stenciled with his name, two bags to carry small objects from the burning premises, a bed-key to dismantle and rescue a man's most essential piece of furniture, and one screwdriver. They were financed by dues and by an elaborate system of "fines." There being no fire insurance, they provided some aid from their funds for distressed members and widows of members. Some of these societies survived as social organizations well into the nineteenth century, long after the professionalization of firefighting made their services obsolete.

The engine companies were distinct from fire societies. They were volunteers and turned out for every fire within their reach. Their duty was to man the engines throwing water on the fire. Other citizens were organized by the firewards into bucket brigades to supply engine tubs with enough water. As early as 1739, a prize was offered by the town for the first company to get a stream of water on the blaze. Money and the spirit of competition made these volunteers more efficient. It was the first step, too, toward a paid department.

For half a century, the 1711 fire remained in men's minds as the greatest calamity Boston had known. But records are made to be broken and the conflagration of March 20, 1760, did just that. The cry of fire woke Samuel Savage just after two in the morning. By the time he had dressed and left the house, he "could scarce see any effects of the flames," but before he was halfway to the Brazen Head tavern on King Street where it had begun, the whole house burst into flames. Adjoining houses caught quickly. Firefighters stopped it on the north and south, but winds drove it irresistibly eastward: down the south side of King Street (State), along Pudding Lane (Devonshire), Quaker Lane (Congress), right down to the docks. By morning, 345 dwellings, warehouses, and shops had been destroyed. The loss hit impartially at rich, poor, and in between. At the height of the fire, Savage found himself on top of Fort Hill (then still a hill). The fire streamed along like some imperious torrent, carrying all before it.

A POEM, descriptive of the terrible FIRE, which made such shocking Devastation in BOSTON,

on the Evening of FRIDAY, April 21, 1787, in which were consumed one HOUSE of Worship, of which the Rev. EBENEZER WIGHT was Pastor, and upwards of one Hundred Dwelling-Houses and other Buildings.— The Loss of Property by this sorrowful Disaster is computed at near £. 70,000.——Composed by H. W.

GENTLE *Clio* calm my Passions,
  Rest my panting Heart a while,
Let me paint this sad Disaster,
  Which will scarce admit Simile.

When refreshing feeble Nature,
  Friends were sitting round their Board,
Curling Smoke surrounds their Dwellings,
  With Commission from the LORD.

Fierce *Æolus* spreads his Pinions,
  Howls along with hideous Groan,
Flaming Arrows tare the Structures,
  All is in Confusion thrown.

Loud as *Ætna*'s bellowing Thunder,
  Or *Vulcano*'s horrid Glare,
Livid Terrors fill their Faces,
  Tumult darkens to Despair.

Clatt'ring Tiles and pointed Chrystal
  Rudely strews the parched Ground,
Children shrieking, Parents groaning,
  Flaming Torrents bursting round.

Hast'ning on like rav'nous Vultures,
  Spread their Trophies thro' each Street,
Clap their Wings and bid Defiance,
  When they Opposition meet.

Hark! the murm'ring *Eccho* * ceases,
  Are the Flames extinct or not?
Cast your swimming Eyes around you,
  Come behold the *sacred Spot*.

Ah! delightful *Seat* of *Worship*,
  All inclos'd with Smoke and Fire,
Burning Shafts promiscuous flying,
  Close attack thy lofty Spire!

Now my trembling Muse forsakes me,
  See the smiling Queen of Night
Throw aside her radiant Vesture,
  Cloath'd with Blood instead of Light.

Famous BOSTON! Seat of Traffick!
  How thy Structures shone like Gold!
Now sits pensive as a Widow,
  An Amazement to behold!

Hundreds left without a Shelter!
  All their Substance lost in Flames,
Aged Widows, helpless Children,
  Now your tender Pity claims!

Rich and Poor salute each other,
  Hand in Hand they mourning go,
No Respect to Age or Station,
  Flames no Mercy on them show.

Once renown'd beloved City,
  How I deprecate thy Loss!
How thy Glory lies in Ashes,
  Soon thy Gold is turn'd to Dross!

Now secure a better Treasure,
  Seek an House not made with Hands,
When all Nature sinks in Ruin,
  Yet that Mansion safely stands.

While each virtuous Heart is bleeding,
  May their Hands bestow Relief,
Heaven an Hundred Fold repay them
  Who assuage another's Grief.

Open wide your Hearts and Houses,
  GOD the cheerful Giver loves,
Now's a Time to act that Temper,
  He rewards and well approves.

May you all with calm Submission,
  Pass the fiery Trial through,
And like Gold come forth more precious,
  Thus my FRIENDS I bid adieu.

* The Rope burnt and the Bell melted before the Sexton made his Escape.

Sold at the Office next Liberty-Pole.

I can say without exageration that I never in my life was in a greater
storm of snow or knew it snow faster than that fire fell all around us.

Like Anne Bradstreet a century before him, he felt this disaster was "the Lord's
doing" as punishment for Boston's sins. Everyone, he said, felt this; and if this
judgment made Bostonians "better" it was a mercy, not a catastrophe.

Exactly what mercy the Lord had in mind on the night of January 24, 1764,
is not so clear. In the middle of a driving snowstorm, Harvard Hall at the
College in Cambridge burned to the ground. Some forty-eight hundred valuable
books in the college library were destroyed, together with rare manuscripts
and the entire "Repositerry of Curiosities." Wailed a contemporary rhymer:

> Down rush precipitate, with thund'ring crash,
> The roofs, the walls, and in one ruinous heap,
> The ancient dome, and all it's treasures lie!

The Lord had nothing to do with the next important fire in the Boston area.
Patriots were more apt to ascribe it to Satan, and the chief arm of Satan at
the moment was the British. For as a by-product of the struggle to gain control
of the Charlestown peninsula, the British set fire to the town of Charlestown,
ostensibly to smoke out snipers and to permit no shelter to the enemy. The
American army in later conflicts would understand such strategy, even if their
rebel forebears did not. An observer at Salem commented on the terrible sight
from that distance: "the western horizon in the day-time was one huge body
of smoke, and in the evening a continued blaze." About four hundred houses
were burned; not a fence nor a tree left standing, said one Charlestownite sadly.
The loss was estimated at £118,000.

Charlestown had been large, handsome, and well built. "Such," philoso-
phized the British *Annual Register* of that year, "is the termination of human
labor, industry, and wisdom, and such are the fatal fruits of civil dissensions."
An American, less philosophical about the loss, exclaimed bitterly over the
act of "those who have so long been friends." Years later, traveling in England,
a Charlestown man, William Austin, saw King George III and said loudly to
a companion, "Do you see that man? He burnt my father's barn."

Fire is no respecter of revolutions, and in 1787, four years after the United
States had shaken off British rule, precisely on the patriotic day of April 19,
Boston had another "Great Fire." Starting in a malt house and backed by
what Parson Belknap called a "dry northeaster," sparks flew from house to
house. Shingled roofs soon acquired moss, and in dry weather, these were
highly combustible. Before it was over eighty-six families were homeless and
one meetinghouse was leveled.

Prompted by the suffering caused by such large fires, when hitherto prosperous families suddenly found themselves destitute, the Massachusetts
Charitable Fire Society was formed in 1792. Its purpose was to provide a
fund to give immediate relief to the distressed. A secondary purpose was to

A woodcut on a broadside of the
fire of 1787 "which made such
shocking Devastation in Boston."
(Courtesy of Massachusetts
Historical Society.)

A FIRE
IN BOSTON
IN 1792

call attention to the need to develop better ways of fighting and preventing fires. Their first idea of how to accomplish this was typically Bostonian: preach a sermon about it. Later, they appointed a Committee on Machines to search out useful inventions.

One of the first products of this committee was a list of Dos and Don'ts, with such advice as servants should go to bed before their masters and not be allowed to carry lighted candles to bedrooms in the garret. The prudent homeowner should prohibit cigar smoking. Further instructions were "never remove hot ashes in a wooden vessel of any kind, and look well to your ash-hole." But if fire came, then "wrap yourself up in a blanket, hold your breath, and rush through the flames. If water be at hand, first wet the blanket." It also advocated "impregnated" water to quench fires. This is one of the earliest references to the use of chemical extinguishers.

Of more practical help was the formation of the Massachusetts Mutual Fire Insurance Company in 1798 by Paul Revere and others. It was the first successful company of this kind and their provision for 80 percent coverage of property for a period of seven years formed a standard other companies adopted. Unfortunately, they were four years too late to help the sufferers from the fire that occurred when the ropewalks on Pearl Street caught fire Wednesday morning, July 30, 1794. In three hours or so, an extensive region from Federal Street to the waterfront was in ashes. Fire or no fire, the execution of three pirates on the Common that afternoon went ahead as scheduled. They were, thought many a smoke-smeared Bostonian, headed for hotter fires than ever afflicted Boston.

(Above) Sketch from a century later of fire-fighting in 1792. (Right) The Rev. Dr. Jeremy Belknap's sketch of the devastation caused by the fire of 1794; the dotted line indicates the section destroyed. (Courtesy of Massachusetts Historical Society.)

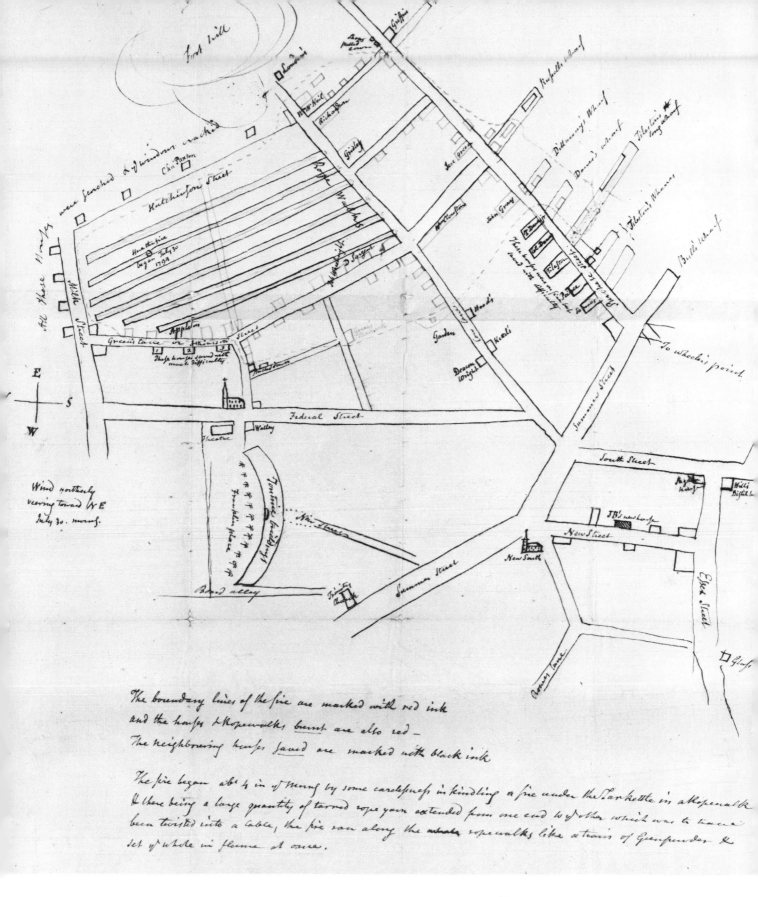

The boundary lines of the fire are marked with red ink
and the houses & Ropewalks burnt are also red —
The neighbouring houses saved are marked with black ink

The fire began abt 4 in ye morng by some carelefsnefs in kindling a fire under the tar kettle in a Ropewalk & there being a large quantity of tarred rope yarn extended from one end to ye other which was to have been twisted into a cable, the fire ran along the whole ropewalks like a train of Gunpowder & set ye whole in flame at once.

129

A watercolor of the old Franklin Engine House in Charlestown by an unknown artist. (Courtesy of The Bostonian Society, Old State House.)

Dockside fire in Charlestown as the 800-ton ship *Bell Rock* (in foreground) and others burned in June 1852.

The new century began with deceptive calm. There were spectacular fires of individual buildings such as that of November 3, 1818, when the town's leading hotel, the Exchange Coffee House, went up in flames that could be seen fifty miles away. More typical of those years was 1820, when Boston's population passed the 43,000 mark, and there were only eighteen reported fires for which the engines were called out—a remarkable record in a town where the entire population cooked and heated by open fires or stoves and used candles or lamps for light. But change was in the air.

In 1822 Boston voted out its historic form of town meeting and became a city. The same factors of growth which necessitated this step also operated in fire protection. Volunteer fire companies, with their social and competitive aspects appealing to rugged young men of the town, had become centers for tumult and political faction. Decent citizens complained of the drinking and gambling that went on in the firehouses, often impairing the ability of the companies to fight fires. And the old spirit of neighborly cooperation was breaking down as well. These engine companies depended on bucket brigades to keep their tubs supplied with water. The bucket brigades were composed of makeshift gangs of spectators drawn to the fire and organized by the firewards. But the larger the city became, the more difficult it was to compel people to help out. A better system had been introduced in New York and Philadelphia; several engines linked up hose lines and pumped water from a water source to the fire. This system was suggested for Boston.

The firemen didn't want to adopt this less exciting method. Moreover, they had grievances of their own concerning pay, jury duty, and militia service. The whole matter came to a head early in Mayor Quincy's administration when on December 1, 1823, all captains of the fire companies, in a power play, resigned. Quincy took over their engines, staffed them with volunteers, and by nightfall could report the fire department "in its usual state of efficiency." Perhaps the mayor's tongue was slightly in his cheek when he used the word "usual."

Two large fires the next year, one on April 7 in the Batterymarch and Kilby street area, and the second on July 7 that burned many fine homes at the lower end of Beacon Street and along Charles and Chestnut, argued that the department needed to be more efficient than "usual." In the second fire, Boston Common was littered with fine furniture hastily dragged from threatened homes of the wealthy. Bottles of wine which "had not seen the light for twenty years" were among the articles brought to the Common for safekeeping. The weary and thirsty firemen, aided by citizen "connoisseurs," made short work of them, "and the scene," a prim Bostonian later recalled, "assumed rather a bacchanalian character."

Quincy worked hard to reform the fire department. Like any proposal for change in the established way of doing things, this occasioned bitter and extended controversy. Some maintained that "the fireproof brethren of the North End" would never submit to it. At a packed meeting of the voters, his plan for reorganization was adopted by a slim plurality. The department was completely overhauled. New engines were obtained, old ones repaired, engine houses relocated. To combat the declining water level in household wells—most noticeable once the mill dam road had cut off the Back Bay from the sea waters—fifteen reservoirs were provided in strategic locations throughout the city. Connections, or "plugs," were made to the pipes belonging to the Aqueduct Company, a private water supply firm. When Quincy left office in 1829, there were twelve hundred men and officers, twenty engines, one hook-and-ladder company, eight hundred buckets, and seven thousand feet of hose in the department.

A demonstration of the Volunteer Fire Company pumping a high spray in front of the house of the late Thomas Melville on Green Street in the West End, June 20, 1832. (Courtesy of The Bostonian Society, Old State House.)

The ease with which the same maneuver was performed by the new steam fire engines twenty years later.

While the center city progressed to a better system of fire protection, the surrounding villages, still essentially rural, did not feel the need of the more elaborate precautions of Boston. Without closely packed business districts, none of them had had large fires destroying whole sections (except the war casualty of Charlestown). That town acquired its first engine in 1724, seventy years after Boston. Medford bought its first engine, "The Grasshopper," in 1763, and it was still in existence, though not in use, ninety years later. Roxbury ordered its first engine, "The Enterprise," in 1784. South Boston purchased the "Mazeppa" in 1814, Arlington, the "Friendship" in 1825, and Chelsea, the "Volunteer" in 1834. East Boston, newly developed, got its first engine, the "Governor Brooks" in 1835, and three years later, Somerville, still part of Charlestown, asked for an engine and was given an old one which they scornfully described as a "cast-off tub." The system of volunteer companies continued in these communities, although East and South Boston were immediately served by the new Boston department.

This created certain problems for the East Boston detachment. Having no land connections with Boston proper, did they or did they not attend fires on the mainland? The general rule was that if fire was in sight and looked widespread, they went over. Here was the opportunity for much argument. It was said the company was composed of three kinds of men: old men, with excellent judgment regarding distances of a fire; middle-aged cripples, exceedingly smart, and wanting to go to every fire; and young men who were uncommonly lazy. At each alarm the engine was dragged out and run down near the ferry landing. Then came the tug of argument. The old men would immediately argue that the fire was either in Charlestown or Cambridge, if in that direction; or, if in the other, it was in Roxbury or Dorchester. "Fire," they observed sagely, "is awful deceptive." The cripples would contend that the fire was near the ferry and stick to it, until the young bloods joined in with the old bloods, and gave it as their opinion that they had all better go into Kendall's tavern and drink on it, which usually carried the day.

Firemen demonstrating their skill at pumping a spray as high as the flagpole and the fountain on Boston Common on a May morning in 1851.

A copy of Robert Salmon's painting of a fire in the Old State House in 1832 was used on certificate of the Boston Fire Department.

A professional fire department was not to be created out of hand, and a considerable "shake-down" period lay ahead. Typical of the freewheeling style of old volunteers was the incident known as the "Broad Street Riot." Some firemen returning from a conflagration in Roxbury on Sunday afternoon, June 11, 1837, collided with a group of young Irishmen waiting for a friend's funeral to pass. A fracas developed; soon firebells rang the alarm, and quickly a full-scale battle between firemen responding to the alarm and mourners in the funeral erupted on Broad and Summer streets. Irish families in tenements on Broad Street tossed missiles on the firemen and the young toughs who had joined them. The latter promptly broke into the houses and sacked them. Torn mattresses thrown out of second-story windows created a feathery storm snowing down on the combatants. Eventually Mayor Samuel Eliot had to bring in the militia to restore order.

Largely as a result of this riot, Mayor Eliot broke up the volunteer fire department, now infected, in Colonel Henry Lee's phrase, with "rowdyism and bumptiousness," and employed a regular paid force. It was a move to professionalism. The next decades saw constant improvements in the new department's firefighting. Lake Cochituate supplied the city with public water in 1848, greatly increasing both the amount and pressure of the supply available to the firemen. A telegraphic fire alarm system was installed in the cupola on City Hall in 1852. Eight years later, the entire department was equipped with steam fire engines, and horses were introduced to pull the hose carriages. Hand companies were gradually phased out.

City of Boston.

(THIS CERTIFIES) that Thomas F. Lyons.

having served for seven successive years

on the FIRE DEPARTMENT of the

CITY of BOSTON

is entitled to all the legal immunities consequent thereon

Given under our hands this   day of   A.D. 18

John E. Fitzgerald

Edw᷎ M White

Fire
Commissioners.

Frederick O. Prince   Mayor.

BOSTONIA
CONDITA D.
1630

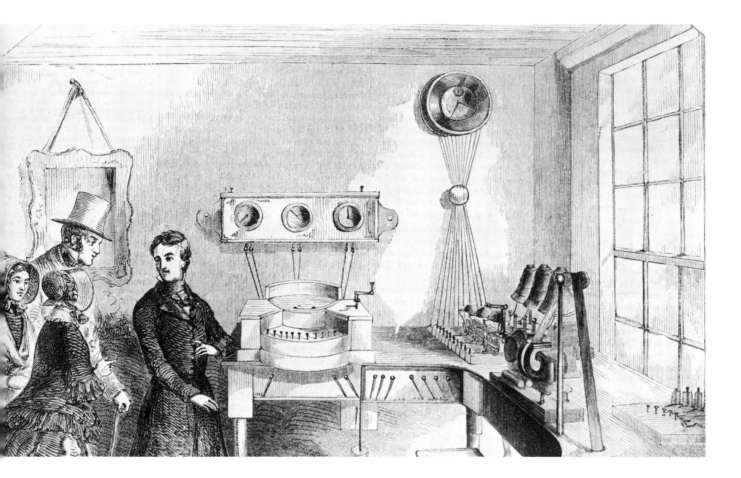

The first central fire-alarm system in Boston made use of the telegraph as illustrated in this woodcut of 1852.

The firebox rules for 1861 show some of the difficulties for the citizen in using this new equipment:

1. If a fire is discovered, go to the nearest box in the District.
2. Turn the crank 25 times, rather slowly at first, and increasing gradually to the last. If possible, wait at the box and direct the firemen to the fire.
3. If you hear no reply at the box or on the bells, turn again. If no reply after the third turning, go to another box in the district.
4. The police, upon hearing the bells, will spring their rattles and call the number of the district and station.

By 1866, the department had acquired a steam fireboat to protect wharf property. The department's "business" increased proportionately, too: 282 alarms in 1848, 497 in 1869. But no improvement was sufficient for the ordeal just ahead.

In late October 1872, Boston horses contracted influenza catarrh, popularly called, "the epizoöty." Few were seen on the streets, and business was almost at a standstill for lack of transportation. For a city whose fire department was

136

horsedrawn, this was a serious crisis. Responding to the emergency, temporary workers were hired, doubling the force. The recollection of the Great Chicago Fire, just a year earlier, when 2,600 acres of that city were leveled, was fresh in all minds.

Saturday, November 9, was a beautiful Indian summer day, the air clear and exhilarating, a gentle breeze from the north, and a gorgeous sunset. The heart of the city was nearly deserted, when a man coming up Summer Street a little after seven o'clock heard the peculiar roaring noise of fire in a large six-story granite building on the corner of Summer and Kingston streets. It had started in the engine room, soared up the wooden elevator shaft, and was now burning fiercely on every floor. Two engines were already in the area at another blaze, and this confusion caused a fifteen-minute delay before the first alarm was turned in at 7:20 on Box 52. By that time the roof had caved in, showering sparks and cinders in a great gush of fire on neighboring buildings, six of which were quickly enveloped in flames. The mansard roofs of wood and tar on top of these granite buildings made them tinder boxes. Four more alarms were rung in, calling out the full department.

137

Only desperate efforts by the firemen saved Old South Church from destruction in the fire.

The Currier & Ives print visualizing the great fire of 1872 as seen from the harbor.

The fire ruins still smoulder in this atmospheric painting by J. J. Enneking. Through the smoke can be seen the steeple of Park Street Church and the dome of the State House. (Courtesy of Massachusetts Historical Society.)

By now, men and machines, hauled to the scene by drag-rope in the old-fashioned way, were concentrated around a block made up of Arch, Devonshire, and Summer streets and Winthrop Square, all of which was burning. Chief John S. Damrell by eight o'clock had telegraphed every town within fifty miles to send help, and sent couriers to towns that couldn't be reached by telegraph. But the more equipment that came in, the more confusion. Hose fittings and hydrant fittings were not standardized. Nor had the hydrants and pipes of the district kept pace with its change from residential to commercial. At the very moment when it seemed as if they might contain the fire, the water supply failed, and the fire roared out of control. Granite facades simply crumbled from the fierce heat. In falling, they broke the principal water and gas mains. By nine o'clock, citizens who had swarmed into the area, were as much of a problem as the fire. They made wild and unreasonable demands on the firemen, even offering large bribes if they would desert one area to defend another. Some store owners opened their shops and invited people to help themselves, rather than watch the flames destroy their goods. People scarcely needed this encouragement to begin widespread looting. The center of the fire was a raging inferno that sucked in air at a speed of thirty miles an hour. So intense was the heat that it was hardly five minutes from the time the first sparks were seen in Pearl Street before the entire block was blazing furiously. People several hundred feet away from the fire found it painful to face it for more than a few minutes.

By eleven, so terrified had the city officials and leading citizens become, they were making all sorts of impossible and irrational demands on fire officials. Blowing up buildings to provide a barrier to the fire was urged, resisted, and finally used. Some credited it with stopping the fire, while others said it only added problems. At the height of the fire, Chief Damrell had 45 engines, 52 hose-carriages, 3 hook-and-ladder units, 1,700 men, and 41,000 feet of hose in action. Even with this force available, the fire raged for eighteen hours uncontrolled. At last, when enough hose could be laid to connect with nearby tidal reservoirs, they could contain it and begin to move in on the heart of the fire. Early Sunday morning people in the suburbs came streaming in. Churches were empty. There was only one topic of conversation. Wild rumors circulated as to extent and amount of devastation. Military units had been called out and were keeping crowds out of the firemen's way. Everything seemed well in hand.

Then Sunday midnight a terrific gas explosion was heard on Summer Street near Washington, and a general alarm was rung in. A building saved the previous night, was now lost to flames. By four hours of "hot endeavor," this fire was kept from spreading.

Figures on the fire show its dimensions. Some 776 buildings were destroyed of which over 700 were brick or stone. Two churches were left in ruins. Nearly 1,000 firms were burned out. Sixty-five acres of land were leveled, and the dollar loss was calculated at not less than $75 million. At least fourteen people

Trinity Church on Washington Street in 1870, two years before the fire. On this site today stands Filene's.

Trinity Church immediately after the fire.

Another view of the destruction in this same area.

had been killed. Troops, barracked in Old South Meeting House, patrolled the city for a week after. Boston, declining offers of outside relief with thanks, raised $350,000, of which a small unexpended amount was returned to the donors. The General Court called upon the city to pass stringent building laws. The fire department was investigated, criticized, and reorganized on October 13, 1873, with Damrell resigning early in 1874. His reputation had not been helped by a second large fire on May 30, 1873, in very nearly the same area that did a million dollars' damage and hit 105 firms, including some that had suffered the previous November. Also the recent annexation of Charlestown, Roxbury, and Brighton had greatly increased the area the department had to protect.

Boston was not the only locality in the metropolitan area big enough to suffer from a devastating fire. Five minutes before noon on November 26, 1889, a fire started in a "nest of wooden buildings" in the center of the Lynn business district. Within fifteen minutes it was out of control. A heavy northwest wind blew big cinders through the air, igniting nearby store awnings, and shortly the whole center of town was in flames, and the conflagration headed toward the waterfront. For miles, the tremendous black cloud could be seen pouring into the sky over Lynn. All cities and towns within twenty miles were called on for aid. By the time it ended, 330 buildings had been leveled, 200 families were homeless, 100 factories were in ruins, 8,000 workers were idled, and damage was well over a million dollars.

Not about to let Lynn get ahead, two days after this fire, on Thanksgiving Day, November 28, a terrible fire hit the Kingston Street area of Boston. Some sixty buildings were destroyed, five people killed, and the loss went to nearly four million. This was the last widespread fire in the city proper, but one more suburb was still to be heard from.

Palm Sunday of April 12, 1908, promised to be a pleasant day in Chelsea. A little before 11:00 A.M. an alarm was sounded for a small blaze in a building near the Everett line. Probably started by sparks from a dump fire, this was soon under control when a building two blocks away burst into flames. Sparks from this building started half a dozen fires. A shed filled with gasoline caught, exploded, and sent burning embers in all directions. A high wind (a forty-mile gale some said) blew the fire south and east. The flames caught house after house and swept down on the central business district. There was terrible confusion, people moving their furniture out into the streets and blocking passage, crying children hunting for their parents. Some women became hysterical and refused to look at the fires destroying their homes. Others laughed insanely at the holocaust. Many residents could not speak English and panicked. Husband and wife fought over what to save as their house burned down around them. One man galloped a wagonload of junk to safety.

The fire now was jumping whole blocks, catching people in between. Hose burned as fast as it was laid. A building that showed no sign of fire would suddenly burst into flames. One large double house was timed and found to have burned flat in eight minutes. People went temporarily insane as the

Victims wander in the ruins of
the Chelsea fire of 1908.

destruction spread. One woman wouldn't leave her house until she had filled her teakettle with water. Some lost the power of speech. One man committed suicide. Smoke was everywhere, blinding, choking, sickening. Runaway horses added to the danger. The strong gale blew women into fences and trees. Furniture rolled down Bellingham Hill. A man in the tower of the mayor's house on top of that hill saw burning boards several feet long fly through the air.

People fled toward Orient Heights in East Boston, but sparks were flying across Chelsea Creek and threatened that refuge. A shift of the wind to the south saved it, however. The main fire in Chelsea finally burned itself out at the water's edge. Inside of ten hours, a section of the city a mile and a half long and three quarters of a mile wide was leveled. Most municipal buildings, 13 churches, 8 schools, and over 2,800 other buildings had gone. Miles of granite curbing had crumbled into little piles of sand and gravel. Three thousand shade trees were ruined. The bodies of two thousand cats were found in the ruins. Eighteen people had been killed—perhaps more. Over three hundred people were injured. The loss was put at $20 million, but in human terms it was greater than the 1872 fire, for some 17,500 families were homeless and needed immediate food and shelter. The state sent in troops and put the city under martial law. Cordoned off, it kept out the many thousands of sightseers drawn to the scene of this enormous disaster. Relief poured in from across the nation. Government and private agencies joined forces to alleviate the effects of what was, at the time, the third largest fire in the country's history.

It may be that the nature of disaster by fire is changing in our modern urban complexes, though it would be foolish to make any predictions. Yet it would seem that in our cities of concrete, steel, and glass, with the progressive elimination of slums, and with the sophistication and efficiency of modern methods of fire control, that there should be fewer fires devastating whole urban areas. The threat may come from a new direction, perhaps prefigured by the tragedy that struck the Cocoanut Grove nightclub in Boston on November 28, 1942.

Shortly after ten that night, a couple in the dimly lit downstairs Melody Lounge, desiring even less light put out a weak bulb near them. A bus boy, told to put it back on, lit a match to see where to insert it. Although he was careful with the match, a spark caught the decorations, all inflammable. Within minutes, blue satin, bamboo, rattan, fiber, and netting were flaring. Fire and thick smoke spread rapidly through the packed room. People panicked and scrambled for the narrow staircase exit, unaware of a second exit behind the bar. But the killing smoke boiled up ahead of most of them and burst into the upstairs dining room and bar, causing a flash fire. People rushed for the few obvious exits. Some were found locked, and the revolving door at the main entrance jammed. Bodies piled up behind it, felled by the deadly smoke. Within twelve minutes, 490 people were dead. After a confused start, the fire department responded fast and performed efficiently. But they were too late to help those killed by smoke.

144

Damaged interior of the Cocoanut Grove nightclub after the 1942 fire. (Wide World Photos, Inc.)

Investigations, indictments, trials, and convictions followed. More important, stricter laws were passed throughout the country to avert similar tragedies: all exits in public buildings must open outward; revolving doors must have swinging doors on either side of them; emergency lighting with its own power sources must be provided; inflammable decorations were outlawed, and, in general, building codes and inspection requirements were tightened. To this extent, the Grove fire has saved thousands of lives. Techniques of treating burns developed in the aftermath of this fire have vastly improved chances of recovery for many who never heard of Cocoanut Grove.

Once again, after the horse thief of fire came by, the barn door of laws was locked. Still, it is worth something to learn from the past—at least we prevent *those* particular disasters from happening again. Yet there is no anticipating where next in our city of skyscrapers "the dreadful cry of fire" will be heard.

Interlude four: Boston to 1800

Quiet nights in old Boston town

. . . haveing an Invitation from the Gentlemen to Dine at Mr. Sheppard's, went Accordingly where was a Company of about 40 gentleman, after haveing Dined in a very Elegant manner upon Turtle &c. Drank about the Toasts, and Sang a Number of Songs, and where Exceedingly Merry Untill 3 a Clock in the Morning, from whence Went upon the Rake, Going Past the Commons in Our way Home, Surprised a Company Country Young Men and Women with a Violin at A Tavern Danceing and makeing Merry, upon Our Entering the house they Young Women Fled, we took Posession of the Room, haveing the Fidler and the Young man with us with the Keg of Sugard Dram, we where very Merry, from thence went to Mr. Jacob Wendells where we where Obliged to Drink Punch and Wine, and about 5 in the morning made our Excit and to Bed.

—Captain Francis Goelet
Journal, October 1, 1750

Boston half burnt up

Alarm'd this morning about 4 o'clock with cry that Boston was half burnt up. With that I got up, and looking out at my window beheld a blaze big enough to terrify any Heart of common Resolution, considering such valuable combustibles fed it—All College up by five. I went to Boston about 9 o'clock and there beheld a most shocking sight! Nigh 300 Houses consumed by Fire! It began at the Brazen Head and spread away to the Bunch of Grapes Tavern in King Street, then over to Fort Hill; burnt the Fort and blew up the magazine, then it also burnt a ship, several sloops and boats. By far the largest fire ever known in New England. It was seen above 30 miles from Boston.

—Nathaniel Ames
Diary, March 20, 1760

A riot of popes

A sorrowful accident happened this forenoon at the North End. the wheel of the carriage that the Pope was fixed on run over a Boy's head & he died instantly. The Sheriff, Justices, Officers of the Militia were ordered to destroy both Sº & North End Popes. In the afternoon they got the North End Pope pulled to pieces. they went to the Sº End but could not Conquer upon which the South End people brought out their pope & went in Triumph to the Northward and at the Mill Bridge a Battle begun between the people of Both Parts of the Town. The North End people having repaired their pope, but the South End people got the Battle (many were hurt & bruised on both sides) & Brought away the North End pope & burnt Both of them at the Gallows on the Neck. Several thousand people following them, hallowing &c.

—John Rowe (1715–87)
Diary, November 5, 1764

Hot words in the coffee house

I went to the Coffee House to pay a visit to Mr. Edington & was most smartly accosted by Capt. Dundass in the following words—"Ha, John are you there—Dammy I expected to have heard of your being hanged before now, for Dammy You deserve it" upon which I made reply "Surely Capt. Dundass, you're Joking"—upon which he answered "No"—Damn him if he was, for you are a Damn Incendiary & I shall see you hanged in your Shoes —& repeated the same—upon which I say to him "Then you are in earnest are you, I was in hopes you were joking"—"No" he repeated "Damn you, I am in earnest, I tell you. You are an Incendiary & I hope to see you hanged yet in your shoes." I took notice who were present as it was spoke about Twelve of Clock at Noon. Mr. Forrest, Mr. Phillip Dumaresque, Mr. Geo. Brinley & several officers of the Army who I did not know in the Coffee Room & entry way—I thought it Prudent not to take any Notice of it just then but came home to dinner.

—John Rowe (1715–87)
Diary, October 2, 1768

Gone with the blast about 1765

"Aunt Polly was, after my remembrance, a confirmed invalid, although tradition says she was the beauty and also the most talented one of the family. Her father used to relate marvels of her courage and perseverance and said, 'although they lived thirteen miles from Boston through woods and uninhabited roads, she would take his horse and chaise in the morning while he was busy with his workmen on his farm, and go that distance alone when sixteen and seventeen years old, call on various gentlemen and transact any business he entrusted her with, often paying or receiving money, and return after dark frequently, and laugh at her mother and sister's fears on her account.' She was also quite a literary genius. In short, her father doted upon her and was exceedingly proud of her. Her health at this time was as perfect as he fancied her in all other respects. No weather ever deterred her from going to town, as it was called, if her father wished. Thus she continued till eighteen or nineteen. About that time her father, who was a real English sportsman as well as farmer, and whose own woods and fields furnished ample game, had been out all day with his friend, Col. Quincy, hunting, had returned in the afternoon for rest and refreshment. They sat in the parlor chatting when, looking out of the window, they perceived Polly reclining on the grass directly under the window, deeply absorbed in a book. Her father, as usual, began his wonted praises of his pet, telling of her wondrous strength of nerve. 'She is not afraid of anything. Why, Colonel! she can fire off a gun as well as you can.' 'Nevertheless,' said the colonel, 'I could frighten her. I'll bet you any wager you please, if you will give me leave.' 'Well, you can try but you will find her proof, I can tell you.' No sooner said than the colonel stepped across the room, took up his gun which stood loaded in a corner, and fired it off out of the window under which the unconscious girl lay. She sprung up, but fainted and fell immediately. The gentlemen both rushed to her assistance, but, alas, one fit after another followed all night. A physician was summoned as fast as the fastest horse could go and return three miles to the nearest village, but a wreck, a sad wreck, was made. Ever after, the slightest noise alarmed her. The sight of a gun would bring on fits, and even after I knew her, the whole family were obliged to move on velvet. Children might play out of doors, but, when within, all their amusements must be quiet, lest they should disturb Aunt Polly. If it thundered, she shut herself up in the darkest and closest room and was in misery until the shower was over. Her boasted nervous system was ruined forever."

—*Grandmother Tyler's Book*

148

Some corner of a foreign field that is forever England

Richard Ames, a soldier of the Fourteenth Regiment, who had deserted since the arrival of the Troops, and taken about 25 miles from Town, was tried on the 22d ult. by a General Court Martial, & found guilty, and on Saturday received Sentence of Death; that the Execution to be on the Monday following: accordingly at 6 o'clock in the morning all the troops were in the Common, and at 7 o'clock, the said deserter was shot according to his sentence; and his body buried at the place of execution. He appeared very penitent; and was attended in his last hours by the Rev. Mr. Palmer, Chaplain of said regiment.

—Massachusetts *Gazette*
Thursday, November 3, 1768

Knock up a Tory

The Act for Tarring and Feathering being repealed, the old Act for nocturnal Painting seems to be revived. A number of executive Officers of the renewed Act made a visit to my House last Tuesday Night; and did me the honor to give my front Door a daub, gratis. I value this favor or savor the more, as the Paint is of our own growth, and what is had from our own BOWELLS. I must acquaint the Gentlemen that I am not insensible of the di-STINK-tion they have shewn me, and therefore request, that the next visit of this sort they make me, however late it may be, that they would knock me up, that I may entertain them according to their real merits.

—Geo. Erving
Notice in the *Boston News-Letter*,
June 2, 1774

Boston on the eve of revolution

March 21, 1775—. . . After breakfast, being a fine day, went to the Common & got upon the top of the High hill at the back of Mr. Hancock's fine house. Upon the top of this hill is a large flag Staff with a Vane; & here I enjoyed the finest prospect I have seen in America. All the Bay of Boston, with the many Islands, & the Harbour with the Shipping, & the water round to the Neck, with Boston neck & the fortifications on it; the whole Town lying below & on all sides, & the country on the other side of the Bay & Harbour to a considerable distance; which from this place makes a very agreable appearance, being entirely cleared & open; consisting of gently rising hills & vallies, thick planted with Churches & country seats. It being about the time of mustering & changing guard, & the troops quartered in the different parts of the town; the Drums & Fifes, with the musick of the different regiments was heard on every side & had a most charming effect.

—Dr. Robert Honyman
Colonial Panorama 1775

A Connecticut Yankee at Bunker Hill

Last Satterday was a day wich New england Never beheld the Scene before Cannons Roaring drums Beating Bells Ringing to Alarm her sons to go fourth in her defense & to spill their Precious Blood to save her from Ruing & misery Last Satterday the Battel began about 2 Clock in the afternoon & Lasted near 3 hours Grape Shot & musket balls as thick as Hail had not the Lord been on our side thousands must have fell but our lives wear spared so that we hope that 50 is the moste that are dead. Aboute as many more wounded their is 4 of our Company missing we suppose one dead 3 wounded Not mortally Wilson Roulinson, Roger Fox, Larance Sullivan Garshum Smith Dead newington people are well excep Daniel Demuns finger Shot of

In battel Some Shot throu their cloaths A remarcable providence that we were preserved For the Regulars stormed our entrenchment we was obliged to Retreat they firing upon us A mile their was above 4000 of the enimy tis supposed. It was thought we took an imprudent step by going so near the mouth of their cannon to entrench For they played upon us on three Sides with cannon.

Charlestown is all burnt down they intend to burn Cambrig.

—Ashbel Seymoure
Letter to Josiah Willard, June 19, 1775

Americans bombard Boston

Oct. 17, 1775—This evening, two floating batteries, accompanied with some boats, went down Cambridge River in order to throw some shot into Boston, to alarm the regular army, and fatigue them with extraordinary duty, and also to endeavor to take a floating battery from them which lay near Boston Neck. They got within three-quarters of a mile of the bottom of the Common, and the firing began between nine and ten o'clock. They fired about seventeen shot into the town; and then a nine-pounder in one of the batteries split: the cartridges took fire, and blew up the covering, or deck, on which several men were standing. Captain Blackley, of Marblehead, who commanded the battery, had the calf of his leg shot off, and was blown, with several others, into the water. A Portuguese sailor was so badly wounded in the thigh, that he bled to death before morning; another had his arm broken, and is very dangerous; four others were slightly wounded. The battery was much shattered, and partly sunk. They towed her up the river by morning. This manoeuvre is not generally approved by thinking people: it seemed to be rather a military frolic than a serious expedition. The camp appears to be a scene of wickedness. The oaths and execrations of the men that went on this frolic were horrid and dreadful. . . .

Oct. 20th . . . By Capt. Mackay, I learnt that the shot fired into Boston from the floating-battery struck the tents on the Common, and killed one man; also the manufactory-house, which is an hospital, which occasioned the removing of the sick; also the Lamb Tavern and Martin Brimmer's house. That both the troops and inhabitants were thrown into great consternation, expecting our army were making an assault upon them.

—Rev. Jeremy Belknap
Journal

Darkness at noon

Friday, May the 19th 1780. This day was the most Remarkable day that ever my eyes beheld the air had bin full of smoak to an uncommon degree So that wee could scairce see a mountain at two miles distance for 3 or 4 days Past till this day after Noon the smoak all went off to the South at sunset a very black bank of a cloud appeared in the south and west the Nex morning cloudey and thundered in the west about ten oclock it began to Rain and grew vere dark and at 12 was allmost as dark as Nite so that wee was obliged to lite our candels and Eate our dinner by candel lite at Noon day but between 1 and 2 oclock it grew lite again but in the Evening the cloud caim over us again   the moon was about the full it was the darkest Nite that ever was seen by us in the world.

—Phineas Sprague
Diary (now lost)

"Wife-swapping"—1784 version

Last Sunday morning I went for a ride in the chaise to the castle a little below Dorchester Point and since it is necessary to cross a small ferry I asked for the boat, but as it was Sunday they did not wish to send it. Patiently I returned over the same road, quite good and pleasant, and when I was about to cross some low ground, found that with the rising tide there was about one foot of water there. A very decent man approached at that moment on horseback with a woman on the haunches. He came up to me and asked if I could take her across in my chaise, as she was afraid. I told him yes, and with that she jumped off the horse, got into my chaise, and I carried her two miles. She then asked me to let her off and remained there in a house waiting for her husband, who came on horseback some distance behind us. Now who is there in Europe who judges so favorably of the human heart as to deliver thus to a stranger his young and beautiful wife? Nor who so crackbrained as to think it a great sin to cross a river on Sunday?

—Francisco de Miranda
The New Democracy in America

A smallpox "holiday" in 1792

It was curious to observe the appearance of the town when innoculation first commenced. Business was in a great measure suspended, and multitudes of all sexes, ages, and conditions were continually flaunting about the streets in their calico loose gowns. So much was the calico gown an appendage of innoculation that a poor fellow who as many others in similar circumstances had the distemper at the Town's expense asked the Selectmen with great simplicity whether the Town found [supplied] calico too? Nothing could be more cheerful and gay than the first appearance. People seemed to think that they were only engaged in a frolic which would amuse and divert them for a few days and weeks, and had no apprehension of the danger to which they were exposed. But alas! . . . it never before proved so distressing and fatal to so great a proportion of those who took it.

> —Rev. Samuel West
> Family Anecdotes And Memories

A rash bill in Woburn, 1792

Woburn Dr. to Daniel Reed Junior, to boarding Sally priest nine weeks at 2s. per week ending— ye 5th of March—

	£.	s.	
	0.	18.	0

to her bringing the itch into my family I leave to your generosity, but money should not hire me to have it.

> Daniel Reed Junior

Woburn March 2 ye 1792
Allowed for Itch

		1—	0.	—0
	£1.	18.	0

> —Woburn Town Records

"Proper" Bostonians, 1797

Now, my brethren, as we see and experience, that all things here are frail and changeable and nothing here to be depended upon: Let us seek those things which are above, and at the same time let us pray to Almighty God, while we remain in the tabernacle, that he would give us the grace of patience and strength to bear up under all our troubles, which at this day God knows we have our share. Patience, I say, for were we not possessed of a great measure of it, you could not bear up under the daily insults you meet with in the streets of Boston; much more on public days of recreation, how are you shamefully abus'd, and that at such a degree, that you may truly be said to carry your lives in your hands; and the arrows of death are flying about your heads; helpless old women have their clothes torn off their backs, even to the exposing of their nakedness. . . . My brethren, let us not be cast down under these and many other abuses we at present labour under: for the darkest is before the break of day.

—Prince Hall
Charge to the African Lodge

Evening on West Boston Bridge*

I strolled in the evening on the bridge which crosses the Charles River to Cambridge. This bridge, together with the dam, is one and a half English miles in length; it is called the West Boston Bridge and is of graceful design, lightsome and elegant. In the middle there is a lock with gates for the passage of boats. There are sidewalks with handrails for pedestrians, the whole is illuminated with splendid lanterns. Never before in any country have I seen a bridge so beautiful, and of such a broad expanse. There the crystal clarity of the water spreads out in wide sweeps beneath the overhanging bridge, to the left are distant fertile hills covered with houses, to the right Charlestown, behind, the old town of Boston and in the forefront gay meadows with the soaring pinnacles of Cambridge

farther off. Every aspect of the view achieves an unsurpassed excellence. During this evening the bridge was crowded with more people than on any single day of the whole year. Whoever had carriage, buggy or horse or could find one for hire, rode in to the famous *Commencement*. Many hackney carriages, buggies, cabriolets and saddle horses wound ceaselessly by. Beside the hackney carriages of the prim and sedate there were others full of negroes, negresses and little black imps. Everyone free, everyone dressed in a similar fashion. There were hackney carriages and cabriolets full of gay young ladies with gentlemen escorts, other young ladies strolled by on foot with their escorts. How far away was the severe Puritan spirit which once held sway in Boston. And thus have strict habits changed today. . . .

—Julian Ursyn Niemcewicz (1758–1841)
Diary, July 19, 1798
(trans. Metchie J. E. Budka)

* Where the Longfellow Bridge now stands.

Ice rides through the streets

The season has been extremely cold and we have had an almost constant succession of snows, which have descended with such regularity and lye so level on the ground that it has rendered it exceedingly useful for carriage travel . . . sleys of every description with their jingling bells and cheerful inhabitants secure in furs from the intense keenness of the air, are continually running by window, and sled-loads of solid ice chill and dazzle the eye as they pass on to their subterranean retreat, the icehouse in town. This ice is produced a few miles from town, formed into massy bodies ressembling the foundation stones of a building, almost clear as crystal, and makes a most beautiful appearance as it moves on glittering in the sunbeams.

—Mary Byles
Letterbook, February 23, 1799

155

CHAPTER FIVE

Hues and Cries

In the beginning there were neither cops nor robbers, but there were drunks. At the earliest Court of Assistants they provided first for the ministers, second for the military, third to keep firearms from the Indians, fourth to protect the corn supply, and lastly to end drunkenness. The punishment for the latter was to be swift and stern: fines, whipping, and "bilbowes"—shackles for the feet. Governor Winthrop set an example by discouraging the custom of giving toasts at meals, a practice he thought sadly overindulged. They were to discover that there was no easy way to put the cork back in the bottle.

Since no community considers itself civilized until it has some group to enforce its will, the Court shortly turned its attention to this matter. Drawing on their English heritage, rather than copying the Indians who had neither police nor crime, they named constables for Dorchester, Roxbury, Charlestown, Watertown, and Salem. In April 1631, they ordered that "Watches" be maintained in Boston every night from sunset. "If any person fire off a piece after the watch is set, he shall be fined forty shillings, or be whipped." The Court was determined to have a quiet night's rest.

The constables were appointed by the Colony government, and not until a February 1636 town meeting, did Boston choose its own watch members. Provision was also made for a "Ward" to keep order in the daytime. Service in the watch and the new ward was unpaid, and was to be performed in turn by the citizens of the town.

At first, the duties of the watch and ward were not specified other than to keep the peace. They were to serve under and assist the constable. His duties, detailed in a 1646 law, included serving warrants, organizing "hues & cries" after criminals, and arresting lawbreakers. The emphasis on the last was given to those "overtaken with drinke, swearing, breaking the Saboth, lying, vagrant persons," and Boston's special bête noire, the "night walkers." As the one active and effective officer of the town, the constable's duties soon went beyond police work into gathering taxes, levying fines and attachments, assisting customs officials, keeping lists of lost goods and straying animals, summoning coroner's juries, notifying voters of elections, and other such miscellaneous jobs.

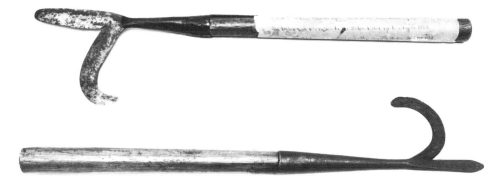

Bill hooks used in Boston by watchmen from at least 1701 until 1854. (Courtesy of The Bostonian Society, Old State House.)

Quite likely when the first two men were hanged in Boston for murder on September 28, 1637, the constable had charge of the business. One was John Williams who had escaped from prison and then murdered his fellow escapee. The other was William Schooler, who brought a bad reputation with him from London. After agreeing to guide a young servant girl to a town beyond the Merrimack River, he had abandoned her in the woods—he claimed. Six months later an Indian found her dead body. The crime was not fully proved against Schooler, but he was hanged anyway. He was the first of a long line that Boston and the Commonwealth would treat as "worthy of murder." Sacco and Vanzetti were to follow in Schooler's footsteps.

The constable's job was an unpopular one. Keeping such a strict eye on his neighbors' business resulted in frequent assaults on the constable. But if they were not prompt and efficient in their duties, they could be, and often were, fined. By 1653, it became difficult to find citizens who would accept the "honor" of being constable, so the General Court fined Boston men a stiff ten pounds if they tried to evade the job.

These early officers were not uniformed, but so that they could be recognized when performing their duties, they were provided with a badge of office. This was a five-foot black staff, tipped with five inches of brass. By statute, the constable was to take it with him "when he goeth to discharge any part of his Office." This could alert people whom the constable was after and let them get away, so later he was not required to carry it on certain special occasions.

Tithingmen were annually appointed by the 1680s. Their principal duty was to seek out and report people who broke the Sabbath laws. Later they shared some of the constables' tasks of supervising their neighbors' behavior. In spite of such assistance, the constables felt overworked and petitioned the Boston selectmen in 1692 to relieve them from collecting taxes. They did not get paid for such an unpleasant job and it prevented their "attendance to those more proper parts of their office." The town, as usual, ignored their complaint.

The first prison in Boston, built in 1635, was a wooden building with barred windows. It was located on the south side of Court Street, then called Prison Lane. Apparently it had an "inner room" for "close confinement" of particularly

157

FIVE ARCH KEYS OF THE BOSTON JAIL ON QUEEN (NOW COURT
IN 1722 & UP TO 1823 MORE THAN 00.000 PRISONERS WERE LOCKED U

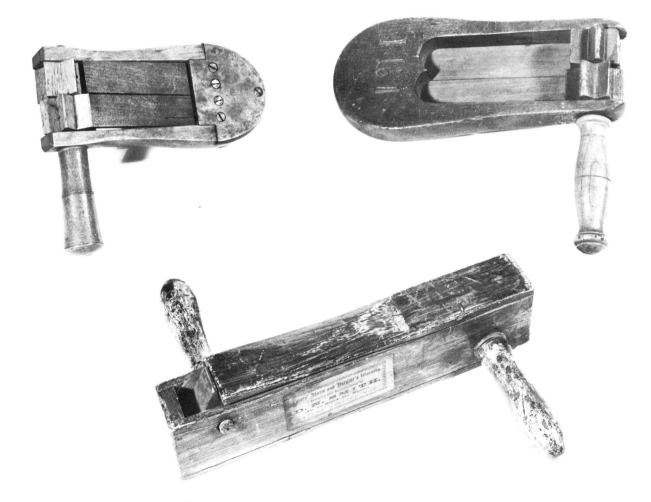

dangerous criminals. Unheated in winter, it was, reported one visitor, a place of "meagre Looks and ill smells." By 1648 it was in need of drastic repairs. There was a fence around the prison, but it was usually falling down and rarely kept friends of prisoners from talking with them through the barred windows and slipping them food and money. Often it was something more useful. One prisoner testified in 1709 that he saw "a Young man come to the Prison Grate . . . and got upon a Ladder and talk'd" to another prisoner for more than an hour. He did not hear what they said "but observ'd they drank Severall halfe pints of Wine together." A female prisoner added that the man on the ladder, she "believed," had thrown in a "Long Case knife with wooden handles & two Edges," and she "supposed" this was how an inmate had escaped.

The jailkeeper reported in 1714 that he had sixteen people in prison, two of them women. Six were in for debt, three for theft, one for "buggary," one for adultery, and five for drinking. Particularly dangerous criminals, however, were not kept in Boston prison, but sent to the fort on Castle Island. Through the seventeenth and eighteenth centuries this fort served as a sort of local Alcatraz, though some judges were reluctant to send prisoners there, fearing that the Crown officials would not honor a writ for habeas corpus.

Jailkeepers had other problems. About 1740 a letterwriter, signing himself "Lover of Virtue," inquired if males and females were being kept apart in jail "as the Rules of Chastity require." The same gentleman wondered if some of the prisoners were being allowed to buy "strong drink" and to spend their time and money "gaming in the prison house or yards." To prevent such evils, he suggested raising the keeper's salary, and instituting a work program for the inmates.

A few years later, William Young, then keeper of the Boston "gaol," complained that several people jailed for debt had brought their families in with them. "Persons are constantly going to and from the prison and have great opportunity of giving assistance to the prisoners to enable them to brake Goale." Further, the building was being damaged "by their Choping fire wood on the Floors." The Court agreed that this was "a very irregular disorderly practice" and ordered it stopped.

From 1712 there had been a system of paid watchmen, "qualified, fixed in numbers, and officered." Watchhouses were built for them in different sections of the town, the ancestors of the modern precincthouses. Quickly, these watchmen became notorious for sleeping on duty. Not disputing the charge, the watchmen argued that low pay forced them to work at other jobs during the daytime to support their families, "sunlighting," we might call it today.

When there was a rash of burglaries in 1789, the watch was castigated from all sides. The entire watch, declared one indignant citizen, had been asleep for seven months. "The captains are generally men in the prime of life, aged from 90 to 100 years, and the crew only average about fourscore, and so we have the advantage of their age and experience—at least, the robbers do."

Lock and keys from the Boston jail on Queen Street (now Court), from the eighteenth century. (Courtesy of The Bostonian Society, Old State House.)

Police and watchmen's rattles, used instead of whistles to sound alarms. (Upper) Type used from at least 1700 to 1855. (Bottom) Two-handed rattle. (Courtesy of The Bostonian Society, Old State House.)

Various suggestions of reform were forthcoming. Parson Belknap, founder of the Massachusetts Historical Society, suggested the most extreme solution. He wanted to divide the town into wards, each ward with an overseer. Every ten houses would have an inspector to visit them each morning before ten, make a written report on specified conditions to the overseer by ten, and he to do the same by noon for the selectmen. It betokened a moral straitjacket unequaled by the strictest dictatorship.

Under an act of the General Court, the Boston watch was completely reorganized in 1796 on a far different plan. The selectmen were given the appointing power. When the architect Charles Bulfinch became Superintendent of Police two years later, he headed a force of 12 constables and 20 watchmen for a town whose population was nearly 25,000. If the same proportions held true today, 1,600 men would have to be dropped from Boston's present force of 2,600.

When Madison took the country into the needless second war with England in 1812, one hundred special watchmen were appointed to patrol Boston in case of riot. If one occurred, "well-disposed citizens" were asked "to place lights in all their front windows." Boys and apprentices were warned to "remain in doors" or they would be "considered rioters." It was two years, however, before the British threatened the town, and then the help of boys and apprentices was urgently solicited to build fortifications that fortunately were never used.

When Boston became a city in 1822, the mayor and board of aldermen administered the police. Boston's new police court first convened on June 20. As new areas were annexed to the city, watches were assigned to them. The pay began to rise, too. The watch had been paid fifty cents a night in 1812. Seven years later, the watch and their friends lingered at a town meeting until most of the other voters had gone, then pushed through a pay raise for themselves to seventy-five cents. The next town meeting quickly rescinded that vote. Gradually they relented, and by 1829 the watch were paid sixty cents a night, and four years later were boosted to seventy-five cents, while the constables had reached one dollar.

More than salaries were changing. The new city was entering a period of spectacular growth. "Enterprise of every description," one Bostonian wrote his son in 1833, was "in its full tide. The rail-roads are building, flats are filling up . . . dwelling houses and stores are shooting up from their foundations and an immense court house is going to be constructed back of the old one." Solomon Willard, architect of the Bunker Hill monument, had drawn the plan, and estimated the cost at $90,000. "Others say it must cost much more." The others proved to be right.

Police duties changed with the city and the times. The daily flow of people in and out of the city and the influx of immigrants, required a day police force separate from the night watch, and was formed under a city marshal in 1838. Some former police functions were given to new departments of the city

Winslow Homer's sketches of Boston Street Characters for *Ballou's Pictorial Drawing-Room Companion*, showing the kind of people the watchmen (center bottom) had to deal with.

LIFE IN TOWN.

CITY SKETCHES

THE CHILDREN OF THE POOR.

THE DOCK LOAFER

THE CHARCOAL PEDLER.

EMIGRANTS.

SKATERS.

THE DUSTMAN.

THE WATCHMAN.

BOSTON STREET CHARACTERS.

[For description, see page 233.]

161

The courthouse in Boston built 1811–12 on School Street on the site of the present Old City Hall, drawn by J. Kidder.

government: health, streets, sewer, and building among them. Criminals became more mobile thanks to the railroad, and their crimes more sophisticated and better organized. Behavior which had been easier to regulate in a small town, became more disruptive in the larger city as it also became less susceptible to control.

The response of one individual to the changing situation was remarkable. John Augustus, after nearly four decades as a shoemaker working with leather, discovered at the age of fifty-seven his true profession—working with people. In Boston Police Court one August morning of 1841, he saw a "ragged and wretched looking man" charged with being a common drunkard. Talking briefly with him, Augustus decided his case was far from hopeless and went bail for him. Three weeks later he brought the man back to court, transformed in appearance and outlook. So impressed was the judge with the results that instead of sending the man to the House of Correction as usual, he fined him one cent plus costs and freed him. Ten years later, Augustus could report the man was still industrious and sober and doubtless saved "from a drunkard's grave."

Before the year had ended, Augustus had bailed seventeen persons for similar offenses and was fully launched on the career which gave him the name of the world's "first probation officer." Soon this thin fidgety man whose skin looked like a wrinkled piece of his own leather was familiar not only in the courts but in "the *very* worst haunts in the city." His warm-hearted impulsive benevolence confronted the vast misery produced in Boston by immigration and industrialism, and at least made a dent in it.

In the eighteen years before his death in 1859, he bailed out nearly two thousand men, women, and children, besides assisting as a sort of one-man charity society more than three thousand females "neglected by the world." One year, for example, he rescued "seven young girls from houses of ill-fame; these girls were from ten to thirteen years of age." Employment agencies had sent them to the brothels. Homeless children, frequently deserted or orphaned and found wandering in the streets, were brought to his house where he and his wife cared for them until they could be placed with responsible families. Once walking through the Leverett Street jail he encountered a crying seven-year-old boy. The charge against him was committing rape on a ten-year-old girl. Augustus asked that the boy be brought to court and bailed to Augustus, who restored him to his parents.

It was not all sweetness and light for this gentle, patient man. Some police and court officials opposed him, feeling his work a hindrance in "clearing the dockets" of these "incorrigible criminals." Further, they lost fees in processing the prisoners. One writer styled them "professional cagers who look upon man-kind as animals to be caged at so much a head." Constables would lose sixty-two cents for taking the prisoner to jail, the clerk twenty-five cents and the turnkey forty cents if Augustus had his way. Thus they had an economic stake in opposing probation. Some citizens felt that strong New England idea of sin— that these people had sinned and should be punished, not helped. Such people called him "Mr. Meddle" and "this Peter Funk philanthropist and pea-nut reformer." Nor did all prisoners respond warmly to his endeavors. One police officer said a drunken woman had spit in Augustus' face.

A woodcut of John Augustus, considered the first "Probation Officer."

> Everybody in court appeared astonished at this act of ingratitude, except Mr. Augustus, who meekly remarked, "Well, what of that; it didn't hurt me; besides she was drunk then. Give me a chance to talk to her when she is sober and I'll answer for it, she won't spit in my face then."

The woman was bailed to him.

Perhaps he was a bit fanatic in his chosen work. His most distinctive characteristic was talking very rapidly. His "tongue . . . appears to be hung in the middle and oiled at each end," said a journalist. Augustus' own 1852 account of his labors does not catch this, although it gives a quaint picture of his work. In the period he surveys, half the sentences to the House of Correction were for being a "Common Drunkard." He had records of more than eight thousand men and women so affected, some of whose names "would create a great smoke and some fire in our city, and could result in no benefit."

As a pioneer, Augustus set remarkable precedents. Keeping detailed records of his "clients," he did not go bail for just anyone, but carefully selected persons who would best respond to his kind of assistance. Delinquent children were placed in suitable homes. People he bailed, he followed up, finding them places to live and work, continuing his guidance and advice. He helped their families, too, and soon was doing "preventive" work with many other people

to the limit of his strength and finances. Scores of people contributed to his work. He continually suggested reforms in the court system, such as the need for public defenders, the establishment of rehabilitation centers, and the necessity for having "the temple of justice watched"—the germ of an ombudsman idea. "The object of the law," he said, "is to reform criminals, and to prevent crime and not to punish maliciously, or from a spirit of revenge."

The response of the city to the new urban conditions was the professionalization of the police. On May 26, 1854, at 6:00 P.M. the Boston Watch and Police passed into history and the Boston Police began. A force of 250 men under a chief of police was formed and were paid at the rate of two dollars a day. They were immediately tested by a call to suppress a riot started when a fugitive slave, Anthony Burns, was arrested by federal officers. They were on continuous duty for nine days and nights before the disturbance was over.

The new department embarked on a program of improvements. The city was divided into divisions and police stations were built or acquired in each division. Telegraphic communication linked them with police headquarters at City Hall. The fee system which had plagued Augustus, was regulated. The old watchmen's rattles, and the billhook, that had been standard equipment, were replaced with short sturdy "billy" clubs. The question of uniforms was hotly debated. Since 1838, they had worn green leather badges on their hats to identify them. Some years later a simple white ribbon with the word "Police"

164

Woodcut of prisoner "signing the pledge" to drink no more used as an illustration in John M. Spears' pamphlet "Labors for the Prisoner."

The new badge of the police in 1853. The hound symbolized watchfulness and activity. It was designed by Mr. E. A. G. Roulston. Before this, the police wore the word "POLICE" in large metallic letters around their hats. The star was called "The Boston Star."

Boston Police Badges, 1853 to 1959. (Courtesy of The Bostonian Society, Old State House.)

lettered in black replaced this. Then in 1846 came a patent-leather badge. A brass badge in the form of a six-pointed star took over in 1853 and was changed to a silver octagon the next year. From then, with few exceptions, the silver badge in some form has prevailed.

Uniforms were another matter. Uniforms would "expose" them to criminals some complained. If police were readily recognizable they would be assaulted by the public. But the advocates of uniforms argued that citizens needed to know how to find an officer when they required one. Discipline would improve, too, since the men couldn't sneak naps or drinks or patronize brothels when in uniform. By 1859, the force was completely dressed in its blue coat with shiny buttons, black vests, and blue pants. Pistols were first provided the police unofficially when the harbor patrol acquired some in 1853. The murder of several police officers soon produced demands that they all be authorized to carry arms. From 1857, some men secured their own weapons and carried them without formal permission. During the conscription riot of 1863, a supply was obtained, and shortly afterward about a third of the force was given a variety of weapons. It wasn't until 1885 that the whole force was officially equipped with uniform weapons—Smith-Wesson double action .38-caliber revolvers.

The police had been unable to escape involvement in the contest over slavery that was soon to shake the union to its foundations. In October 1842, constables had seized George Latimer, an escaped slave, on the streets, but abolitionists

Above, left to right, Francis Tukey, Esq., City Marshal of Boston, Wendell Phillips, and Thomas Sims, the slave. Opposite, police conveying Sims to the vessel.

bought him from his master and freed him. In February 1851, under the new Fugitive Slave Law, another slave, Shadrach, was captured. But a crowd of free Negroes broke into his place of confinement and freed him. Three months later Thomas Sims was not so lucky. Embarrassed by their earlier failure, Marshal Tukey of the Boston Police made an all-out effort, and Sims had the dubious honor of being the first fugitive slave returned to servitude by the Boston Police. But Marshal Tukey, who was a "tough cop," eventually lost his job, partly as a result of his excessive zeal on this occasion. The last fugitive case before the Civil War was Anthony Burns in May 1854.

On the twenty-fourth of that month, the United States marshal arrested Burns, lately fled from Virginia, on the Boston streets on a trumped-up charge of larceny. The Antislavery convention was meeting in the city that same week and emotions peaked fast. Rev. Theodore Parker wrote inflammatory posters. "Kidnapping again!" they screamed. "Shall Boston steal another man?" "See to it that no free citizen of Massachusetts is dragged into slavery." A huge protest meeting packed Faneuil Hall and Parker cleverly whipped their fury to fever pitch calling them "fellow citizens of Virginia." Then he demanded "are we to have deeds as well as words?" Out into the night they streamed. Another minister, Rev. Thomas Wentworth Higginson, later to lead a black regiment in the war, led the attack on the courthouse where Burns was being held—but everything went wrong. Higginson got his chin split open; one courthouse guard was shot. The crowd hesitated. Bronson Alcott walked around in a transcendental mist. Then troops arrived and restored order. The grand assault had failed. For ten days and nights the courthouse was guarded by soldiers, marines, and at the end by the police. Legal efforts to save Burns failed when Commissioner Loring opened every loophole in the law to send Burns back and closed any loophole that might have freed him.

Two thousand soldiers, preceded by two hundred Boston policemen, marched Burns through Boston streets packed with crowds taunting them, to

166

the ship that took him back to slavery. Burns, wearing a new suit given him for the occasion, thought that was "a lot of folks to see a colored man walk down the street." The cost to the government to keep Burns a slave was put at $100,000. It was money wasted, as Burns was bought by the abolitionists and given his freedom. Commissioner Loring lost his state job as judge of probate and was dropped from the Harvard faculty. The legislature passed laws to fine and jail peace officers who cooperated in the capture of fugitive slaves.

Slavecatchers might come and go, but drunkards, it seemed, went on forever. Police Chief Edward Savage reported that the year 1861 was the worst year for drunkenness from 1854 to 1871. He laid it to the war, but liquor could be bought everywhere. Hotels, groceries, barrooms, "jug-rooms"—more than three thousand places existed, one outlet for every eighty-five persons. He made a personal survey of twelve hundred drunkards in the summer of 1872, asking what they were arrested for; most said being drunk or "tight," some said "find out," and others said they had the "horse disease" or "got corned." Savage solemnly reported this information in his yearly report. When he asked them what they drank, most said whiskey or beer, but other intoxicants listed included ether, Wheeler's Bitters, benzine, indigo, hyacinth, male berry coffee, pigweed, and "cut-nails," and ninety-one answered "everything."

When Garrison, Douglass, and other abolitionists tried to celebrate the anniversary of John Brown's execution, a group of anti-abolitionists took over their meeting and expelled them from Tremont Temple, December 5, 1860. (*Harper's Weekly,* December 15, 1860.)

Some reformers were tempted by the existence of a strong police force to hope that their views of morality could be imposed upon the community. Several attempts at prohibition were made but failed. Although the community backed away slightly from such rigidity, it continued to license liquor dealers even more strictly. The police department continued to regulate public morals, but did not try to effect fundamental reform.

The politics of who controlled this force became increasingly important. From 1853 to 1878, the department was commanded by a chief of police appointed jointly by the mayor and aldermen. That year the system was changed to a board of three police commissioners appointed by the mayor. As domination of the city slipped from the old "Yankee" element, this did not sit well with them. "It is as certain," one Republican proclaimed, "that the force will be used for partisan purposes as it is that the mayor is a politician. Whoever knew a Democratic politician to lose such an opportunity?" With such visions of what could happen with Mayor Prince and his Democratic board of aldermen running the seven-hundred-man force, the Republicans in 1885 pushed a bill through the state legislature taking control of the department away from Boston and putting it under a three-man commission appointed by the governor. At least he was still a Republican!

State control of the Boston Police lasted from 1885 until 1962. The form changed in 1906 to a single commissioner appointed for a five-year term by the governor. In 1962, the power to appoint and remove the police commissioner was restored to the mayor of Boston. The security of tenure enjoyed by the commissioners under state control was unequaled by any other American police department.

Under the state-appointed commissioners, some popular but nonpolice functions were discontinued. One of these was the soup kitchens, a charity ladled out to the poor at the stationhouses and costing $5,000 by 1876. Overnight lodging was provided in police stations for 63,000 penniless vagrants the same year, 51,000 of them nonresidents. The police took on such unpopular duties as covering strikes, not often on the side of strikers. Improvements went on: matrons were provided at the stations to assist when women and children were arrested. Four park policemen were put on bicycles in 1896, and by 1900 the department was equipped with nine police ambulances.

The first state commissioner, Stephen O'Meara (1906–18), made a strong and successful effort to keep the police free from political influence. High standards were maintained, although the department did not encourage imagination and experimentation: it became deeply conservative and traditional

Not until 1880 were people allowed to smoke in public in Boston. Previously, smokers were liable to arrest if found smoking in the streets or even on the Common except in a special section set aside for that purpose and named "the Smoker's Circle," as shown in this 1851 view.

169

during this period. Still, Raymond Fosdick could say of O'Meara's force that it "was conducted with a disregard for political considerations rarely encountered in American cities."

Also established in 1906 was the Boston Juvenile Court, under Judge Harvey H. Baker. Many had long realized the need for better methods of dealing with juvenile delinquency. The House of Refuge for Children dated from 1826. An 1870 law required Suffolk County court to hear cases against children under sixteen "separate from the general and ordinary criminal business." Under Judge Baker, and his immediate successors, Frederick P. Cabot and John Forbes Perkins, the court became widely recognized for pioneering more intelligent and psychologically sound ways of dealing with juvenile offenders. Under Cabot's leadership, a clinic was established and named in honor of his predecessor, for "the intensive study of baffling cases which fail to respond to ordinary probationary treatment." Their examinations aid the judge of the court in deciding what disposition of the cases before him will best serve both the child and the community.

The second commissioner was Edwin U. Curtis, a former Boston mayor and wealthy Republican "Brahmin." He was efficient, honest, courageous, but also autocratic and stubborn. Less than nine months after he was appointed, Boston Police went on strike. On Tuesday, September 9, 1919, at 5:45 P.M., after weeks of unsuccessful negotiation, 1,117 of Boston's 1,544 policemen turned in their badges and struck for the right to have a union. Other grievances included wages and working conditions. Not much more than a quarter of the force was left to protect Boston that Tuesday night.

The Mayor, Andrew J. Peters, was that oddity, a Yankee Democrat. He was a reform mayor serving between the first and second terms of James Michael Curley, and had been elected on a "Good Government Association" platform. Curley called them the "Goo-Goos." Peters asked Gov. Calvin Coolidge to mobilize units of the State Guard, but Coolidge refused on assurances from Curtis that he was "ready for anything." The Tuesday evening *Transcript* headline said "Boston's Protection Arranged." For one thing, Harvard was sending seven hundred student volunteers.

It didn't take the crowds long to discover that Boston, even with Harvard's help, was largely unprotected. A holiday mood spread. The Common blossomed out in illegal crap games. Later the mood turned ugly. Stones were thrown through store windows. Trucks were overturned. Mattresses and railroad ties blocked the streetcar lines. Suddenly people realized there were no police to restrain them. Rowdies swaggered through South Boston streets, which were soon covered with broken eggs. Others joined them to loot. On Washington Street, in the business district, men were backed against the wall and relieved of their wallets and watches as the crowd looked on. The main rioting took place in and around Scollay Square. Several women were dragged into dark doorways and raped. Professional criminals swarmed into the city and began a methodical looting. The few policemen who tried to stop them were badly beaten up. Four Harvard students were almost lynched near Cornhill.

170

The Commonwealth of Massachusetts.

By His Excellency

CALVIN COOLIDGE
GOVERNOR

A PROCLAMATION

There appears to be a misapprehension as to the position of the police of Boston. In the deliberate intention to intimidate and coerce the government of this Commonwealth a large body of policemen, urging all others to join them, deserted their posts of duty, letting in the enemy. This act of theirs was voluntary, against the advice of their well wishers, long discussed and premeditated, and with the purpose of obstructing the power of the government to protect its citizens or even to maintain its own existence. Its success meant anarchy. By this act through the operation of the law they dispossessed themselves. They went out of office. They stand as though they had never been appointed.

Other police remained on duty. They are the real heroes of this crisis. The State Guard responded most efficiently. Thousands have volunteered for the Guard and the Militia. Money has been contributed from every walk of life by the hundreds of thousands for the encouragement and relief of these loyal men. These acts have been spontaneous, significant and decisive. I propose to support all those who are supporting their own government with every power which the people have entrusted to me.

There is an obligation, inescapable, no less solemn to resist all those who do not support the government. The authority of the Commonwealth cannot be intimidated or coerced. It cannot be compromised. To place the maintenance of the public security in the hands of a body of men who have attempted to destroy it would be to flout the sovereignty of the laws the people have made. It is my duty to resist any such proposal. Those who would counsel it join hands with those whose acts have threatened to destroy the government. There is no middle ground. Every attempt to prevent the formation of a new police force is a blow at the government. That way treason lies. No man has a right to place his own ease or convenience or the opportunity of making money above his duty to the State.

This is the cause of all the people. I call on every citizen to stand by me in executing the oath of my office by supporting the authority of the government and resisting all assaults upon it.

GIVEN at the Executive Chamber, in Boston, this twenty-fourth day of September, in the year of our Lord one thousand nine hundred and nineteen, and of the Independence of the United States of America the one hundred and forty-fourth.

CALVIN COOLIDGE.

By His Excellency the Governor.

HERBERT H. BOYNTON,
Deputy, Acting Secretary of the Commonwealth.

God Save the Commonwealth of Massachusetts.

Coolidge's "belated" proclamation against the police strike.

Police dispatchers on duty answering emergency calls. (Phil Stack.)

Coolidge spent the first part of the evening waiting for something to happen. When it got near his bedtime and he had heard nothing, he dismissed the State Guard unit he was keeping at the Armory and went home to bed. Nobody, he later claimed, told him anything about the rioting until the next morning. The mayor spent the night at his home in Brookline. He kept in touch with the crisis by telephone, but he felt his hands were legally tied; there was nothing he could do. By morning, however, he decided that he was authorized by two statutes to act under law to suppress tumults, riots, or violent disturbances of the public order. He assumed control of the police force and called out local members of the State Guard, asking the Governor for at least three more regiments. Coolidge called out the rest of the Guard. By Wednesday night, the Guard and volunteer police had controlled the situation, but by then six persons had been killed. By Thursday morning order had been restored to most of the city.

With law and order reestablished, Coolidge suddenly acted boldly. He took control of the police force away from Peters and put Curtis back in power, lest Peters might compromise the dispute with the striking policemen. A confused public opinion supported the Governor. President Wilson called the strike a crime; a New York paper termed it "civic treason." Local newspapers, ministers and priests, the Chamber of Commerce, all denounced the strikers. "All America backs Boston," headlined the *Transcript,* who warned their readers against the savagery of the riot ("an orgy of robbery and destruction"). They detected the foul smell of communism in the whole business, and said the strike was a "stab at the heart." It did not help matters when the bartenders threatened to strike in sympathy with the police.

The public contributed $500,000 to compensate the volunteer police and the State Guard for their services. Curtis took advantage of a legal loophole to discharge all the striking police, claiming they hadn't struck, but had "deserted." The rest of his short term he spent recruiting and training replacements. "Police officials," said one authority, "felt that they were doing well if they kept the system from breaking down completely."

To avoid the breakdown, the city approved a number of reforms including a pay raise, which if granted earlier might have prevented the strike. Coolidge summed the situation up in a simple catchphrase that caught the public mind: "There is no right to strike against the public safety by anybody, anywhere, anytime." The public's superficial understanding of the crisis and Coolidge's role in it, had oddly focused attention on him as the "hero." "By doing little more than nothing," said one commentator, "he managed to project himself into the national limelight." So the man who some maintained was "the laziest man who was ever Governor of Massachusetts," who was said to smoke a cigar and read the *Herald* mornings and nap afternoons, was rewarded with the Vice Presidency and then succeeded to the Presidency. He proved as busy in Washington as he had been in Boston.

The next several commissioners constantly modernized the force. They faced peculiar problems because of national prohibition and the increasing use of automobiles. Six women were added to the force in 1921. Ballistics and photographic sections were added to the detective service. Prowl cars were bought. The signal system was improved. Training classes for patrolmen were introduced. New methods employed to help ease chronic traffic problems included parking meters and off-street garages. Automatic traffic signals at dangerous intersections were introduced in 1951.

In recent years, the department has undergone several searching studies to increase its efficiency, notably the finance committee survey in 1941 and the Quinn Tamm report in 1964. The national prominence given to such events as the 1962 TV *Biography of a Bookie,* gangland murders, the Brinks case, and the "Boston Strangler" case, suggests that crime runs rampant in John Winthrop's old town. While the shortcomings make headlines, on the whole the twenty-six-hundred members of the Boston Police do their work well, bravely, and efficiently.

Middlesex County put up its Court House in East Cambridge, the Lechmere Point area, to accommodate Andrew Craigie, a land speculator with holdings in that area.

When compared with the average of about two hundred American metropolitan areas, Boston has half the murders, half the rapes, half the larcenies, one-third the assaults, and two-thirds the burglaries. The only area of major crime in which Boston's record is bad is auto theft. The long-term trends also show that the city's rate for major crimes is consistently low, arguing that agencies supporting law and order are doing a relatively commendable job. Still, there is always room for improvement, and arguments are heard for a Metropolitan Police Force. Within the Route 128 area, there are some forty-eight cities and towns, with forty-eight police chiefs at the head of forty-eight independent police departments, and with forty-eight different policies and standards of police work. "This," said one observer, "is home rule with a vengeance."

Could even a metropolitan police cope with Boston's oldest crime—drunkenness? Still a crime in Massachusetts, half the people in prison are there for this offense. Half the arrests in Boston and the state are for this cause. Well over nineteen thousand such arrests were made in Boston in 1966. Drunkards are the "greatest recidivists." Some have had more than one hundred arrests for this one offense. Three hundred and fifty years later, the words of that early General Court would still seem to apply, that there is "an excess of drinking & unto drunkennes it selfe."

Gentlemen of the Bench and Bar

THOMAS LECHFORD   Can be called the first Boston lawyer. Arrived in town about 1638. Some of his writings declared heretical; denied church membership and could neither vote nor hold office. Made a living as copyist and drafter of petty legal documents. Accused of trying to influence a jury and forbidden to plead in court. Returned to England, 1641. Published "Plain Dealing; or, Newes from New-England" in 1642. His "Notebook" gives valuable legal information on this period.

RICHARD DANA (1700–72)   Leader of the bar. Graduated Harvard, 1718. Great influence in public affairs. Active for the town in law cases. In the "Sons of Liberty." Advised patriots on legal and constitutional matters. Under the Liberty Tree in 1765, Justice Dana administered oath to Secretary Oliver that he had not and would not distribute the stamps enforcing the Stamp Act.

JEROME GRIDLEY (1702–67)   Called "Father of the Boston Bar." Graduated Harvard, 1725. Taught grammar school, occasionally preached. Edited *The Weekly Rehearsal*, 1731. Encouraged professional education and ethics. "Pursue the study of the law rather than the gain of it. Pursue the gain of it enough to keep out of the briers; but give your main attention to the study of it." Formed a law club, the "Sodalitas" in 1765. Attorney General shortly before death.

EDMUND TROWBRIDGE (1709–93)   "Perhaps the most professional lawyer of New England before the Revolution." Harvard, 1728. Attorney General of the Province, 1749. Later on Superior Court. Tory predilections, but presided with impartial fairness over "Boston Massacre" trials. Resigned in 1772, retired to Bedford during revolution. Had finest law library in the Commonwealth. For a part of his life called Edmund Goffe.

JAMES OTIS (1725–83)   From a patriotic and legal family. Harvard, 1743. Studied under Gridley. Argued eloquently against Writs of Assistance, 1761. Abandoned own business for public affairs. Served in Stamp Act Congress, 1765. Principal leader of malcontents until his reason failed in 1769. Most quoted American abroad. Struck dead by lightning—a manner in which he had wished to die.

JAMES SULLIVAN (1744–1808)   Of Irish descent. Lame. Lawyer with large practice. Judge of Admiralty, Probate, Superior, and Supreme Courts of Massachusetts. In legislature, council; Attorney General, Governor. Promoter of Middlesex Canal. Wrote political tracts and law text on land titles. Interested in history of law in America. Ablest and most powerful Democrat of the period in Massachusetts.

THEOPHILUS PARSONS (1750–1813) Began career in Newburyport. Expert in prize and admiralty law, a lucrative branch. To Boston, 1806. Remarkable memory, never used a brief. Never took fees from widows or clergymen. Brevity, force, simplicity, and success his trademarks. "He put one foot on his chair, and with an elbow on his knee, leaned over and began to talk about the case as a man might talk to a neighbor at his fireside." When a Justice, speeded up court cases. Very autocratic; overdid his judicial authority. Federalist. Slouching appearance, unclean in dress and person. Once in action to recover insurance on a shipwreck, painted vivid picture of horrors of disaster at sea. Accidentally said the wind blew off a leeshore. Sullivan interrupted, "How could that be?" Thundered Parsons, "It was an Irish hurricane, brother Sullivan."

LEMUEL SHAW (1781–1861) Graduated Harvard, 1800. Advised in important commercial enterprises. Had principal part in writing Boston city charter, 1822, that lasted until 1913. In effect, invented form of municipal government for American cities. Chief Justice 1830–60. Harsh on counsel. Not strong in criminal or equity law, but made law on such matters as waterpower, railroads, public utilities. Probably no other state judge so greatly influenced commercial and constitutional law. Thorough, systematic, patient. Called "the Chief" by members of the bar.

RUFUS CHOATE (1799–1859) Graduated Dartmouth, 1819. Joined Massachusetts bar, 1822. A magician of the bar. Fervid oratory. Sometimes spoke so vigorously that he perspired freely and had to be wrapped up in two or three overcoats afterward to prevent chills. Successful practitioner; no client of his in Essex County ever convicted in criminal proceedings. Almost hypnotized juries. In Terrill case, set up the defense of somnambulism. Once losing a case, declared "Every judge on that bench seems to be more stupid than every other one, and if I were not afraid of losing the good opinion of the court, I would impeach the whole batch of them." Described a certain politician as "self-sufficient, all-sufficient, and in-sufficient." Said "the lawyer's vacation is the space between the question put to the witness and his answer." Single-minded interest in the law. Reluctantly drawn into public affairs. Helped organize Whig party. Served as U.S. Senator. Bronze statue by Daniel Chester French now in Boston Courthouse.

BENJAMIN ROBBINS CURTIS (1809–74) Harvard, 1829. Leading lawyer of Boston bar for seventeen years from 1834. Prepared exhaustive, exact cases. Held conservative position on slavery. 1851 went to U.S. Supreme Court and edited its decisions. Dissented on Dred Scott case. Resigned, 1857, returned to the bar. Successfully defended President Johnson during his impeachment in 1868.

HORACE GRAY (1828–1902) Harvard, 1845. Court reporter until 1861, finished Cushing's reports and prepared sixteen volumes that bear his name. To Massachusetts Supreme Court 1864. From 1873 Chief Justice. Wrote 1,367 opinions in seventeen years and four months on the court. To U.S. Supreme Court 1882. Martinet as a judge. Good equity lawyer. Expert in international law. Most learned American judge of his generation.

The 1852 version of the paddy wagon, "Black Maria," called the prisoner's own omnibus.

A SHORT SAMPLER OF BOSTON CRIME

Foreign Trade—Richard Hopkins was severely "whipt, & branded with a hott iron on one of his chcckcs, for selling peeces & powdr & shott to the Indeans."

—1632

Down on the Farm—William Hatchet found guilty of "Beastuality" and sentenced "to bee hanged, & the Cowe to bee slayne & burnt or buried."

—1641

A Piece of Rope—Edward Sanders, charged with rape, found "not guilty of death, but deserving a high and severe censure; sentenced to be whipt and henceforth to wear a rope about his neck hanging down two feet long, to continue during Court's pleasure; if found over 40 rods from his own house without the rope to be whipt for each offence."

—1654

Speaks for Itself—Joseph Gatchell, guilty of Blasphemy, "to stand in pillory, have his head and hand put in & have his toung drawne forth out of his mouth, & peirct through with a hott iron."

—1684

Signs and Stripes—Hannah Newell—"Adultery by her owne confession."—"Fifteen stripes Severally to be laid on upon her naked back at the Common Whipping post." Lambert Despar, the codefendant, was given twenty-five lashes "and that on the next Thursday Immediately after Lecture he stand upon the Pillory for the space of the full hower with Adultery in Capitall letters written upon his brest."

—1694

A Windy Warning—William Fly, Samuel Cole, and Henry Grenville, hung for piracy. Two days before execution they were taken to Mr. Colman's church, to listen to a sermon, for which they cared little. Fly was hung in gibbets on an Island in the harbor. The wind whistling through his bones many months after, was a warning to sailors passing in and out of the harbor.

—1726

Bread and Stones—"Went after dinner upon Boston Neck and saw John and Ann Richardson set on the gallows for cruelly and wilfully endeavoring to starve their children; the man behaved in the most audacious manner, so that the mob pelted him, which was what he deserved."

—John Rowe's Diary
October 4, 1764

A Day's Work—At the session of the Supreme Judicial Court, the following sentences passed: "One burglar to be hung; five female thieves to be whipped; four male thieves whipped; two big thieves to sit on the gallows; one counterfeiter to stand in the pillory, and have right ear cut off."

—September 9, 1787

"The Old-Fashioned Burglar" with his dark lantern and jimmy, about his business of "breaking and entering."

Two for One—Mary Kentland applied for a warrant against John M'Deed:

Court.	What has he done?
Mary.	He bate me and abused me, and almost broke me arum (proceeding to strip up her sleeve.)
Court.	I have no wish to see it. How did it happen?
Mary.	He called me a bad name, which, saving your prisince, it's not dacent to repate.
Court.	What then?
Mary.	I struck him wid me fist.
Court.	Well—what next?
Mary.	He hit me a thump, and bruised me arum so that I can't fetch it over the wash-tub.
Court.	Is that all?
Mary.	Yes, yer honor.
Court.	Well, as you committed the first assault, he is entitled to the first warrant, if he comes here and demands it; and if I issue a warrant in your case too, the result will be, that you will both be fined, so you had better consider of it.

Mary did not like the aspect of things very well, and considered it best to avert tit-for-tat proceedings, by evacuating.

—Boston *Morning Post*
circa 1835

Black and White—Henry Day—the gigantic black bully of the Hill, and duly acknowledged by force of might to be the legitimate successor of his late Colossal Majesty, Big Dick the First—was charged with all the sins "that flesh is heir to." Besides other heinous offences—such as drinking and fighting—it was alleged that he associated with, and even preferred the society of white women to black. Day denied, with the strongest symptoms of revulsion and indignation, that he had ever dishonored himself by such a degraded association; but it was proved that one of his most particular favorites was as white as a lily, though she was known by the ebon name of Miss *Coal.* This fact made it a dark day for Henry Day; for, in his defence, he seemed to admit that, if they proved he had ever kept company with white girls, he ought to be sent to the House of Correction—whither he was sent for four months.

—Boston *Morning Post*
circa 1835

Splitting Hairs—John Daress, a red-haired blacksmith, was fined $3.00 and costs, for hammering the life half out of James Rice, a bald-headed carpenter. Rice undertook to lay a new floor in Daress's cellar, but did not do it to his satisfaction. Rice said, "it was laid well enough for a d——n Paddy." Whereupon Daress gave him a tremendous Paddy-whack in the eye, and spilt him entirely down upon the new flooring. Moral to be deduced from this case:—It is not healthy to curse a red-haired man to his face!

—Boston *Morning Post*
circa 1835

Fast Cure—John Donovan got so drunk in Sea Street that he couldn't see Sea Street. Two one dollar pills and a dose of cents were administered. The medicine did not seem to set well.

—Boston *Daily Times*
January 3, 1854

A Dream Walking—Mary Ann Daily, a delicate creature of the tender age of forty, and with a fairy form of about 180 pounds, was accused of being of a poetical turn of mind and fond of moonlight rambles. It was also insinuated that, when it got late o'nights, she would solicit the protection of the sterner sex and induce them to walk home with her. Mary Ann has gone South for six months and will return in season to see the procession next fourth of July.

—Boston *Daily Times*
January 10, 1854

Just Testing—Thomas Clapp and Sarah Gilman were complained of being guilty of the crime fornication. They were fined $15 and half the costs each. They both plead guilty. Thomas said that he and Sarah intended to be married and he thought it would be well enough to get the "hang of the new school house" in season. He was very jocose about the matter, and admitted that he had only slept with Sarah one week. Sarah, who is quite a withered specimen of antiquity, in admitting the maze, informed the Court that "some very peculiar circumstances prevented their marriage until spring."

—Boston *Daily Times*
January 12, 1854

Prosit—Mary Hardy, alias Long, for sucking the daylights out of a black bottle, was fined $5 and costs.

—Boston *Daily Times*
January 12, 1854

The Heart of the Matter—Bridget Bennet, for assault upon Cecelia Miller and Charles A. Miller, was sent three months to the House of Correction. If the Court understood the case, it did more than we could. It was one of those complicated, conglomerated, and mixed-up Irish squabbles, where it is difficult to tell who is the assailant, if, indeed, there is an assault at all. In this case, there appeared to be two women and a boy, a broomstick, a dress, a petticoat, a flight of stairs, and a backyard. Bridget slapped the boy across the face with the backyard, and Cecelia hit Bridget with a pair of stairs; then Bridget seized Cecelia's dress or petticoat, or neither, and run down the broomstick or stairs into the cooking-stove or wood-shed, and then the boy was pitched or turpentined down or up the backyard or the broomstick or the stairs, but which we could not learn. By this time, the affair got snarled up in an hard knot and stood still.

—Boston *Daily Times*
January 14, 1854

Pickpocket on a Brookline streetcar, an illustration from the 1897 book by two Boston policemen titled *Our Rival, The Rascal.*

Interlude five: Boston to 1850

Plaguing the pigs

As the principal business street is very narrow, and most of the buildings are occupied by the families of the shopkeepers, it is often rendered nearly impassable by a large congregation of boys of all ages, who, in addition to occupying a great part of the sidewalk for their various games, will, in rainy weather, vary their amusement by making ponds in the carriage-way between. And when a drove of pigs passes through the streets there is a grand rush after them, the boys shouting "Here comes the Charlestown folks," catching the smaller pigs by their tails and throwing them over the others, or into the shop-doors and entry-ways, as well as scattering them over the sidewalks in the way of pedestrians, who, in addition to their other annoyances, are sometimes greeted with a shower of feathers or flour thrown from some upper window by some of the smaller children.

—Anonymous foreign visitor,
early nineteenth century

Going to bed in Chelsea, circa 1805

I picture to myself the bustle of going to bed, which, to be sure, always used to be carried on in great style at home. I remember first comes my father's "Well, child, it's nine o'clock!" So, then, my mother starts some new subject, which lasts until half after nine; then the cap is sent for, and the head bound up, and a pin put in here and then another there. Then comes "toasting feet." Then the watch is duly handed to my father, which used to be my office. Then good-night to my father; presently after to my mother; then a knocking, not heard because Tom's so furious in his argumentation, laying down the law with his left hand. Then it's surmised that there has been a knocking; *that's by Margaret.* Then the knocking is repeated. Harriet then makes a sort of half motion, as if she would go and see what it was for, though (faith!) not a step before the expediency of the thing is proved. Then the bowl of tea, which was forgotten, is carried up (which is sure to be brought down next morning untouched, and drank by some unlucky wight). Then comes down aunt Hill, with an anxious face, for Blois has been quite naughty. Then follows a little discussion on education, and then I say good-night.

—Henry Cary
The Cary Letters

I could have danced all night

I well remember my first ball. It was at Mrs. Higginsons'. Mother was not well and father said he would take me instead. It was important that I should go. I had my hair done up long before hand in the way they did then, very high above my head. It was tied up so tight that it made my head ache. I felt horridly, but they said I should get used to it. I felt very shy in going upstairs, past the crowded rooms, and I thought everybody was looking at my head. When I got to the dressing-room there was nobody there but a lady who was lying on the bed, groaning. It was Mrs. Allston, wife of the painter. She had fainted downstairs and they brought her up and left her. She felt very sick and asked me to get her some warm water. I rang and rang and at last a chambermaid came and I got her to bring the water and then she went off in great haste. So I had to stay. I had a horrid time with the poor lady, but I could not leave her. At last after a long while Mr. Allston came up and carried his wife off; but I dared not go down alone, so I stayed there till finally Father hunted me up. He had gone into the card-room and had been playing there all the evening, supposing that I had gone down to the ballroom. He took me home and then I could get my hair down. I could have cried from relief!

—Eliza Perkins (Cabot)
Reminiscences (about 1806)

Fired by a millionaire

March 26, 1814—A day or two ago we parted with our black boy, Abraham Francis, who has lived with us about two years and a half, and proved a very excellent servant, till within a few days, when he took it into his head that he must have wages.— He is but seventeen years old—and we thought he had not judgment enough to spend money for himself—beside which he has an idle father who would probably insist on his wages.—Mrs. Brooks has sent him to Prime Saunders' school this winter to learn to read well and write and we think it has been a great injury to him: for it has not only put this notion of wages and independence into his head,— but has led him into company, and made him fond of staying out at night, and given him airs of familiarity very different from what he was wont to have. —From whatever cause it may arise, it is, I believe, a fact that very few blacks have conduct enough to support themselves.

—Peter C. Brooks
Manuscript account book
Mass. Hist. Soct.

A prison tour

In the afternoon we all walked over to Charlestown to see the State's Prison . . . I cannot describe my feelings upon entering this place of punishment. When we entered the yard there were several sentinels pacing round with their guns. We finally got admittance and were led by the keeper through the workshops where in a three story building were all sorts of mechanical business going on (besides a great number of prisoners being employ'd in the yard wheeling dirt, etc. and gardening) and here I was sadly struck at the miserable sight of so many of my fellow creatures suffering bondage for their crimes and could not help heaving many a sigh for them. Many of them were fine looking young men who appeared as if they might have been an ornament instead of a disgrace to their Country. [Miss Callendar was 22 years old.] I was particularly struck with a youth of 15 who was spinning and confined for *Life!* his crime theft, what a prospect for him dreary indeed. Their appearance was different, some both black and white fit for "treason, strategems, and spoils," whilst others looked so mild, so meek, so contrite that it was difficult to think they deserved being there. We passed through their eating-room where their suppers was preparing; it all looked nice neat and clean; in some of their tin dishes was hasty pudding and molasses, while in others there appeared to be molasses and water with a good piece of brown bread by the side of it; we went into some of the cells all looked clean. There were three beds in some, all the prisoners were dressed in red and blue, there were 19 refractory ones in the solitary cells where it is entirely dark, where the keeper told us (in a very unfeeling manner I thought, and which made me shudder) they kept them on bread and water if they would not work and if that did not answer they chain'd them down with fifty weight of iron! I no longer wondered at their industry. They have a fine pleasant chapel and I think their situation *far far* preferable to being in a common jail.

—Eunice Callendar
Diary, June 3, 1809

A little too much rum in Lynn, 1816

Blackstrap [rum] sold for 16 cents per quart and Satarday every apprentice an boy laid in his half a gallon for Sunday. One Sunday I with another boy had 2 gallons. This we stowed in a field adjoining the turnpike road. About 12 o'clock in the day both of us being drunk we resolved to have some sport as we called it. When the meeting was let out, we stripped off our clothes and like naked savages in their barbarous state, persued all the girls as they came along from meeting. Colonel Brimblecoms dauthers I chased into their house and nothing was said to me about it, only as a joke.

. . . In L[ynn] tidemen went around every Sunday to keep people from walking about in church time. It so happened that one of these came across a young fellow by the name of James Phineous Winthrop and my self. He asked us why we want in church. I told him I did not make a practice of going there. "If your not in Church this afternoon you must suffer the consequences," said he, and left us. In the afternoon he came into a shoemakers shop were we were drinking and ordered us to Church. We took him neck and heels and put him out door. The next morning I received a note saying he was willing to settle it by my paying 16 dollers. I had not 16 cents in the world to bless myself, my clothes most all gorn and I nothing before me but a prison.

We immeadiately sold our tools, but not all of them keeping one set for our selves. All the money we could raise was two dollars with hardly a shift of clothes to our back. We scarcely had got our tools packed before the High Sherrif and his brother a constable made their appearance. Snatching up what we had got we fled to the hills and traveling through Sagus we crossed the ma[r]shes and arrived in Boston that night. My partner had been to sea. Taken me to a sailors boarding house we got supper and lodgeing. That night we played cards for *Rum* and lost all our money but one quarter of a doller. In the morning we got a pint of black strap, some tobacco, a few smoked herring, and brisket—which took all our money and we started for Providence penniless.

—James Holley Garrison (1801–42)
Profligate brother of William Lloyd Garrison
from *Behold Me Once More*

Harvard commencement

Commencement day pleasant and fine as usual Town all alive. The People crowding together. Tents creating shows, many-headed monsters, Negroes, Sailors, Coaches, literati, Peddlars, rope-dances, pies, cakes, melons, eggnog brandy rum and confusion on confusion all muddled together announced Commencement.

—Aaron White
Diaries, July 30, 1817

Cambridgeport in the 1820s

The greater part of what is now Cambridgeport was then (in the native dialect) a *huckleberry pastur*. Woods were not wanting on its outskirts, of pine, and oak, and maple, and the rarer tupelo with downward limbs. Its veins did not draw their blood from the quiet old heart of the village, but it had a distinct being of its own, and was rather a great caravansary than a suburb. The chief feature of the place was its inns, of which there were five, with vast barns and court-yards, which the railroad was to make as silent and deserted as the palaces of Nimroud. Great white-topped wagons, each drawn by double files of six or eight horses, with its dusty bucket swinging from the hinder axle, and its grim bull-dog trotting underneath, or in midsummer panting on the lofty perch beside the driver (how elevated thither baffled conjecture), brought all the wares and products of the country to their mart and seaport in Boston. These filled the inn-yards, or were ranged side by side under broad-roofed sheds, and far into the night the mirth of their lusty drivers clamored from the red-curtained bar-room, while the single lantern, swaying to and fro in the black cavern of the stables, made a Rembrandt of the group of ostlers and horses below. There were, beside the taverns, some huge square stores where groceries were sold, some houses, by whom or why inhabited was to us boys a problem, and, on the edge of the marsh, a currier's shop, where, at high tide, on a floating platform, men were always beating skins in a way to remind one of Don Quixote's fulling-mills.

—James Russell Lowell
Fireside Travels

The voice of the snow—about 1827

As a boy I lived on Beacon Street. My father's breakfast-room overlooked the street. In mid-winter the country sleds, loaded with hickory and walnut, drawn by oxen whose muzzles were all icicles, whose smoking flanks were covered with hoar-frost, whose nostrils sent forth great puffs of hot breath in which the particles of starry congelations glittered; the drivers farmers, muffled in neck wrappers with warm caps and buckskin mittens,—all went up the street in slow procession for the wood market, each sled uttering that strange, unpronounceable, enchanting snow voice of deep winter. I and my brothers heard it with such joy at breakfast. It was the herald of perfect coasting, of the finest skating, the assured promise of the dry, keen, north-west, inspiring, intoxicating atmosphere, full of tingling health, that made the day one long joy. . . . You see the music requires a heavy sled, a wooden runner— oak, I think,—rather broad, not shod with iron, and the snow must be very dry and compact; there is no bird melody finer than the snow-harp of nature.

—William Minot (1817–94)
Letter of January 26, 1893

Old Theatre Alley

As I first remember it, commerce had not encroached upon its precincts; no tall warehouses shut out the light from its narrow footway, and its planks were unencumbered by any intrusive bales or boxes. . . . The stage door of the theatre was in the alley, and the walk from thence, through Devonshire Street, to the Exchange Coffee House, which was the great hotel of Boston at that time, was once well known to many whose names are now part of the history of the drama.

The two posts which used to adorn and obstruct the entrance to the alley from Franklin Street, when they were first placed there, were an occasion of indignation to a portion of the public, and of anxiety to Mr. Powell, the old manager. That estimable gentleman had often been a witness to the terror of the children and of those of the weaker sex . . . who sometimes met a stray horse or cow in the alley; so he placed two wooden posts just beyond the theatre, to shut out the dreaded bovine intruders. But the devout Hibernians who used to worship at the church in Franklin Street could not brook the placing of any such obstacles in their way to the performance of their religious duties; and they used to cut the posts down as often as Mr. Powell set them up, until he took refuge in the resources of science, and covered and bound them with iron bands which imprisoned them up to a very recent period.

Old Mr. Stoughton, the Spanish consul, used to occupy the first house in Franklin Street above the alley, behind which his garden ran back for some distance. How little that worthy gentleman thought that his tulip beds and rose bushes would one day give place to a dry goods shop! . . .

Mrs. Grace Dunlap's little shop was an institution which many considered to be coexistent with the alley itself. . . . The snuff and tobacco which Mrs. Dunlap used to dispense were of the best quality, and she numbered many distinguished persons among her customers. The author of the History of Ferdinand and Isabella was often seen there replenishing his box, and exchanging kind courtesies with the fair-spoken dealer . . . Mrs. Dunlap herself was a study for an artist. Her pleasant face, her fair complexion, her quiet manner, her white cap, with its gay ribbons, rivalling her eyes in brightness, were all in perfect keeping with the scrupulous neatness and air of repose that always reigned in her shop. Her parlour was as comfortable a place as you would wish to see on a summer or a winter day. It had a cheerful English look that I always loved. The plants in the windows, the bird cage, the white curtains, the plain furniture, that looked as if you might use it without spoiling it, the shining andirons, and the blazing wood fire, are all treasured in my memory of Theatre Alley as it used to be.

—Charles B. Fairbanks
Aguecheek

Within a budding grove

Went yesterday to Cambridge & spent most of the day at Mount Auburn, got my luncheon at Fresh Pond, & went back again to the woods. After much wandering & seeing many things, four snakes gliding up & down a hollow for no purpose that I could see—not to eat, not for love, but only gliding; then a whole bed of Hepatica triloba, cousins of the Anemone all blue & beautiful but constrained by niggard Nature to wear their last year's faded jacket of leaves; then a black capped titmouse who came upon a tree & when I would know his name, sang *chick a dee dee*[;] then a far off tree full of clamorous birds, I know not what, but you might hear them half a mile. I forsook the tombs & found a sunny hollow where the east wind could not blow & lay down against the side of a tree to most happy beholdings. At least I opened my eyes & let what would pass through them into the soul. I saw no more my relation how near & petty to Cambridge or Boston, I heeded no more what minute or hour our Massachusetts clocks might indicate—I saw only the noble earth on which I was born, with the great Star which warms & enlightens it. I saw the clouds that hang their significant drapery over us.—It was Day, that was all Heaven said. The pines glittered with their innumerable green needles in the light & seemed to challenge me to read their riddle. The drab-oak leaves of the last year turned their little somersets & lay still again. And the wind bustled high overhead in the forest top. This gay & grand architecture from the vault to the moss & lichen on which I lay who shall explain to me the laws of its proportions & adornments?

See the perpetual generation of good sense:

Nothing wholly false, fantastic, can take possession of men who to live & move must plough the ground, sail the sea, have orchards, hear the robin sing, & see the swallow fly.

—Ralph Waldo Emerson
Journals, April 11, 1834

Street cry

Fresh mackerel! Fresh mackerel!
  Oh! what a dismal doom is mine!
To hear each morn that horrid yell
  Bellow'd from four o'clock till nine.
When up the eastern arch of blue,
  Dan Phoebus drives his fiery wain,
Slumber and dreams and rest, adieu!
  I court the drowsy god in vain;
For hark! the cry,—I know it well,
  Fresh mackerel! Fresh mackerel!
        —Samuel Kettell
        Yankee Notions, 1837

Dickens at the Asylum for the Blind, 1842

. . . I sat down in another room, before a girl, blind, deaf, and dumb; destitute of smell; and nearly so of taste: before a fair young creature with every human faculty, and hope, and power of goodness and affection, inclosed within her delicate frame, and but one outward sense—the sense of touch. There she was, before me; built up, as it were, in a marble cell, impervious to any ray of light, or particle of sound; with her poor white hand peeping through a chink in the wall, beckoning to some good man for help, that an Immortal soul might be awakened.

Long before I looked upon her, the help had come. Her face was radiant with intelligence and pleasure. Her hair, braided by her own hands, was bound about a head, whose intellectual capacity and development were beautifully expressed in its graceful outline, and its broad open brow; her dress, arranged by herself, was a pattern of neatness and simplicity; the work she had knitted, lay beside her; her writing-book was on the desk she leaned upon.—From the mournful ruin of such bereavement, there had slowly risen up this gentle, tender, guileless, grateful-hearted being. . . . Her name is Laura Bridgman.

. . . She had, until now, been quite unconscious of the presence of visitors; but, having her hand placed in that of the gentleman who accompanied me, she immediately expressed his name upon her teacher's palm. Indeed her sense of touch is now so exquisite, that having been acquainted with a person once, she can recognise him or her after almost any interval. This gentleman had been in her company, I believe, but very seldom, and certainly had not seen her for many months. My hand she rejected at once, as she does that of any man who is a stranger to her. But she retained my wife's with evident pleasure, kissed her, and examined her dress with a girl's curiosity and interest.

—Charles Dickens
American Notes

A royal skate on Jamaica Pond

(Sunday)—Saturday afternoon I drove out with Mr. Benjamin to Jamaica Pond, and had a royal skate. The whole pond was as smooth as a looking-glass. There was a beautiful sunset, whose brilliant red and purple was reflected from the ice as from water; and after that came the clear moonlight, silvering the whole scene. We skated two or three hours with little fatigue. The ice was so smooth and hard, and the pleasure of it added one more argument in favor of Jamaica Pond for our future home.

—William Minot
Letter of December 23, 1844

Portrait of the historian as philanthropist, 1848

I strolled about the city for half an hour, and on my way back, passing through Broad street, where the Irish congregate, met one Michael Sullivan whom I knew. He seemed to be in trouble, and I inquired what ailed him. He said he had been sick and out of work, and had no money, and his family was starving with cold. I went with him to the den where he lived, and found his wife and three or four small children in a wretched loft over a warehouse, where they were lying on the floor, huddled in a pile of straw and shavings, with some rags and pieces of old carpet over them. The only furniture in the room was a chair, a broken table, and a small stove in which were the expiring embers of a scanty handful of coal, which they had begged from neighbors equally poor. The mercury was below zero out of doors, and the dilapidated apartment was not much warmer than the street. I had no time to spare, and the detention, slight as it was, prevented me from getting back to Mr. Prescott's till a quarter-past one. His MSS. lay on my desk, and he was walking about the room in a state of impatience, I knew, though he showed none, except by looking at his watch. As I warmed my chilled hands over the fire, I told him, by way of apology, what had detained me. Without speaking, he stepped to a drawer where scraps of writing paper were kept, took out a piece, and laying it on my desk, told me to write an order on Mr. ——— (a coal dealer with whom he kept an account always open for such purposes) for a ton of coal, to be delivered without

delay to Michael Sullivan, Broad street. He then went to his bell-rope and gave it a vehement pull. A servant entered as I finished the order. "Take this," he said, "as quick as you can, to Mr. ———, and see that the coal is delivered at once. What is the number of the house in Broad street?"

I had neglected to notice the number, though I could find the place readily myself. I therefore suggested to Mr. Prescott, that as there were probably twenty Michael Sullivans in Broad street, the coal might not reach the right man unless I saw to it in person, which I would do when I went to dinner, at 2½ o'clock.

"Thank you, thank you," he said, "but go at once, there will be time enough lost in getting the coal."

I reminded him of the letters. "Go, go! never mind the letters. Gayangos and Circourt will not freeze if they never get them, and Mrs. O'Sullivan may, if you don't hurry. Stay—can the man be trusted with money? or will he spend it all in drink?" He pulled out his pocketbook. I told him he could be trusted. He handed me five dollars. "See that they are made comfortable, at least while this cold spell lasts. Take time enough to see to them, I shall not want you till six. Don't let them know I sent the money, or all Broad street will be here begging within twenty-four hours."

—Robert Carter
Recollections of W. H. Prescott

194

CHAPTER SIX

Much Preached At—Part I

Boston has always been a very "churchy" place. The voice of the turtledove may not be loud in the land, but the voice of the clergy has never been silenced. A limerick put it rather concisely:

> Here's to the town of Boston
> And the turf that the Puritans trod,
>   In the rest of mankind
>   Little virtue they find,
> But they feel quite chummy with God.

Chummy, yes; simple, no. A Bostonian's relationship with his God, has always been an endlessly complicated affair. Yet Boston's religious history has been remarkably uncomplicated. For the first half of the 350 years since European settlement, its orientation was toward Protestant Congregationalism; for the last half of that period its orientation has been toward Catholic Romanism. Along the way, in the cracks as it were, it grew several "home-made" religions. These were an odd group: the Universalists who claimed God was too good to damn men, the Unitarians who declared men were too good to be damned, and the Christian Scientists who insisted it was all immaterial.

CONGREGATIONALISTS   In the beginning, Puritans were the "establishment," and permitted no competition. The settlers' first official act was to provide for their ministers. Only after that did they discuss military needs, food supplies, and drunkenness. Puritan theory held that they were a people in covenant with God and that this contract bound everyone living within the Commonwealth. Dissenters were, in effect, breaking a contract and implying that the Puritan church was a false one. This was not to be tolerated. All the inhabitants were encouraged, even compelled, to attend services and hear "the word of God," but only the "visible saints" were permitted to take the sacraments.

The position of ministers was curious. They were paid from public taxes, and disrespect to them was punished by the state, but they were not elected (by custom, not law) to public office. There were no church courts, and state authorities probated wills, performed marriages, and authorized divorces.

The Rev. Richard Mather in 1675 from John Foster's woodcut. (Courtesy of Massachusetts Historical Society.)

The First Church in Boston in its third home, which was called the Old Brick Meeting House, on what was later called Washington Street, west of the Town House (Old State House). It was taken down in the year of the engraving (1808) which is after the drawing by I. R. Smith.

Marriage was a completely secular function. Ministers might attend, and were sometimes allowed, reluctantly, to say a few words. The state jealously guarded what it considered its sovereign rights.

Shortly after landing, the settlers formally organized a church, thus the anomaly that the First Church in Boston was actually formed in Charlestown where they held their first religious services outdoors under a large tree. The Reverend John Wilson was their minister. After they moved across to the Boston peninsula, worship was held on alternate Sundays on either side of the Charles River. By 1632, First Church had built its first building. It had a thatched roof and was on State Street.

That same year the first division occurred, as members still living in Charlestown requested they be "peaceably dismissed" so they might have a church there and avoid the tiresome ferry trip. When the Reverend John Cotton arrived from England in 1633, he joined Wilson in ministering to First Church, and quickly proved so influential in both civil and ecclesiastical matters that he has been known as "The Patriarch of New England." In 1640, the congregation decided to build a more commodious meetinghouse at the head of State Street. This was destroyed in the fire of 1711, and a third structure, which came to be called "Old Brick," took its place, lasting until 1808. The fourth building of First Church was erected on Chauncy Place that same year, designed by Asher Benjamin, and was remodeled in 1843. In 1868 they dedicated a new Gothic church designed by Ware and Van Brunt on the corner of Marlborough and Berkeley streets, which was destroyed by fire in March 1968. Construction of its sixth building in 340 years began in 1970. The new building was designed by Paul Rudolph.

From the loins of First Church sprang new congregations. The Second Church in Boston, or "Old North," was "gathered" in 1650 and located at the head of North Square. Its first building burned in 1676, and was replaced on the same spot with a solid wooden building which lasted until British soldiers took it down to use as firewood during the siege of Boston. Some have claimed this was the Old North where lanterns were hung to inform Paul Revere which route the British were taking to raid the military stores in Concord; others claim it was from the belfry of Christ Church. After that war, Second Church united with other groups and moved to various locations further and further from the old North End, until it ended up in Audubon Circle in the Fenway. In 1969, with most of its parishioners active in suburban churches, it brought more than three centuries of religious history full circle by rejoining First Church. Its notable ministers included the father and son team of Increase and Cotton Mather, and that lean romantic philosopher Ralph Waldo Emerson.

Sometimes the divisions were not accomplished peacefully. Old North under the Mathers had borne in 1714 a "New North" of less genteel people, "seventeen substantial mechanics," who got no help from their wealthier brethren in building their church except "prayers and good wishes." But when New North decided in a few years to ask the Reverend Peter Thacher of the Weymouth church to be an associate minister, a fierce controversy erupted. In those days a minister stayed with a church for life; it was unheard of for a wealthy church to lure away a minister from a poorer country church. Thacher was voted in, but so violent was the opposition that when he was installed, he had to be sneaked into the church. When the protesters learned they had been tricked, they stormed in to the service, occupied the galleries, and, as a lady present reported with much asperity, spoiled her new velvet hood by sprinkling "a liquor, which shall be nameless" upon the congregation below. Another observer described the commotion as worse than any beer garden.

Not content with pouring urine over the heads of their fellow Christians, the discontented members got out and in 1719 organized another church. Land was bought on Hanover Street and in 1721 what was called "New Brick" opened its doors. Some called this the "Revenge Church" or the "Cockerel," for on its steeple it had a weathervane in the shape of a golden cockerel designed by Shem Drowne. When the weathervane was put up, one member climbed up, straddled the metal bird, and loudly crowed thrice, in mockery of Peter Thacher.

For a hundred years, the First Church in Roxbury (1631) was the only church in that general area. From its beginning it has been located on what is now named Eliot Square after its first minister, the well-beloved Apostle to the Indians. Eliot served the church for sixty years, was renowned for his charity and Christian love, and at a time when Jesuits were held in anathema in Boston, once entertained a Jesuit priest in his house for a whole winter. He translated the Bible into the Indian language with the help, as he put it,

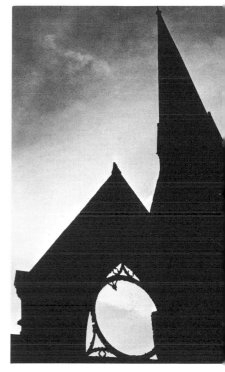

The tower of First Church after fire ruined it in 1968. (Daniel S. Brody photograph.)

The Curtis House in Jamaica Plain where the Rev. John Eliot lived. This building was erected in 1639 and taken down in 1888. (Courtesy of The Society for the Preservation of New England Antiquities.)

of "a pregnant witted young Indian" who knew English. Education for Indians and English alike was a main concern of his, and in 1645 he founded Roxbury Latin School. From First Church came the West Roxbury Church and the Jamaica Plain Church, while the parent church continues to meet in its fifth house of worship (built in 1804) on the spot where worship first began in Roxbury.

The founding of the First Parish in Dorchester preceded the Boston church by some months. Since it was organized in England and in theory sailed across the Atlantic with its congregants, it can be said to be Boston's most traveled church. They landed near Hull, but soon settled in a section the Indians called Mattapan, now Dorchester Neck, a good distance from the present Mattapan. There was no other church in Dorchester until 1806. From 1670, its edifices have been on Meeting House Hill, and the present building, erected in 1896, is practically a reproduction of their 1816 meetinghouse. Richard Mather, the father of Increase, filled its pulpit in the seventeenth century. In Cambridge, first called New-towne, there was a church under Thomas Hooker from 1633. When he and his flock left for Connecticut, another First Parish was founded in 1636 under Thomas Shepard. His influence was one of the reasons Harvard College was located in Cambridge and not Marblehead as originally proposed. The Cambridge pastor for many years had a strong influence on the student body. Until 1814, students were required to attend services at the First Parish, and college commencements were held in the church until 1873.

Although often called a theocracy, the Massachusetts government was not really ruled by clergymen, but since most of the state leaders had a sense of religious mission, were intent on planting the Gospel in the new land, and took the Biblical Israel as a model for the state they wished to create, they

felt themselves to be agents of God, responsible for preserving His Church and His Religion. Holding such beliefs, leaders of the new colony were constantly challenged by newcomers. First they had trouble with the Church of England minority among them, who either were forced to conform or were driven out. Then they consistently had problems with the nonreligious element among the settlers. Robert Shawe who gloried in cursing was whipped (1632); Hugh Buets was banished for maintaining he was free from original sin (1640); Roger Scott was rebuked for falling asleep in church and then hitting the man who woke him up (1642); Allester Grimes was punished for hoeing on the Sabbath (1665) as was John Baker who shot birds on that sacred day (1630). And in 1643 Henrie Walton of Lynn was taken to court for flatly asserting "he had as Leeve to hear a Dogge Barke as to heare Mr. Cobbett Preach."

However, the most difficult group of all to keep in line was their own. Mrs. Anne Hutchinson, a woman "of ready wit and bold spirit" according to her opponent John Winthrop, had arrived in the colony with husband and children in 1634. Soon settled in a comfortable home about where the Old Corner Book Store now stands, she soon had fifty to eighty people coming to hear her interpret the weekly sermons. Boston was not ripe by several centuries for a Mrs. Eddy.

The principal part of Mrs. Hutchinson's problem was that she was interpreting scripture. She maintained that saving grace went only to those who were justified by faith (the "covenant of grace"). Those so saved were then beyond the need of such shallow symbols of piety as going to church, and saying prayers (the "covenant of works"). No amount of good deeds could prove one had been saved. Her religious opinions were dividing the town, the clergy, and even the political leaders. That she was a woman added particular

199

annoyance. After a bitter struggle, the orthodox group which included Winthrop prevailed, suppressed dissent, and eventually—in 1638—drove Mrs. Hutchinson out of town.

Hardly was one dissident gone, than another appeared. In 1640, Dr. Robert Child, an intelligent physician, made his second visit to the Bay Colony. A Presbyterian, in a period when the English Parliament was under Presbyterian influence, he was unhappy with the local congregational establishment. He spearheaded a daring attempt to somewhat enlarge the boundaries of religious freedom, and to extend the voting franchise beyond the limited membership of the church. By 1646 the General Court had decided against him. Child took his case to England where he might have won, but other events brought an end to Presbyterian influence, and he lost. Congregational polity now dominated the churches in New England and was confirmed by a synod of the ministers which accepted the so-called Cambridge Platform of 1648. Within three years all the local churches had assented to that Platform.

Life, however, has a way of making all such platforms shaky and insecure. A speeding up of the religious history of the last half of the seventeenth century would show all kinds of dissenters shoving and pushing against the establishment's platform: Ranters, Seekers, Muggletonians, Fifth-Monarchy Men, as well as the longer-lasting Baptists and Quakers. Two Quaker "ladies" in 1658 broke bottles over the head of the Reverend John Norton to prove to him his "emptiness." All these groups, the Puritans felt, had (as Cotton Mather said of Roger Williams) "a wind-mill" in their heads. Puritans were quick to tilt at those windmills, however, using more effective instruments than Don Quixote: whips, prisons, mutilations, and the gallows. Decades later, these proved as futile as the befuddled don's lance. But before the Puritans learned this, the hysteria of the Salem witchcraft trials and killings had stained both the church and government authorities.

Boston and Massachusetts had long since outgrown the structure of a trading company ruling with sovereign powers and attempting to mold the plantation into a God-ruled society. Sometimes slowly, sometimes sharply, the old ways were modified. Under royal sponsorship and protection, the Anglican church was introduced; Baptist churches were permitted, and gradually others allowed to worship. Citizenship had been broadened in 1664. The "Half-Way Covenant" allowed children of nonchurch members to be baptized although they were not permitted full membership and communion. Other changes made their painful way into acceptance: elders disappeared and deacons took their place; the pastor's and the teacher's office were merged into one; "associations" were formed which assumed moral (but not legal) responsibilities for their neighboring churches.

Other changes were even less happily received by the clergy. These were the new customs, new manners, and seemingly new morals of the third and fourth New England generations. An emotional religious revival, marked in western Massachusetts by the earnest, urgent sermons of Jonathan Edwards, was triggered in New England during the mid-eighteenth century. It spread to other colonies, and was helped along by the fervid preaching of an Anglican clergyman, George Whitefield, who attracted huge throngs wherever he went. An estimated twenty thousand crowded onto Boston Common to hear him on one occasion—more than the entire population of the town. This "Great Awakening" as it was called, brought many into the churches, and spawned new churches. But its effect in Boston was limited, for Harvard College and such local ministers as Charles Chauncy of the First Church, held out against the bath in emotionalism, keeping their faith in the human mind and what it reasonably and rationally could encompass.

Not all the Boston ministers were so restrained. Andrew Croswell, called a "Merry Andrew" by some and by others simply a madman, saw a "New Light" in the incandescent sermons of Whitefield. He set off on a preaching tour in 1742 to spread this new light through darkest New England. He succeeded in splitting the Plymouth church, the oldest in the colony, and wound up putting on a magnificent show in his hometown church of Charlestown. There, as a friendly observer described his performance, he "wailed and howled," tore off his clothing—"though not quite naked"—and went "skipping about like a ram from pew to pew and from seat to seat, even from the upper gallery to the floor of the house." Outside in the streets they could hear him shouting "Lo here, a Kingdom of God that cometh with observation." The *Ballad of Boston Ministers* jibed at him: "the man means well, but none can tell, With what his noodle's stored."

Ministers and people in the Boston area skipped to a different drum than did Master Croswell. Generally, it was one of an increasingly liberal theology, away from the old Calvinism. Shortly after the clarion call to a "Great Awakening," over thirty ministers in Boston and vicinity were declared by conservatives to be "unsound in the faith." The first antitrinitarian book in America was published in Boston in 1756. Shortly, the divinity of Christ was being disputed and disbelieved. The doctrine of eternal punishment and original sin was looked at critically. Dr. Charles Chauncy, for sixty years minister of First Church (1727–87) and Dr. Jonathan Mayhew at West Church, spoke out in their sermons against the old doctrines. Mayhew preached against the Trinity as early as 1753. Although the coming of the American Revolution diverted popular attention from such theological conundrums, liberal sentiments continued to grow.

After the Revolution, these "heresies" were distinctly stated by ministers and accepted by congregations. By 1785, King's Chapel—for a time in these postwar years known as the Stone Chapel—was in fact a Unitarian church. Quite simply, Unitarians were those who could not accept the Caesarian dictum that "All God is divided into three parts." This movement toward a unitarian theology proceeded rather quickly in Salem, more slowly in Boston. The Federal Street Church dropped all trinitarian references from its hymn book in 1795. By the end of the century all but one of the Boston ministers were unitarian in thinking and were supported in this belief by their congregations.

Banner of the Boston Young Men's Total Abstinence Society, formed in 1843. (Courtesy of The Bostonian Society, Old State House.)

But it was not to be a quiet revolution. Calvinists disputed the new doctrines. When a professorship at Harvard fell vacant, matters came to a head. A Unitarian was proposed for the position and the orthodox clergy, led by Dr. Jedidiah Morse* of Charlestown, the lone local supporter of the trinitarian position, fought bitterly against his nomination. When the Unitarian was elected in 1805, and soon afterward a liberal president appointed and several other liberal professors selected, it was clear to the orthodox that Harvard College had been "captured." The dissidents formed their own Theological Seminary at Andover, legally bound to hold their theological positions forever, or so they intended. By 1908 it had allied itself once again with Harvard Divinity School. When this was later contested in the courts, the restrictions were somewhat modified, but the alliance with Harvard came to an end, and in 1931 Andover affiliated with the Newton Theological Institute.

With the Boston Congregational churches gone Unitarian in what amounted to a religious landslide, orthodox Congregational churches had to be reestablished in the city if their doctrines were to be heard. By 1809, the Park Street Church had been organized and the next year dedicated its Peter Banner-designed building on what quickly became known as "Brimstone Corner" thanks to the hellfire doctrines preached inside.

Park Street Church has been missionary-minded almost from the day it opened its doors. After 150 years, it supports on its own nearly a hundred missionaries around the world. Many organizations have been founded in this church including the Handel and Haydn Society, the Prison Discipline Society, the American Temperance Society, and the Animal Rescue League. Almost sold in 1902 to real estate developers, a public outcry prevented that desecration. In 1914, the white paint that had long covered the exterior was removed and the warm red worn brick allowed to show again. Since the houses above it on Park Street were numbered beginning with one, the Church is officially located at Zero Park Street.

The only church in Boston proper remaining within the Congregational tradition was the Third Church (1669) that had long met in Old South Meeting House (built in 1729) on Washington Street. In 1875 they moved to a handsome building on Copley Square designed by Cummings and Sears. Here, during the long ministry of Dr. George A. Gordon—rated with Phillips Brooks as one of Boston's outstanding preachers—they too gradually moderated the harsh features of the old Calvinism.

Congregational churches in the Boston area have long supported evangelistic campaigns such as those of Lyman Beecher, the Chapman-Andrews team, Gypsy Smith, Billy Sunday, and Billy Graham. They also have financed for more than a century and a half the domestic evangelism of the City Missionary Society (founded in 1816). The concern of this Society at first was to convert new immigrants from their "heathen" Roman Catholicism. Gradually,

---

* Morse's son, the painter and inventor of the telegraph, Samuel F. B. Morse, later became a radical Unitarian.

The old Congregational House on the corner of Beacon and Somerset Streets, later moved across and up the street.

Famed Unitarian divine, William Ellery Channing.

however, they professionalized their work and concerns and now deal with the social and secular, as well as spiritual, concerns of the twentieth century.

UNITARIANS At first, the Unitarian churches did not use that name to describe themselves. They considered themselves the same churches as before, except that they had brought their beliefs up to the level of "modern" thinking. Dr. Morse fastened the name Unitarian on them in 1815 despite William Ellery Channing's arguing that they were not disciples of Priestley and Belsham and were only liberal Christians. The new name stuck and Channing, minister of the Federal Street Church, became the leading Unitarian in America after he preached his definitive "Baltimore Sermon" in 1819.

Two years later, the weekly *Christian Register* was founded as a forum for this liberal viewpoint. Soon, other denominational machinery was in existence, and by 1825 the American Unitarian Association was organized. Ten out of the eleven Boston churches joined this Association as did ninety others in Massachusetts alone. It was a disaster for historic American Congregationalism. The Unitarians continued their former democratic policies, and since they were moving with the liberal spirit of the age, attracted the "makers and finders." Such men as Emerson, Lowell, Everett, Parkman, Holmes, and Parker were Unitarians and played a prominent part in the "flowering" of New England. For a long period, anybody who was anybody in Boston was a Unitarian.

But should such free spirits as the Transcendentalists be included among the "elect"? Some were doubtful. Inspired by advanced German and English philosophers, the romantic Transcendentalists wanted to continue theological

A "country church" — the old Unitarian meeting house in North Chelsea.

reform. They also fought many of the ills of society—poverty, slavery, war, ignorance, crime, and intemperance. They came to prominence in their magazine *The Dial*, and more actively in the Chardon Street Convention of 1840, where these social problems were raised. They prompted the effort made the next year at Brook Farm in West Roxbury under the leadership of the Reverend George Ripley to solve all the problems by creating a loving community that would give immediate substance to a better world.

Emerson's address at Harvard Divinity School in 1838 had particularly inspired one of his listeners, Theodore Parker. This short, sturdy, massive-headed man, rapidly becoming bald, was twenty-eight years old at the time, and preaching in West Roxbury. He wanted Unitarianism to go farther than it had: to develop its "unconscious truth," to reject completely the supernatural elements of popular Christianity, and all the other "rubbish" which "polluted" the message of Jesus. Such language did not endear him to his more moderate colleagues. An 1841 sermon, *The Transient and Permanent in Christianity*, developed this vigorous thesis and brought Parker controversial fame. Orthodox ministers labeled him an "infidel" and "blasphemer." Even conservative Unitarians excluded Parker from traditional pulpit exchanges, not foreseeing that later generations of Unitarians would hail him as one of the denomination's great prophetic voices.

Despite his colleagues' verdict, popular appeal brought Parker to Boston to preach regularly at the Melodeon Theater on Washington Street. So successful was this that he left his West Roxbury parish the next year to preach to the group now organized as the Twenty-eighth Congregational Society. By

Theodore Parker's library.
(Courtesy of The Bostonian
Society, Old State House.)

the 1850s this Society had moved to the Music Hall. On Sundays as many as
three thousand people crowded in to hear his sermons. Younger Unitarians by
then were preaching his brand of Unitarianism. When he died in 1860 most
Unitarians had reluctantly accepted his importance.

Brought out of their theological diddling by the advent of the Civil War
and its demands, Unitarianism expanded after the war from a "Boston religion" to a national one. For the rest of the century, though some scoffed at it
as the "feather-bed of falling Christians," it enjoyed a period of great influence
in Boston and elsewhere. Popular and able ministers filled its Boston pulpits:
Cyrus Bartol, Edward Everett Hale, James DeNormandie, Charles Gordon
Ames, James Freeman Clarke, and Henry Wilder Foote.

In the twentieth century Unitarianism in Boston had seen its solidification
as a continental church, served by such Bostonians as Samuel Atkins Eliot, Frederick May Eliot, and Dana McLean Greeley, from its continental headquarters
in Boston in a 1927 Bulfinch-reproduction building on Beacon Street. In the
city itself, most of its once numerous churches have succumbed to the population changes, and not many more than half a dozen remain in the center
city. In 1961, its merger with the Universalist Church brought those two similar faiths together to coordinate their mutual concerns and to strengthen their
locally dwindling constituency.

EPISCOPALIANS   It is sometimes forgotten that Anglicans (or Episcopalians)
were in the Boston area before the Puritans arrived. William Blaxton, the first
white settler on the Boston peninsula, was an inactive priest. Samuel Maverick

was "strong for the prelatical power." Thomas Morton on his plantation Mare Mount, or Merry Mount, near Quincy, ran a prosperous fur trade, had thirty servants, lived elegantly for the time and place, and—worst sin of all in the eyes of the Pilgrims—daily read from the Book of Common Prayer. Illegally, they invaded his territory and sent him packing to England for allegedly arming the Indians. Regarding his Pilgrim and Indian neighbors, Morton was quite blunt: he preferred the Indians. "These I found most full of humanity, and more friendly than the other."

Nor did the new immigrants under John Winthrop prove any more desirable neighbors to Anglicans than had the Pilgrims. The Salem ministers had set the trend in 1629 by abandoning Church of England ways, asserting that a proper ministry was based on an inward call from God and an outward call from a congregation. Blaxton quietly watched his Puritan neighbors build their government and church on the Shawmut peninsula to which he had invited them. He neither objected to, nor attended their services, but finally decided the neighborhood was becoming too crowded and run down by such people. He moved to Rhode Island, acidly observing that he had left England because he didn't like the "lord-bishops" and had no greater inclination to live "under the lord-brethren."

As Puritan power grew, Anglicans were not welcomed into the new colony, and more than a hundred adherents already living in the region were given the choice of conforming or leaving. Most returned to Old England. When a book of John Winthrop's, that contained both the Book of Common Prayer and the New Testament, was eaten by mice, they only chewed up the former. Winthrop interpreted this as God saving the New Testament. It did not occur to him that it could as easily have been interpreted that the Book of Common Prayer was more nutritious.

With Charles II's restoration, efforts began to return Anglicans to New England. Charles proceeded so cautiously that nothing had been accomplished at his death. When the Bay Colony was made a Royal Province by James II, the Reverend Robert Ratcliffe accompanied the new governor (President) and again conducted Anglican services in Boston. Refused the use of the three churches in town, they took a temporary room in the Town House. Finally the new governor, Sir Edmund Andros, commandeered the use of the South Meeting House for part of Sunday. This caused so many complications and bad tempers, that construction was begun in late 1688 for what came to be King's Chapel. First services were held in it in June 1689. When Anne was on the throne it was called Queen's Chapel. The present building dates from 1754.

From then on the Church of England had legal protection and encouragement from the ruling authorities. Communicants grew rapidly enough so that by 1723 the foundation was laid for Christ Church in the North End. In five years this church counted eight hundred communicants. Trinity Church was founded in 1740 and built on Summer Street, while outside Boston several churches started: at Braintree in 1713 and at Marblehead in 1716. Christ

Church in Cambridge was organized in 1759, and Martha Washington attended one service there at the beginning of the Revolution.

The Revolution shook the foundations of the Church of England, tied so intimately as it was to the King of England (although three-fourths of the signers of the Declaration of Independence were Church-of-England men). Samuel Parker at Trinity Church openly supported the Revolutionary cause, but the rector of King's Chapel evacuated with the British and took the records of that parish with him; they were returned years later.

Not all Congregationalists were rebels. The witty Mather Byles of the Hollis Street Church was a staunch Loyalist, though he did not leave with the British. An incorrigible punster, he was placed under house arrest by the victorious rebels. He called his guard, his "Observ-a-tory." Once, wanting his sentry to go fetch some milk, the sentry objected, "Who will guard you?" "I will," answered Byles. He took the sentry's gun, and faithfully marched up and down until the sentry returned with the milk. When his sentry was removed, replaced, and finally removed again, Byles commented that he had been "guarded, reguarded, and disreguarded."

One result of the war was a change at King's Chapel. Lay reader James Freeman, refused ordination as an Episcopal priest because of his unitarian views, was ordained by his senior wardens. He rewrote its prayer book. An Englishman who attended King's Chapel once in the nineteenth century complained that the service was "expurgated": President Eliot of Harvard gently corrected him: "Not expurgated, *washed*." The congregation became a Unitarian church, winning a lawsuit which upheld their right to the property.

Nationally, the Church of England was making readjustments occasioned by separation from England, taking the familiar name of Episcopalian and modifying its rituals. The modifications were apparently not enough for some; parishioners of St. Paul's in 1825 complained that Sunday services ought to be shortened by ten minutes so that they could "get to the Post Office in time for their letters—as soon as gentlemen of other congregations."

Internationally, the Anglo-Catholic movement developed, splitting Episcopalians into the ritualistically rich High Church, plain Low Church, and in-between Broad Church. The Church of the Advent (organized in 1844) insisted with its rector, the Reverend William Croswell, that there was room in Boston for High Church as well as Low, and after much distress and infighting, its sister churches agreed with it. A monastic order, the Cowley Fathers, was connected with this church for a period after 1872. Now they are associated with the Mission Church of St. John the Evangelist on Bowdoin Street.

Trinity Church, which had been destroyed in the 1872 fire, was rebuilt in Copley Square in an elaborate dust-catching Gothic manner by architect Henry Hobson Richardson and was consecrated in 1877. Phillips Brooks, born in Boston in 1835, returned to his home city to minister to this church in 1869. An immediate preaching success, he had, said a reporter, "the humanity of Channing with the creed of Jeremy Taylor and strikes at the shirks and shams of our day with the dashing pluck and the full blood of Martin Luther." His ministry reached all classes, and when he died at fifty-seven, probably from diphtheria, only fifteen months after his consecration as Bishop, mourning was general in Boston. Copley Square was packed with mourners who could not get into the church for the funeral. Eight husky Harvard students had been specially drilled in the Harvard Gym with "three hundredweight of iron in a coffin" so that they would not drop the corpse as they carried it in and out of the church. Brooks in his prime stood six feet four and weighed over three hundred pounds. Both in size and example he stood out among his contemporaries.

One of the surprising Episcopalian responses to the Christian Socialism of the nineties had been aided by Brooks who had encouraged the formation of the Church of the Carpenter in April 1890 with the Reverend William Dwight Porter Bliss as rector. Bliss also organized a Brotherhood of the Carpenter in the church. This blend of Christian Socialism attracted the interest of a lively group of people including Hamlin Garland, William Dean Howells, Edward Bellamy, and Vida Scudder. She described their Sunday night meetings where they sang Socialist songs and the Magnificat, had "wonderful supper, true agape, when the altar at the back of the little room was curtained off and we feasted on ham and pickles and hope of an imminent revolution." Within two years the Church and the Brotherhood had disbanded and revolutionary hopes were salted away with other youthful dreams.

The new century saw Brooks' successor, as Bishop, William Lawrence, establishing St. Paul's Church as the Cathedral of the diocese in 1912. That same year Christ Church was restored architecturally. This is presently the oldest church building left in the city. Lawrence had been succeeded as Dean of the Episcopal Theological Seminary at Cambridge (begun in 1867) by George Hodges, a Christian Socialist, and the church continued its ambitious responses to the new century.

In 1906, the pastors of Emmanuel Church introduced a healing ministry which made use of the skills of psychiatrists and other physicians. This work came to be called the Emmanuel Movement and proved helpful to hundreds of distressed people. It was widely copied throughout the country, making, said one commentator, the healing ministry once again "an integral element in the gospel and normal in the life of the church." The Emmanuel Movement was one kind of ministry, the preaching of Phillips Brooks another, and the work of the Brotherhood of Carpenters, perpetuated in the charitable endeavors of the Episcopal City Mission during the depression years, yet another. Within its low, broad, and high reaches, the Episcopal church has endeavored to contain and continue all three.

BAPTISTS   "Chummy" as the Puritans might feel toward an impalpable God, palpable neighbors were a wholly different order of being. Anglicans they eventually had to endure, others they did not. Particularly if, as with Roger Williams, their opponents' standards were even more stringent than their own. From the moment the tall, handsome, intelligent Williams arrived in Boston in 1631, he found he disagreed with the local "establishment" both on specifics and generalities of doctrine. He believed in the entire separation of church and state, equal protection to all forms of religious worship, no compulsory church attendance, and the abolition of church tithes and taxes. These were far from the views of seventeenth-century Bostonians. After a few uncomfortable years in Salem and Plymouth, or traveling among the Indians, Williams was tried and condemned by the Puritans, escaping in 1635 to the Rhode Island region where he began a new colony.

Here, Williams founded what became the first Baptist Church in America, though he soon moved beyond any particular Christian church in his seeking after truth. People from this Providence Church began infiltrating back into the Boston area. Three men were arrested in Lynn in 1651 for worshiping in a private house. Brought to Boston they were cruelly flogged. Since they denied the saving power of infant baptism, John Cotton denounced them as "soul-murderers" using the same logic and words which several centuries later would be used to denounce abortion reforms.

To the Puritans, Baptists (or Anabaptists as they were sometimes called) were the anarchists of the day: "the incendiaries of commonwealths." So they were horrified in 1654 when the President of Harvard College, Henry Dunster, openly embraced the belief that infant baptism was "unscriptural." Harvard is always distressing somebody. Dunster was ousted and retired to die in obscurity in Plymouth Colony, but the doctrine did not disappear so easily. In 1665 a group of Baptists organized in Charlestown a church that subsequently came to Boston but had difficulty holding meetings. Yet in the next decade many people accepted the doctrine. In 1680 they had their own building with John Russell as pastor, but the General Court ordered its doors nailed shut and shut they stayed until England passed the Act of Toleration in 1689. Barely tolerated at first, they soon gained some acceptance. When the next Baptist minister, Elisha Callendar, was ordained, Cotton Mather preached his sermon and Increase Mather gave him the right hand of fellowship. In the climate of the day these were dramatic reversals, yet their growth was slow. The second local church did not begin until 1743, and then it was stimulated by the Edwards-Whitefield revival.

The gradual achievement of religious liberty is the story of these years. As in the matter of birth control, Massachusetts had fallen far behind all other states in these matters. In 1728 both Baptists and Quakers gained exemption from Massachusetts poll taxes. By 1781 the Baptist church in Arlington successfully got a rebate on their ministerial taxes. The Universalists had joined these groups in combating the restrictions on religious freedom. Still, it was not until 1833 that the General Court finally approved an amendment recognizing the separation of church and state, although such had been part of the federal constitution since 1791.

At the beginning of the nineteenth century there were two strong Baptist churches in Boston. Dr. Samuel Stillman had ministered at First Church for thirty-five years and was considered a popular extemporaneous preacher. The Massachusetts Baptist Missionary magazine began publication in 1803 and claims to be the oldest church periodical in the world. The Baptists started their theological school at Newton in 1825. A student at Newton, Samuel Francis Smith, wrote the patriotic hymn, "My Country 'Tis of Thee," in half an hour. It was first sung at Park Street Congregational Church on July 4, 1832.

Boston Baptists have been much concerned with being "Heralds of Salvation" and preaching "in heathen lands." A Missionary Society was founded the year before the magazine and Adoniram Judson, Jr., became one of its noted early workers. A national foreign mission was formed in Boston in 1871, and a home mission society six years later.

During the first part of the century, Baptist churches grew fast. Tremont Temple, in the heart of the city, was built then. But as population changes came, churches had to follow their parishioners out to the suburbs, or organize special churches for Negro members or Swedes as the case might be. A prominent Baptist layman in this period was the publisher Daniel Sharp Ford who spent lavishly to advance Baptist interests. He left the Baptist Social Union nearly a million dollars for them to do something for the welfare of the laboring classes. They built Ford Hall on Ashburton Place and for some years this housed the stimulating and controversial Ford Hall Forums, which now are held at Jordan Hall, the old Ford Hall long having been taken down. In recent years, Baptists have been adjusting, like all churches, to the new interests and urgencies of the twentieth century. Perhaps this has been symbolized in the careers of two Negro Baptists, the singer Roland Hayes, and Martin Luther King, Jr., who trained at the Theological School of Boston University.

THE BLACKS   Since there were blacks in Boston as soon as there were whites, and since Puritans required everyone to attend church, the question arose of where the black slaves and servants would sit. At first, they shared the rear pews with boys and poor people. Later, when galleries were built, the blacks were seated one flight nearer heaven. Yet church membership did not depend on wealth, social status, or skin color, so Negroes were occasionally admitted to the company of "visible saints." Winthrop reports of a Negro maidservant welcomed into the Dorchester church in 1641 because of her "sound knowledge and true godliness." This was more than many whites could attain.

The old African Church on Smith Court off Joy Street on Beacon Hill. Built by Afro-Americans and dedicated in 1806. In its sanctuary the Anti-Slavery movement was founded in 1832. From being the Independent Baptist Church, it later became a Jewish Synagogue.

Because Negro slavery was legal in Boston until after the Revolution, though the practice had been dying out before, it made it difficult for the church fellowship to accept Negroes as fellow Christians inside the church and as slaves outside it. Separate worship developed about the time of the Revolution. In 1789 the selectmen voted to allow "the Blacks to have the use of Mr. Vinal's school for public worship on the afternoon of the Lord's Day." As soon as they could afford to build and support their own church, like all other ethnic groups, they did so. This "African Church" was on the back slope of Beacon Hill. In 1806 a brick building was erected on what is now Smith's Court. It continued to serve a black congregation until after the middle of the century when it was sold to a Jewish congregation, the blacks having moved elsewhere. Before the Civil War it had been frequently used for abolitionist meetings, attended by such noted persons as Harriet Tubman, Frederick Douglass, and Sojourner Truth.

Once begun, separatism grew. White churches did not welcome blacks, just as Protestant churches did not welcome Catholics. When a wealthy Boston merchant escorted a well-dressed but very black gentleman into his pew in Federal Street Church one Sunday in the 1820s, it caused great consternation. The merchant answered the protests of his fellow worshipers with the satisfactory explanation that although the visitor was indeed black, he was also "worth a million." Yankees, who were willing to be chummy with God, were even more anxious to be chummy with a million dollars.

Yet a black gentleman who bought a pew in Park Street Church in 1835 did not fare so well. His fellow Christians nailed up the door of his pew and so many threatened to leave the society that the trustees were forced to revoke his deed. Forewarned, another Boston church immediately inserted a clause in *their* pewdeeds stating that they could only be held by "respectable white persons."

As the Negro population increased, various denominations began to serve their religious needs. A Negro Methodist congregation took over the white Baptist church on Charles Street in the nineteenth century. In the 1900s this group followed its congregation to Roxbury, selling their building, but keeping their name. Thus, on Warren Street one will find the Charles Street African Methodist Episcopal (AME) Church. In the 1870s two well-known Negro Baptist churches were founded in the South End: Ebenezer Baptist and Day Star Baptist, of which the former survives on West Springfield Street.

In all the change and movement, some things remain constant: the old perplexity of whether one was eating in the meetinghouse or meeting in the eatinghouse is still with us. During the Depression there was a Father Divine's Peace Mission on Canton Street in the South End which featured chicken dinners for fifteen cents; dessert was a nickel extra. Presently, Muhammad's Mosque No. 11 has its Shabazz Restaurant, where it permits no drinking or smoking, out-middle-classing the middle class.

Churches serving the Negro population of Boston today have been active in the contemporary civil rights movement, and have included such varied denominations as St. Mark's Congregational Church, Twelfth Baptist, Union Methodist, St. Monica's Episcopal, and St. Hugh Roman Catholic. Nor should the Blue Hill Christian Center and the determined Reverend Virgil Wood be overlooked. This contemporary social action of Christianity has been documented in watercolors by black artist Allan Rohan Crite, setting the madonna and child down among the elevated tracks and bars of Boston's slums. It is also visible in the new Ecumenical Center on Crawford Street.

PRESBYTERIANS   Presbyterians have had difficulty in making any large religious impression on Boston. They were too close in sentiment to the dominant Congregationalists. Although Presbyterians from Scotland were among the earliest settlers (forming the country's oldest charitable group, the Scots Charitable Society, in 1657), their first real church, started by the Reverend John Morehead in Henry Deering's barn on Long Lane (Federal Street) in 1729, was made Congregational by the members. Subsequently it evolved into the Unitarian Federal Street Church where Channing preached, and later moving into the new Back Bay it took the name of the Arlington Street Church. A group of French Huguenot refugees had earlier established a Presbyterian church on School Street in 1686, but this soon died out and was sold to Congregationalists, and eventually served as the first Roman Catholic chapel in Boston.

It was not until 1825 that the First Presbyterian Church was incorporated in Boston, but the persuasion never took firm root. Even though a hundred years later there were ten active Presbyterian churches in the city, including the Gloucester Memorial Congregation of Negroes, the depression, population changes, and moving to the suburbs eliminated them after mid-century from the center city. The Church of the Covenant on Newbury Street is the principal survivor, and that, too, merged with a Congregational Church.

The Third Presbyterian Church on West Springfield Street, shown in a Hawes photograph about the middle of the last century, by 1950 was the home of the Ebenezer Baptist group.

UNIVERSALISTS   Universalism might well be thought of as a home-grown Boston religion, although its nominal founder was an immigrant Englishman who first preached his version of James Relly's doctrine of salvation for all souls in New Jersey in 1770. Three years later he was making trips into New England and Boston where he found a small core of interested believers in the new teaching. After a brief fling as chaplain during the siege of Boston, John Murray settled in the Cape Ann community of Gloucester, although making frequent trips to spread his ideas. By 1793 he had made Boston his headquarters, where he felt he could be more influential.

A year after Murray's death in 1815, another Universalist church in Boston called the most prominent Universalist leader of the period to its pulpit. For nearly thirty-five years, the Reverend Hosea Ballou, an ex-Baptist, brought the message of Universal Salvation, as he had drastically modernized it, to New England from his pulpit on School Street and in debates and writings. As editor from 1819 of *The Universalist Magazine*, he began what is now the oldest continuous religious publication in the country, though it has been

The Asher Benjamin church built for the Third Baptist congregation in 1807, later became the First African Methodist Church, and after restoration work in the 1930s now houses the Charles Street Meeting House (Unitarian Universalist). The depiction is by Percy Grassby, about 1936.

through many mergers and name changes. Boston became headquarters of the denomination that grew from revisions of Calvinism. After much effort, the national denomination founded the nonsectarian Tufts College on Walnut Hill in Medford in 1852. Numerous churches developed in Boston and its environs during the last part of the nineteenth century, with perhaps the most noted minister being Alonzo Ames Miner, later president of Tufts College.

Miner was one of the chief advocates of temperance. He underlined the Universalists' interest in social problems. Another, the Reverend Charles M. Spears, had been active in prison reform and the Reverend Adin Ballou had united various small reform efforts in founding the Hopedale Community. Under the impact of the social gospel and the leadership of the Reverend George L. Perin, the Shawmut Avenue Church in Boston developed a full "institutional" program in 1894, calling itself the Every-Day Church. Out of Perin's endeavors grew the Franklin Square House for working girls, now serving today as a center for the elderly. Reverend Clarence R. Skinner preached and practiced this same social concern up to the middle of the twentieth century, both from his pulpit at Community Church which he and a small group founded in 1920 and from his teaching and deanship at Tufts' School of Religion.

As the population changed, most local Universalist churches closed or moved to the suburbs. At the time the denomination merged with the Unitarians in 1961, there was only one active Universalist church in the core city, although that was the remarkably experimental group under the leadership of the Reverend Kenneth L. Patton at the Charles Street Meeting House.

METHODISTS John Wesley's brother Charles was briefly in Boston in 1736, when various Methodist evangels included the city as one of their stopping places on their preaching circuits. Bishop Francis Asbury, chief founder of Methodism in America, made many swings through Boston as early as 1790, though he found Lynn more cordial than Boston. The first church was built between 1795 and 1797 with ministers of several denominations contributing to its construction. It has since been known as the "Mother of Bishops" because of the number of its clergy who were raised to that office. With the same penchant for nicknames, the Tremont Street Methodist Church has been called the "cradle of the Women's Foreign Mission Society."

This growing Methodist group, like other churches, started a weekly newspaper, *Zion's Herald,* in 1823, still in existence, which holds the distinction of being one of the two New England papers to protest the violent "mob" which attacked William Lloyd Garrison in 1835. Their most popular preacher in Boston then was Edward T. Taylor, "Father Taylor," of the Boston Seamen's Bethel, which he had taken charge of in 1828, operating it as a nonsectarian religious home for sailors, and largely supported by Unitarians. Father Taylor served as the model for Melville's preacher in *Moby Dick.*

The Unitarians also became involved in another Methodist project: Henry Morgan, an eccentric philanthropist and revivalist, organized a Boston Union Mission Society in 1859 that eventually developed into an institutionalized

214

church. When he died his property was bequeathed to the Benevolent Fraternity of Unitarian Churches (founded in 1834), familiarly called "Ben Frat," while the religious work of the Mission remained in charge of the Methodists. In 1912, representatives of other denominations were appointed to the Mission's controlling board and the group is responsible today for the Morgan Memorial organization that aids the poor. Through its Goodwill Industries it collects and reclaims cast-off articles from Greater Boston homes. It also sponsors a Church of All Nations.

In 1869, Methodists founded Boston University, which though now non-sectarian and coeducational bears a strong Methodist imprint, particularly in its theological school. The other major contribution of this group to the Boston scene was the New England Deaconess Hospital, an important adjunct to Boston medical care.

SWEDENBORGIANS Rescuing Emanuel Swedenborg's *Arcana Coelestia* from a remote dusty corner of Harvard College Library in 1816, a young student, Thomas Worcester, became so interested in its doctrines that two years later he helped to organize the Church of the New Jerusalem (Swedenborgian) in

The Old West Church in Boston on the corner of Cambridge and Lynde Streets as painted by Maurice Prendergast, early in the twentieth century.

215

Samuel Chamberlain's 1947 photograph of the New Jerusalem Church on Bowdoin Street, since replaced.

Boston. For forty-nine years he served it as its pastor. After meeting for years in rented halls, in 1845 they built a church on Beacon Hill near the State House. Remodeled in 1926, it was replaced with a high-rise apartment building—Boston View—in 1966, the ground floor of which houses the new sanctuary of the church. Several suburban societies have branched off from the Beacon Hill Church. Almost continuously since 1827 it has published a periodical now titled the *New-Church Review*. A theological school, once located in Waltham, then Boston, since 1889 has been in Cambridge.

LUTHERANS   Lutheranism came to Boston with German immigrants who formed a church in 1839. As other immigrants with a Lutheran background arrived in the city—Swedes, Danes, Norwegians, Letts—churches were organized by them. As these people dispersed to the suburbs, their churches went with them or became extinct. A social service project, the Martin Luther Orphans' Home, established in West Roxbury in 1870 on the site of Brook Farm, continues today as the Lutheran Brook Farm Home, working with emotionally disturbed children. The principal surviving Lutheran church in the city is housed in a modern building on the corner of Berkeley and Marlborough streets.

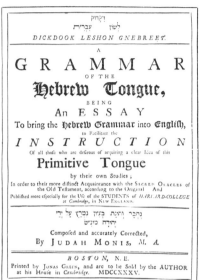

וקרוק
לשון עברית
DICKDOOK LESHON GNEBREET.

A

GRAMMAR
OF THE
Hebrew Tongue,
BEING
An ESSAY
To bring the Hebrew Grammar into English,
to Facilitate the
INSTRUCTION
Of all those who are desirous of acquiring a clear Idea of this
Primitive Tongue
by their own Studies;
In order to their more distinct Acquaintance with the SACRED ORACLES of
the Old Testament, according to the Original And
Published more especially for the Use of the STUDENTS of HARVARD-COLLEGE
at Cambridge, in NEW ENGLAND.

נחבר ונתת בעיון נבון על ל ידי
יהודה בן אל

Composed and accurately Corrected,
By JUDAH MONIS, M. A.

BOSTON, N.E.
Printed by JONAS GREEN, and are to be Sold by the AUTHOR
at his House in Cambridge. MDCCXXXV.

When Temple Israel was brand new, shown in this stark photograph from the Boston Public Library.

The title page of Judah Monis' pioneering Hebrew Grammar, 1735. (Courtesy of the American Jewish Historical Society.)

JEWS   Many early New England ministers spoke Hebrew—"the language of God" as they thought—but the first known Jew who visited Boston seems to have been Soloman Franco who passed through briefly in 1649. Charles Chauncy, President of Harvard from 1654 to 1672, was said to have had a Jew living with him for about a year, with whom he daily conversed in Hebrew. However, the interest of the early ministers was not so much in speaking Hebrew as in converting them. "Simon the Jew" was the first of these to become Christian, on September 13, 1702, taking the name Simon Barnes (or Barns). Other conversions followed in the next decades, the most important being that of Judah Monis in 1722. Two years before, Harvard gave Monis the first and only honorary degree given a Jew before 1800. For thirty-eight years Monis instructed students in Hebrew, as well as running a shop on the side. In 1736, Harvard published his Jewish grammar.

Only a few other Jewish individuals lived in Boston until just before the middle of the nineteenth century. By 1842, there were enough families to form the first congregation, which was formally organized in 1843 and incorporated in 1845 as the Congregation Ohabei Shalom with Henry Selling as its rabbi. Two groups developed from this first congregation, which was mainly Polish in background: a group of German Jews withdrew in 1854 to become what is today Temple Israel, and another group separated in 1858 to form Mishkan Israel.

Temple Israel's innovative Rabbi Solomon Schindler.

Interior view of the Smith Court Synagogue shown in 1949 photograph by Arthur G. Haskell. (Courtesy of the Society for the Preservation of New England Antiquities.)

Temple Israel chose Solomon Schindler as rabbi in 1874 bringing to Boston this innovative German immigrant, who reformed and Americanized the old-world rituals. He introduced the family pew, the choir, the organ, a new prayer book, and abandoned the wearing of hats. He tried to erase prejudices between Jew and Gentile, even sanctioning intermarriage, and moved beyond specific Jewish tenets to an acceptance of the validity of all religions. He considered each religion would contribute whatever was "immortal" in them to the religion of the future. Rabbi Joshua Loth Liebman, a generation later and from the same pulpit, continued much of Schindler's spirit of outreach both in his work and in his religious bestseller, *Peace of Mind*, published in 1946 and probably the best of the inspirational books it prompted.

Like other small congregations serving various ethnic groups, these Jewish synagogues successfully became part of the larger Boston community. Suddenly they were swamped under the huge Jewish immigration that began in the 1880s when the Russian pogroms started. Many newcomers flocked in to the West and North End, and small congregations formed to meet their religious needs. At the turn of the century there were twenty-one congregations in Boston plus two in Chelsea and one in Lynn. The subsequent story of these synagogues is their migration and merger as their members moved away from Boston proper into the suburbs, particularly Roxbury and Dorchester, and then into Brookline and the Newtons.

Clustering around these congregations came associated organizations: the B'nai B'rith was in Boston from 1855; burial grounds were bought almost as soon as each community was organized; active Zionist groups were founded from 1900 on; various Chevras to study the Talmud, promote Jewish education, and provide charitable assistance were formed; the United Hebrew Benevolent Society was organized in 1864; the Federation of Jewish Charities after 1889; and the first periodical (the short-lived *Jewish Watchman*) from 1882. It was not until the *Boston Jewish Advocate* began in 1902 (as the *Mt. Sinai Monthly*) that the local Jewish community gained a prominent and respected voice still heard today. Mt. Sinai Hospital was founded by these Jewish groups in 1902, to be succeeded by the highly successful Beth Israel Hospital in 1917. Brandeis University in Waltham, named in honor of the most distinguished Jewish citizen of Boston, dates from 1948, and quickly became, under Dr. Abram Sacher, one of the country's leading universities.

The anti-Semitism expressed so vocally in Boston during the 1930s and 1940s by supporters of Father Coughlin (who boasted he received most of his financial support from Boston) and the pro-Nazi activities of Francis P. Moran's Christian Front—they took over the 1941 South Boston Evacuation Day parade —have largely evaporated. In part this is because the intolerance has turned upon the aspirations of the local Negro community. That Negroes should share the anti-Semitism of their oppressors is one of the crueler ironies of the time. To what extent the "cult of interfaith banqueting and head-tableship" has contributed to the removal of prejudice is doubted by some observers. But in true Boston spirit, the town has not one but two leagues of Christians and Jews, and an era of "bigger and better goodwill banquets" seems ahead.

Front page of first issue of *Truth*, early Jewish newspaper in Boston, 1895. (Courtesy of the American Jewish Historical Society.)

Justice Louis Brandeis (Courtesy of Brandeis University).

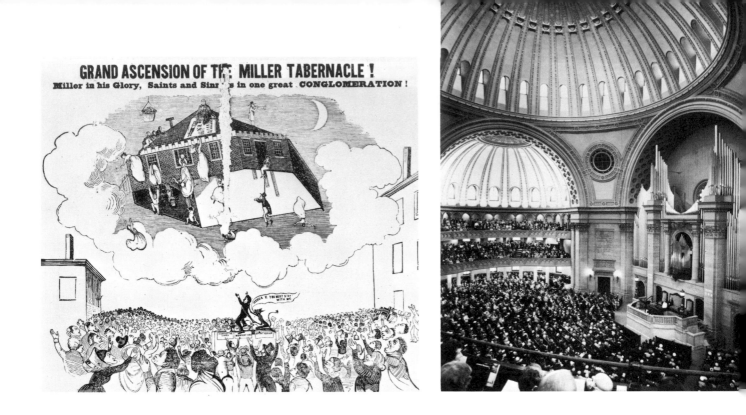

SEVENTH-DAY ADVENTISTS   One of the bizarre incidents of the 1840s was the
excitement stirred up by a Baptist farmer-preacher named William Miller who
had predicted that the world would end soon after March 21, 1843. The
millennium would then begin for all who had accepted Christ. The rest of
mankind would perish. Among the emotional, the poorly educated, and the
orthodox believers in scriptural literalism, these doctrines aroused fear and
conviction. From 1839 on, the Reverend Joshua V. Himes, pastor of the
Chardon Street Chapel, publicized Miller's theory in his paper, *Signs of the
Times,* later named the *Advent Herald.* Such promotion plus some unusual
astronomical occurrences, including a comet in 1843, convinced many the end
of the world was approaching. A large tabernacle where the message could be
preached was built in May 1843 on Howard Street in Boston (where the Old
Howard Burlesque Theater was to entertain another kind of devotee).

Enthusiastic disciples predicted various dates for the final holocaust. Boston
Millerites determined it would be October 10, 1843, at 4:00 P.M. and that day
Millerites gathered inside the tabernacle, with a large crowd outside waiting
"to see 'em go up." Just before four o'clock, the leaders changed their pre-
diction to October 22. Many followers came in to sleep in the tabernacle until
the fateful night, some having sold all their possessions since they would
no longer be needed. The story of the Millerites donning white "Ascension
Robes" was probably fabricated by scoffers. The twenty-second came—and
went—but the Millerites didn't. Most believers now abandoned the movement,
though a few persisted, eventually forming the Seventh-Day Adventist denomination and several other sects. Several Seventh-Day Adventist churches
are active in the Boston area, as is their large New England Memorial Hospital
in Stoneham.

CHRISTIAN SCIENCE   Religion has been essentially a male monopoly, the place of woman largely being restricted to bearing the messiahs, saints, and prophets, but not *being* them. They were also encouraged to work on fairs and sewing circles and "Ladies' Aid." But Boston ladies from time to time have wanted to do more than aid, much to male distress. The solution at first was to banish them (Mrs. Hutchinson) or hang them (the Quaker ladies), but womanly persistence has a way of wearing down the strongest male objections, and Bostonians finally learned the wisdom of "If you can't lick 'em, jine 'em."

The lady who taught them that lesson was a New Hampshire girl, born Mary Baker in 1821. Widowed at twenty-three from George Glover, she became a semi-invalid subject to nervous attacks. In 1853 she married a dentist, Dr. Daniel Patterson, who deserted her in Lynn in 1866. They were divorced in 1873. In 1862, however, she had discovered the teachings of Phineas Parkhurst Quimby, a Belfast, Maine, handyman, who cured himself of semi-invalidism by hypnosis, then set up as a healer in Portland, Maine. Mrs. Patterson visited him and became a disciple. After Quimby's death in the same year as her husband's desertion, she slipped into loneliness and invalidism. A bad fall on the ice threatened to make her a helpless cripple, but she healed herself with Bible reading and a system she worked out over the next years called "the Science of divine metaphysical healing." Its principle was an insistence that neither disease nor matter existed; "both were fictions of blinded minds."

In 1875 she published her treatise on this discovery, *Science and Health*, later revised several times to make it "clearer" and the phrase "with Key to the Scriptures" added to the title. The next year she had gathered a small band of disciples, one of whom, Asa Gilbert Eddy of Lynn, she took as her third husband in 1877. Soon she extended her work into Boston, lecturing Sunday

221

The Christian Science Publishing House. (Courtesy of The Christian Science Publishing Society.)

afternoons at the Shawmut Avenue Baptist Church. In 1879 the Church of Christ (Scientist) was chartered. Three years later, Eddy, a small mild man, died of mesmeric poison, and Mary Baker Glover Patterson Eddy remained a widow the rest of her life. Her remaining years were busily devoted to spreading her teachings and building up the institution that grew out of them.

After several early schisms, Mrs. Eddy and twelve selected disciples formed the "First Church of Christ, Scientist, in Boston, Massachusetts"—the "Mother Church"—erecting their first edifice in 1895 in the Back Bay. So quickly was this outgrown that a huge extension, seating five thousand and costing $2 million, was built and dedicated in 1906. A series of religious publications was started, the best known of which is the international daily newspaper, the *Christian Science Monitor*. This was begun in 1907 when Mrs. Eddy was a vigorous eighty-six years old. This award-winning newspaper made a niche for itself by avoiding the staple diet of many other newspapers: scandal, sex, and sin.

With Mrs. Eddy's death in 1910, a prolonged struggle began for control of the church apparatus, ending in 1921 with a decision for the absolute rule of the central Board of Directors. Today they preside from Boston over an international organization with nearly twenty-five hundred churches, ten thousand practitioners, and an estimated three hundred thousand members. Besides their institutional accomplishment, they have been canny real estate owners, and are playing a major role in rehabilitating their section of the Back Bay.

222

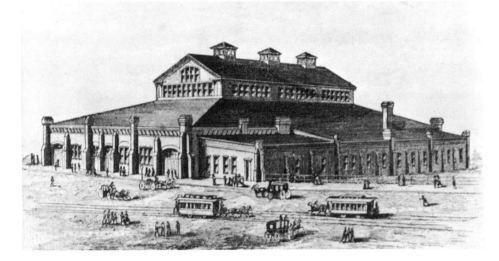

Moody and Sankey Tabernacle in Boston in 1877 on Berkeley Street.

Spiritual Temple built on the corner of Newbury and Exeter Streets in Boston, now home of the Exeter Street Theater.

QUAKERS Quakers were early active in the Boston area. Deborah Wilson in 1662 walked through the streets of Salem "naked as the day she came into the world" to dramatize to the stubborn Puritans the "nakedness" of their religious doctrines. A Friends' meetinghouse stood in Boston from 1694 to 1865. For a few years after that, Boston Quakers went to Lynn for their silent meetings. Then they were reestablished in Roxbury from 1894 to 1926. When the Roxbury group closed, they joined with the Friends meeting which had been held in Cambridge since 1911.

At one time or another, short- or long-lived, almost every tint in the religious spectrum has shone on the Boston scene. For nearly sixty years after the arrival of Robert Sandeman in Boston in 1764, his followers—Sandemanians—met in various buildings in the North End, finally vanishing without a trace. Salvation Army units have trumpeted their message of salvation on Boston streetcorners since the 1880s. Immigrants from Eastern Europe brought their ancient and colorful rites with them and soon Orthodox Catholic churches following Greek or Armenian customs were being built in the South End where many of these immigrants settled. Here on a Sunday, the Mass could be heard in Russian, Ukrainian, Albanian, ancient Syriac, Arabic (the Mechites), Greek, and Armenian.

It should not be forgotten that in any period of Boston's religious life there is a "fourth faith," the uncommitted, the unchurched, the non-believers, the non-attenders. These represent a large number of people, but since they are not organized, they are silent and usually disregarded. And names of other religious groups could be included in this survey of the religious scene. All of them have made some impact on their adherents and left ripples even on the apathetic majority. But such lists could go on and on. The poet Whittier, a Quaker, summed up the important fact:

From scheme and creed the light goes out,
The saintly fact survives.

Interlude six: Boston to 1900

Boston is barrels

"When I go to Boston, I go naturally straight through the city down to the end of Long Wharf and look off, for I have no cousins in the back alleys. The water and the vessels are novel and interesting. What are our maritime cities but the shops and dwellings of merchants, about a wharf projecting into the sea, where there is a convenient harbor, on which to land the produce of other climes and at which to load the exports of our own? Next in interest to me is the market where the produce of our own country is collected. Boston, New York, Philadelphia, Charleston, New Orleans, and many others are the names of wharves projecting into the sea. They are good places to take in and to discharge a cargo. Everybody in Boston lives at No. so-and-so, Long Wharf. I see a great many barrels and fig-drums and piles of wood for umbrella-sticks and blocks of granite and ice, etc., and that is Boston. Great piles of goods and the means of packing and conveying them, much wrapping-paper and twine, many crates and hogsheads and trucks, that is Boston. The more barrels, the more Boston. The museums and scientific societies and libraries are accidentals. They gather around the barrels, to save carting.

—Henry D. Thoreau
Journal, December 25, 1853

The Boston woman—1857

The Boston woman draweth down her mouth, rolleth up her eyes, foldeth her hands, and walketh on a crack. She rejoiceth in anatomical and chemical lectures. She prateth of Macaulay and Carlyle, belongeth to many and divers reading-classes, and smileth in a chaste, moonlight kind of way on literary men. She dresseth (to her praise be it spoken) plainly in the street, and considereth india-rubbers, a straw bonnet, and a thick shawl, the fittest costume for damp and cloudy weather. She dresseth her children more for comfort than for show, and bringeth them up also to walk on a crack. She maketh the tour of the Common twice or three times a day, without regard to the barom-eter. She goeth to church twice or three times on Sunday, sandwiched with Bible-classes and Sabbath-schools. She thinketh London, Vienna, or Paris—fools to Boston; and the "Boulevards" and "Tuil-leries" not to be mentioned with the Frog Pond and the Common. She is well posted up as to poli-tics—thinketh "as Pa does," and sticketh to it through thunder and lightning. When asked to take a gentleman's arm, she hooketh the tip of her little finger circumspectly on to his male coat-sleeve. She is as prim as a bolster, as stiff as a ram-rod, as frigid as an icicle, and not even matrimony with a New Yorker could thaw her.

—"Fanny Fern" (Sara Willis Farrington)
Fresh Leaves, 1857

Blacks in Boston, spring 1860

You see not near as many black persons in Boston as you would expect. They are not near as plenty as in New York and Philadelphia. Their status here, however, is at once seen to be different. I have seen one working at the case in a printing office (Boston Stereotype Foundry, Spring Lane) and no distinction made between him and the white compositors. Another I noticed, (and I never saw a blacker or woolier African) an employee in the State House, apparently a clerk or under-official of some kind—at the eating houses, a black when he wants his dinner, comes in and takes a vacant seat wherever he finds one—and nobody minds it. I notice that the mechanics and the young men do not mind this either. As for me, I am too much a citizen of the world to have the least compunction about it. The blacks here are certainly of superior order—quite as good to have in contact with you as the average of "our own colour." There is a black lawyer named Anderson, (a resident of Chelsea) practicing here in Boston, quite smart, and just as big as the best of them. And in Worcester, they are now put on the jury list, two of the names put on being black men, one of them a fugitive slave who has purchased his freedom.

—Walt Whitman

A moving experience on Beacon Street, circa 1865

At that stately door, the one with the side windows, through which the hall might be reconnoitered, one day in the middle Sixties two young men rang the door-bell. The maid opened the door.

"We have come for the sofa!" said one of the youths, a slight fair lad with earnest, impressive look. So impressive was he that the maid, at his gesture, stood aside. The two lifted the hall sofa—I see it as a long, light settee of cane and teak—and with a word of acknowledgment walked off with it, out of the door, down the steps, down the street. The maid may have worn a puzzled expression as she closed the door; she certainly did not look after them. They carried the sofa a few rods, poles or perches, then rang at another stately door. This being opened by another maid—

"We have brought the sofa!" said the quiet fair lad with the earnest look. This young woman, too, impressed, stood aside; the sofa was deposited against the wall; a pleasant gesture of satisfied accomplishment, and the youth departed with his companion. All the rest of the day, his soul frolicked with its coat off; he dined and supped on mirth. A great, a monumental joke; to be described amid tempests of laughter to the other members of the Frozen Pudding Club, that mystic Four, the chief aim of whose life at that time was the perpetrating of jokes.

—Laura E. Richards
My Boston

Sliding down Fort Hill (Roxbury)

Roxbury was my home for five years of the most romantic period, from eleven to sixteen. I knew all the poetry of its groves, its absurd rocks, its incredible cliffs. On Parker Hill, before the digging of the old reservoir that has recently been filled up, I hunted Indians. I discovered and explored the land of enchantment that is now Franklin Park. I shuddered at Bussey's Woods, scene of a horrid murder which I always identified with the story of the Babes in the Wood. . . . And I viewed the world from Fort Hill, beside the Standpipe, the rallying-place of our gang.

Down Fort Hill, with its long, steep, dangerously right-angled incline, I used to coast in winter, in preference to the more frequented Honeysuckle Hill. There it was that Jimmy Burns involuntarily saved my life; for at the perilous corner of the coast, my sled, which had skidded on the ice, ran into his, and was thereby prevented from plunging over a precipice fifty feet high. To me it was evident that Jimmy had been fore-ordained to perform this service, that such was the real purpose of his seemingly meaningless existence; but I never could bring him to look upon the incident in that light. Indeed, to him a trifling bruise on his thigh, where my runner struck him, looked more important than my salvation. The stone tablet subsequently erected on the summit of the hill, however, commemorated not this momentous episode, but something or other connected with the siege of Boston; and a whole line of its inscription had to be cut out and done over, because "siege" was misspelled.

—Charles Hall Grandgent
Prunes and Prism

The sin of slums

I pass . . . as I ride into the city and return, squares of newly built tenant houses erected on lands which the high tides can hardly fail to overflow and every rain inundate—near a slaughterhouse moreover, rendering them unfit for human dwellings at any season. The capitalist doubtless pleads his legal right to use his money or lands in any manner he please, and the poor occupant perhaps considers him a benefactor in furnishing a shelter even in such unwholesome quarters, while he can pay his rent for it; though his wife and children, if not himself, fall victims to his surroundings, unless they chance to be sound and virtuous.

Cities, like Cain, may not hope to shield their crime by legislation, excusing themselves from being their "brother's keeper" thereby, nor hold any guiltless who disregard, for gain, the health, comfort, or virtue of a single citizen.

—A. Bronson Alcott
Journals, July 31, 1870

Sundays in King's Chapel, 1870

. . . it was a relief to be safe within the high enclosure of the family pew, huddled in his cushioned corner (the very one where his father had sat) out of sight of everyone, even of the minister still hidden behind his lofty pulpit, while the organ softly played a few quavering arpeggios. The music was classical and soothing, the service High Church Unitarian, with nothing in it either to discourage a believer or to annoy an unbeliever. What did doctrines matter? The lessons were chosen for their magical archaic English and were mouthed in a tone of emotional mystery and unction. With the superior knowledge and finer feelings of today might we not find in such words far deeper meanings than the original speakers intended? The sermon was sure to be pleasantly congratulatory and pleasantly short: even if it began by describing graphically the landscape of Sinai or of Galilee— for the Rev. Mr. Hart had travelled—it would soon return to matters of living interest, would praise the virtues and flatter the vanity of the congregation, only slightly heightening the picture by contrast with the sad vices and errors of former times or of other nations. After church Mr. Alden could enjoy the mid-day sunshine as he walked home to his Sunday roast beef and apple dumpling, confirmed in all his previous ways of thinking.

—George Santayana
The Last Puritan

By horsecar to Boston in 1880

From just above our Channing Street [in Cambridge], on either side of us, catering thus to both Brattle Street and Mt. Auburn Street, a line of street-cars ran to Harvard Square and Boston. . . . As I remember it took several changes of horses and approximately two hours to run a car to Boston and back again on either the Brattle Street line or the Mt. Auburn Street line.

Between the two car routes however a very distinct social line was drawn.

Though cars and service on both routes were almost identical, the fact remained that generally speaking nobody except day-laborers ever patronized the Mt. Auburn Street line at either morning or night, if he could help it.

Bristling with sticks and staves, pronging with pitchforks, glinting with shovels and hoes, our brawny, jovial Mt. Auburn Street neighbors just naturally commandeered the traffic to themselves.

The Brattle Street line on the contrary was patronized almost entirely by the élite, leisurely ladies bound on some shopping or social errand, leisurely gentlemen faring forth to college classroom or law office, quiet-mannered children on their way to or from their private schools. . . .

In winter for warmth and comfort, straw was heaped into the center of the car, and we children were only too glad to cuddle down into its sumptuous depths. Even so I remember perfectly well the cold and discomfort of the long winter ride into Boston and back. There was however an actual "silver lining" even to this.

Sometimes in the straw or hay we found pennies, nickles, or dimes, that heedless people had dropped from their wallets. . . .

The grown people of course never looked for anything in the straw except warmth for their feet. No matter how high in the clouds these Brattle Street heads were reputed to be, the owners of them always seemed very glad indeed to keep their winter feet in the straw though by some miraculous dispensation of Providence they never emerged from the car with the slightest trace of hay-seed upon their immaculate persons to betray to any ribald eye the fact that to all intents and purposes they had been traveling in a portable barn.

—Eleanor Hallowell Abbott
Being Little in Cambridge

A Marxian view of Boston, 1888

Aug. 28—Boston is just a village, sprawling far & wide, but more human than New York City, Cambridge even very pretty, quite European continental to look at.

Aug. 31—Yesterday in Concord, in the reformatory and the town. We liked both. A prison in which the prisoners read novels and scientific books, form clubs, meet and discuss without the presence of officials, eat twice a day meat and fish and with it as much bread as they like, have ice water in every shop, running fresh water in every cell, the cells decorated with pictures etc., where the inmates dressed like common laborers look one squarely in the eyes without the hang-dog look of the ordinary criminal-prisoner, cannot be found in the whole of Europe, for that the Europeans, are, as I told the Superintendent, not bold enough. And he quite American-like answered: well we try to make it pay, and it does pay. There I got great respect for the Americans.

Concord is very lovely, in good taste as you would not expect it after New York and even Boston, but a perfect little place to be buried in, but not alive! Four weeks there and I would go to pieces or go crazy.

My nephew Willie Burns is a fine fellow, clever, energetic, with body and soul in the labor movement. He is doing well, he is employed by the Boston and Providence Railroad (now Old Colony), makes $12.—weekly, has a nice wife (brought with him from Manchester) and three children. He would not return to England for anything, he is just the boy for a country like America.

—Frederick Engels (1820–95)
Sorge Collection, N. Y. Public Lib.
translated by Dirk J. Struik

A Chestnut Hill Thanksgiving, 1887

In the morning we went to church. P.M. we played Prisoner's Base on Hawthorne Street. In the evening we went to the Farm to dinner. Seventeen were there. First course, raw oysters; second course, thick and thin soups; third course, two kinds of fish; fourth, patties; fifth Turkey, cranberries, celery, potato and peas; sixth, ducks, rice birds and salads; seventh, Plum Pudding, four kinds of pie, wine jelly and Charlotte Russe; eighth, ice cream and cocoanut cakes; ninth, fruit and candy. Julie, Amos, and I sat at a little table. In the middle of dinner Amos had to run up and down the stairs so that he could eat some more and he also took his vest off, it got so tight.

—Marian Lawrence Peabody
To Be Young Was Very Heaven

A pleasing encounter with a pickpocket

Dec. 21, 1892—I was in town the other evening, walking by myself, at my usual rapid pace, and ruminating, in all likelihood, on the military affairs of the Scythians, when, at a lonely street corner not adorned by a gas-lamp, I suddenly felt a delicate stir in my upper pocket. There is a sort of mechanical intelligence in a well-drilled and well-treated body, which can act, in an emergency, without orders from headquarters. My mind, certainly, was a thousand years away, and is at best drowsy and indifferent. It had besides, no experience, nor even hearsay, which would have directed it what to do at this thrilling little crisis. Before it was aware what had happened, and in the beat of a swallow's wing, my fingers had brushed the flying thief, my eyes saw him, and my legs (retired racehorses, but still great at a spurt) flew madly after him. I protest that from the first, though I knew he had under his wicked thumb the hard-earned wealth of a notoriously poor poet, . . . yet I never felt one yearning towards it, nor conceived the hope of revenge. No: I was fired by the exquisite dramatic situation. . . . I was in for the chase in the keen winter air, with the moon just rising over the city roofs, as rapturously as if I were a very young dog again. My able bandit, clearly viewed the instant of his assault, was a tiger-lily of the genus "tough"; short, pallid, sullen, with coat-collar up and hat-brim down, and a general air of mute and violent executive ability. . . . As I wheeled about, neatly losing the chance of confronting him, and favored with a hasty survey, in the dark, of his strategic mouth and chin, the one sentiment in me, if translated into English, would have uttered itself in this wise: "After years of dulness and decorum, O soul, here is some one come to play with thee; here is Fun, sent of the immortal gods!"

This divine emissary, it was evident, had studied his ground, and awaited no activity on the part of the preoccupied victim, in a hostile and unfamiliar neighborhood. He suffered a shock when, . . . I took up a gallop within an inch of his nimble heels. Silently, as he ran, he lifted his right arm. We were soon in the blackness of an empty lot across the road, among coal-sheds and broken tins, with the far lights of the thoroughfare full in our faces. Quick as kobolds summoned up from earth, air, and nowhere, four fellows, about twenty years old, swarmed at my side, as like the first in every detail as foresight and art could make them; and these darting, dodging, criss-crossing, quadrilling, and incessantly interchanging as they advanced, covering the expert one's flight, and multiplying his identity, shot separately down a labyrinth of narrow alleys, leaving me confused and checkmated, after a brief and unequal game, but overcome, nay, transported with admiration and unholy sympathy! It was the prettiest trick imaginable.

—Louise Imogen Guiney
Patrins

Bird hunting in Arlington

May 18, 1893—Faxon and I to-day heard two Least Bitterns cooing in the upper Arlington reservoir where the Grebes breed. Both were among cat-tails, one at the inlet, the other on an island in the pond about 300 yards from the inlet. The latter bird cooed at frequent intervals during the entire day. When we first heard him, he was near the southern extremity of the island in a bed of broken-down, last year's flags which covered an area only a few yards square. After fixing the spot from whence the sound came with all possible accuracy and most satisfactorily, I sculled the boat to it slowly and silently and just as the bow was on the point of crashing into the flags the Bittern, a beautiful male with steel blue back and crown, rose from a bunch of flags within 15 or twenty feet of us and directly ahead of the boat.

—William Brewster
Concord River

231

Professor James on drugs, circa 1895

One spring morning his first remark was: "Mrs. James is house-cleaning to-day. You know that awful upheaval—and she says I can't come home to luncheon. Won't you all come over to the club and have luncheon with me?" The question seemed to us a valuable creative idea, and in due time we were gathered round the table of a delightful host. In the midst of the cheerful conversation he turned to me and said, in a confidential tone: "Did you ever take enough of anything stimulating so that you felt yourself just going off, letting go of the present and grasping for a moment a real conception of the unity of the universe?" Having been brought up in a conservative New England village, I had never even seen any one grasping for cosmic unity in just that way; so I replied with a hesitating negative. Then our host went on to describe certain emotions he had experienced while experimenting with strange drugs.

Occasionally he would report these experiences in class and quote the words he had spoken as they were carefully taken down by his devoted wife.

Two that I remember are: "The only differences in the world are differences of degree between degrees of difference and no difference at all"; and: "School, high school, normal school, law school, divinity school, school, school. Oh my God!" Perhaps the last of these psychological experiments he tried the following year with mescal. A medical friend sent him a bud telling him that it would give the most glorious visions of color and gild every common object with splendor. The net result was nothing but twenty-four hours of dangerous illness—and no visions.

—Mary E. Raymond
Memories of William James

The landlady comes for the rent, Dover Street, 1897

Surely as sorrow trails behind sin, Saturday evening brought Mrs. Hutch. The landlady did not trail. Her movements were anything but impassive. She climbed the stairs with determination and landed at the top with emphasis. Her knock on the door was clear, sharp, unfaltering; it was impossible to pretend not to hear it. Her "Good-evening" announced business; her manner of taking a chair suggested the throwing-down of the gauntlet. Invariably she asked for my father, calling him Mr. Anton, and refusing to be corrected; almost invariably he was not at home—was out looking for work. Had he left her the rent? My mother's gentle "No, ma'am" was the signal for the storm. I do not want to repeat what Mrs. Hutch said. It would be hard on her, and hard on me. She grew red in the face; her voice grew shriller with every word. My poor mother hung her head where she stood; the children stared from their corners; the frightened baby cried. The angry landlady rehearsed our sins like a prophet foretelling doom. We owed so many weeks' rent; we were too lazy to work; we never intended to pay; we lived on others; we deserved to be put out without warning. She reproached my mother for having too many children; she blamed us all for coming to America. She enumerated her losses through nonpayment of her rents; told us that she did not collect the amount of her taxes; showed us how our irregularities were driving a poor widow to ruin.

My mother did not attempt to excuse herself, but when Mrs. Hutch began to rail against my absent father, she tried to put in a word in his defence. The landlady grew all the shriller at that, and silenced my mother impatiently. Sometimes she addressed herself to me. I always stood by, if I was at home, to give my mother the moral support of my dumb sympathy. I understood that Mrs. Hutch had a special grudge against me, because I did not go to work as a cash girl and earn three dollars a week. I wanted to explain to her how I was preparing myself for a great career, and I was ready to promise her the payment of the arrears as soon as I began to get rich. But the landlady would not let me put in a word. And I was sorry for her, because she seemed to be having such a bad time.

At last Mrs. Hutch got up to leave, marching out as determinedly as she had marched in. At the door she turned, in undiminished wrath, to shoot her parting dart:—

"And if Mr. Anton does not bring me the rent on Monday, I will serve notice of eviction on Tuesday, without fail."

We breathed when she was gone. My mother wiped away a few tears, and went to the baby, crying in the windowless, air-tight room.

—Mary Antin
The Promised Land

Lord! The wonder of the subway!

. . . I had to go to town on account of my celebrated back-tooth, which has been a source of income to dentists since 1833. It finally broke off and came out one day lately, and I repaired to Piper to have it repaired. He got into my mouth along with a pick-axe and telescope, battering-ram and other instruments, and drove a lawn-cutting machine up and down my jaws for a couple of hours. When he came out he said he meant wonderful improvements, and it seems I'm to have a bridge and a mill-wheel and summit and crown of gold, and harps, and Lord knows what, better than new. After this, and to comfort me for not being able to bite anything but the inside of my cheek, George took me to Hoyt's "Black Sheep," of which the scene is a bar-room in Tombstone, Arizona, and coming home, we went through the new Touraine, Young's Hotel, on the corner (opposite Pelham), which was all blown up last year, you know. It is perfectly gorgeous. Kings don't know what they are talking about when they speak of living in palaces. This is really beautifully furnished, you pass from Louis Quartorze to Elizabeth Rococo, all hung with

Ambuson and Ormola. There is a great library with real books bound in calf, and make-believe old gentlemen sitting reading in them. Then we took a compass to Park Street and came home through the Subway. Lord! such a wonder. Broad steps lead down to the bowels of the burying-ground, but there it is all white and brilliant and spotless clean; a wind sweeps through the chasm, and open cars and shut cars, Brookline cars and Reservoir, shoot to and fro; you spring on, and with one dash whirl through an avenue of sparkling lights to the feet of Charles Sumner, where you are once more un-earthed, and all for five cents, in three minutes. 'T is wonderful; methinks my father's hair would stand on end to see the sight.

—Susan Hale
Letter of September 19, 1897

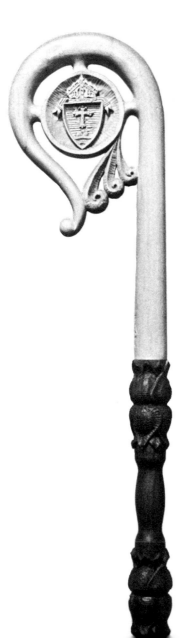

CHAPTER SEVEN

Much Preached At—Part II

Three periods can be discerned in the local 180-year history of the Roman Catholic church. First, a period of roughly forty years when that church was considered by the dominant Protestants as simply another sect of Christians with rather special practices, in an era when many such minority groups were establishing branches in Boston. Second, a period of about sixty years when the flood of largely Catholic immigration pushed that church to a dominant position in the community. This brought open conflict with many orthodox Protestant groups. During the last period of some eighty years the Roman Catholic church represented the beliefs of the great majority of Boston area residents. What use it made of its power and influence makes this period particularly interesting.

The French were the first to attempt to "plant the Faith" in New England, particularly among the northern Indians. English victory in the French and English intercontinental wars not only doomed that effort, but stigmatized Catholics as both religious and political enemies of the Protestants.

In Boston, one form this prejudice took through most of the eighteenth century was the celebration of "Pope Day." Each fifth of November—Guy Fawkes Day in England—gangs from the North End of Boston fought pitched battles with gangs from the South End for possession of effigies of the Pope which each carried into combat. These were bruising affairs and could be deadly. In 1764, a five-year-old boy was killed when he was run over by a wheel of the float carrying the Pope's image. Just before the Revolution, some of the anti-Catholic feeling was diverted toward the Tory ministry in London.

The Revolution softened the anti-Catholic prejudices of many. Hopes for Canadian support in the fight with England and the actual alliance with Catholic France prompted a constitutional change in Massachusetts, granting Catholics religious freedom. Masses were soon held in Boston by chaplains from the French fleet. Regular services, which the Congregational minister, Reverend Jeremy Belknap, termed "mummery" and "a puppet show" for the "curious and idle folk," began in 1788. In what must amount to one of the least fulfilled predictions of all time, he declared the outcome would prove "a source of ridicule."

236

This first small congregation was organized in a congregational manner, with monthly meetings to decide parish business. Under three different priests who "wanted talents, character, or perseverance" (in the words of Catholic historians) nothing of consequence was achieved until the arrival of a theological professor from France, Father Francis Anthony Matignon, in 1792. Under his tactful, prudent administration, schisms were healed, debts paid, and calm settled on the troubled parish. They adopted the pew-rent system of the Protestants, annually elected three wardens to run their temporal affairs, and everyone was admonished "never to bring or to suffer any dogs in the church." In 1796, Father Jean Louis Anne Madeleine Lefebre de Cheverus arrived to help Matignon. Young and vigorous, the two made a compatible team. All New England was their parish. At first, Cheverus spent much time outside Boston, ministering to the Maine Indians, and making missionary journeys to places like Newburyport and Plymouth.

In Boston, Matignon determined to leave the rented church on School Street and committed the congregation to building a new edifice on Franklin Street opposite the Boston Theater. Bulfinch designed their building without charge, President John Adams gave $100, and Protestants contributed 20 percent of the building cost, estimated at $17,000. Sacrifices of the poor congregation made up the remainder. On September 23, 1803, when Bishop Carroll from Baltimore dedicated the new Cathedral, about one thousand Catholics lived in Boston. Quickly after this pioneer venture came a new house for the priests, a new prayer book, a new church organ (a Goodrich installed in 1804), more communions, more devotions, establishment of the Confraternity of the Blessed Sacrament, a growing membership and *converts*—always a subject of consuming interest to American Catholics.

The growing importance of this northern province of American Catholicism led to the appointment in 1808 of Cheverus as Bishop of the Diocese of Boston, after Matignon refused the honor. The new Bishop was consecrated and installed in 1810. His small stature prompted the affectionate epithet, "the least of Bishops." He was a genuinely popular person in Protestant Boston, being witty, brilliant, and sociable. It was said he always carried a handful of sugarplums in his pocket for children.

Pastoral Staff of Archbishop Medeiros. (Courtesy of Phil Stack, *The Pilot.*)

Cathedral of the Holy Cross on Franklin Street, designed by Charles Bulfinch and dedicated in 1803.

Gilbert Stuart's portrait of Bishop Jean-Louis Le Fabure de Cheverus, leader of the Boston see from 1808 to 1823. (Courtesy of Museum of Fine Arts, Boston.)

Matignon died in 1818. By then many of the founding members of the church were passing on, and being replaced by a slowly increasing stream of Irish immigrants. A new church was erected for them in South Boston the next year. In 1820, four Ursuline sisters were brought to Boston and a convent for them set up next to the Cathedral. The same year, Roman Catholics were granted full political liberty. When Cheverus left in 1823 to accept a See in France, he left many of his books to the Boston Athenaeum in token of his regard for the town. The church seemed on a firm footing, but there was a thorn on the rose.

Baptists and Methodists were among the rising sects in those same years. They and the orthodox Congregationalists, now minus the liberal-minded Unitarians, stood strongly against "Popery" and the "Papists." Historians have yet to fathom this attitude. This might have been harmless enough religious infighting, except that increasing immigration from Catholic countries brought thousands of foreign Catholics to Boston. As the Catholics slowly assumed a majority position in the community and the state, their Protestant neighbors experienced job competition and the always disturbing effect for many people of changes in custom. The administrations of the next three Roman Catholic prelates were all shadowed by this virulent controversy with many of their Protestant neighbors. Bishop Joseph Fenwick, who led the diocese from 1825 to 1846, took office when the Catholics made up 5 percent of the city's population; when he died the figure had risen to 25 percent. He had to cope with this prejudice in its most violent form, while he also struggled desperately to contain the many Catholics, almost all Irish, who were pouring into New England. He had to provide them with churches, priests, and religious services, and also to put down what was virtually a decade of Catholic lay attempts to gain temporal control over their local churches.

Fenwick tried to counter this rising intolerance by establishing in 1829 a newspaper, *The Jesuit or Catholic Sentinel*, which unfortunately exhibited all the sins of its opponents in the use of tirades and invective. From 1831 he printed pamphlets (the Catholic Tract Society dates from the same year), lectured, and debated, mainly against the intemperate harangues of Lyman Beecher, but nothing stopped a series of anti-Irish riots. There was an attack by toughs in Ann Street in 1823, what is termed the first Broad Street Riot in 1826, two days of tumult in South Boston in 1828, and disturbances on Merrimac Street in 1832.

The most dramatic incident was the burning of the Ursuline convent on Mount Benedict in what was then West Charlestown and is now part of East Somerville. Building a handsome brick building on what had been Ploughed Hill of Revolutionary fame, amidst very orthodox Protestants was dangerous. The ten-acre plot was bought through straws and the nuns were moved in secretly at 4:00 A.M. It served as a boarding school for girls and was too expensive for most of the local Catholics, but extensively patronized by many rich Unitarian girls.

Bishop Joseph Fenwick (1825–1846).

The Ursuline Convent on Mt. Benedict in Charlestown (now Somerville). Opened in 1826, it was destroyed in 1834 by a mob.

Rumors that women were held in the convent against their will seemed true when Sister Mary John ran away from the building on July 28, 1834, and sought shelter with Protestants. She was apparently emotionally disturbed and when she recovered her reason she voluntarily returned to the convent, but tales that she was being kept captive there nevertheless were spread throughout Charlestown. Crowds held meetings in nearby brickyards and threatened to burn down the buildings if she were not "freed." They were persuaded to wait, but on Sunday, August 10, placards were nailed up in Charlestown and Boston further inflaming Protestant prejudices. Monday afternoon the Charlestown selectmen made a three-hour inspection of the convent, finding nothing wrong. That night, after eight o'clock, before their official report could appear in the Tuesday papers, crowds gathered on Winter Hill Road in front of the building's main gate. Responsible people tried unsuccessfully to disperse them. The Mother Superior, Sister Mary Edmond St. George, a stout, hot-tempered, regal lady, who liked a pinch of snuff now and then, faced down one small contingent of toughs about 9:30 P.M., but another group went for tar barrels and by 11:00 P.M. had a big bonfire going near the convent.

Half an hour later, certain there were no male defenders on the premises, and enlarged by several rowdy fire companies, the crowd assaulted the convent. Nuns and children fled out the back door, while the mob ransacked the building, and then set fire to it. All the other buildings on the property were burned: the Bishop's Lodge with its library, the barn, stables, farmhouse, and what they could of the icehouse. Even the mausoleum was broken into and coffins opened. No effort was made by local authorities to prevent the assault or bring it to an end. No marines from the Navy Yard, no militia were called out, as might easily have been done. During the night the nuns and children were sheltered about half a mile away at the home of Mr. and Mrs. Joseph Adams, two kind Protestants. In the morning Bishop Fenwick sent carriages to bring them into Boston.

Great indignation was felt through the community the next day, and many feared a racial and religious war. Packed public meetings in Faneuil Hall, Cambridge, and Charlestown condemned the act, and Boston's Mayor Lyman appointed an investigation committee. For the next few nights, volunteers patrolled the streets to prevent further violence. Bishop Fenwick and his priests kept guard in the Cathedral. Mobs were prevented on Tuesday night from marching on Harvard and burning down its library. Wednesday night they were kept out of Boston by raising the draw of the Charlestown bridge.

Twelve men were indicted, but only one convicted at the trial in December. He was only peripherally involved, but he was given a life sentence. Bishop Fenwick and Madame St. George headed the list of those who asked that he be pardoned, which was granted. An indemnity was sought from the legislature for damages, but the General Court merely passed a resolution deploring the crime. Later attempts to indemnify the Ursulines were defeated. The ruins were allowed to remain as a visible symbol of the effects of prejudice until 1875. Between then and the end of the century the hill was leveled and its soil used

The "Donahoe" building on Franklin Street where *The Pilot* was published in the middle of the last century. A fine example of French Renaissance architecture, this building was designed by Gridley B. F. Bryant and Louis P. Rogers. The drawing is by Rheimunt Sayer.

to fill in the Middlesex Canal and the marshland along the Mystic River.

The Broad Street and Montgomery Guard Riots of 1837 were a continuation of the Native American movement of these years, which focused most of its hostility on the Irish and "their" religion. "Catholics in those years," says the standard account, "were constantly exposed to vituperation, invectives, insults, assaults, and arson. Groups of rowdies infested the streets of Boston . . . eager to insult and beat up the 'Paddies.'" The situation was similar to the early years of the second world war when young Catholic toughs did the same things to Jews in Dorchester, and to pacifists in South Boston during the Vietnam conflict. Intolerance always follows the same pattern, unfortunately; only the names change. It was even difficult to get fire insurance for the one Catholic church in Charlestown; so it proved for the Arlington Street Church in Boston during the Vietnam war.

Fenwick and his people responded with dignity and nonviolence to these outrages. This greatly impressed sensible people. Dr. George Shattuck, an eminent Boston physician and a Protestant, left the Boston Bishop $500 in his will in token "of the great injustice done by the unindemnified destruction of the convent." Meantime, Fenwick was busy providing new churches for Catholic immigrants both in Boston and neighboring suburbs. Churches opened in Cambridge, Roxbury, West Quincy, Chelsea, and Lynn. He fought "Trusteeism" in his churches, a continuation of the lay struggle to participate in the direction of the temporal affairs of their churches. By 1836, the *Jesuit*, after several changes of names, had become *The Boston Pilot*, and under Patrick Donahoe was beginning to make a distinguished name for itself in Catholic journalism.

Bishop John B. Fitzpatrick
(1846–1866).

A detail from one of D. C. Johnston's cartoons satirizing the committee inspecting Nunneries and Convents.

Investigation of the dormitory. What was here discovered, has not yet been revealed.

When Fenwick died in 1846, after a life so busy he once complained, "I have not even time to sneeze," fifty thousand people came out to see his body lying in state in the Cathedral. Even as the Catholics had tolled their bell for the funeral of William Ellery Channing in 1842 (the only non-Unitarian church to do so) so did the Federal Street Unitarian Church return the honor for Fenwick's funeral.

Bishop John B. Fitzpatrick, Fenwick's successor, inherited his twin problems of keeping up with the growth of the diocese now limited to Massachusetts, and battling new outbreaks of prejudice. The Great Famine of 1846 in Ireland brought forth large contributions from the Boston Irish for the relief of their stricken kin. They were aided by most Protestants in Boston; a famous local merchant, Capt. Robert Bennet Forbes, captained a relief vessel to Cork in 1847.

Some Americans were eager to help the Irish as long as they stayed in Ireland, and didn't come to the states. Come they did, however, and this brought a new wave of anti-Catholicism, known in history as the Know-Nothing movement of the 1850s. The influx of Catholic children into the public schools, which had been almost exclusively Protestant in outlook, was one area of friction. Protestants feared Catholics would demand public moneys to support private schools, yet at the same time they made public schools more difficult for Catholic parents to accept. Compulsory Bible readings and school prayers were voted in by an anti-Catholic Know-Nothing legislature in 1855. The Boston School Committee, in the hands of Protestants, set up a series of devotional exercises for schoolroom use which were openly Protestant in nature. Bishop Fitzpatrick protested strongly against any such "act of public worship" in public schools, deploring it as "promiscuous worship." Nor would the School Committee concede anything to the Catholic minority, much in the same spirit of a hundred years later when an obdurate Catholic school committee opposed any concessions to Negro parents. On March 14, 1859, a young Catholic pupil, Thomas Wall, was brutally whipped for half an hour by a bigoted Protestant teacher because he refused to repeat the Ten Commandments in the Protestant translation, which his father had forbidden him to do. The incident was too common. When charges were brought against the teacher, the School Committee blandly defended him. A century later such incidents would be repeated with Irish teachers whipping young Negro pupils for equally insane reasons.

These early years of Fitzpatrick's incumbency saw many such incidents directed against what one bigot termed "the papal population of the city." For a time the Boston City Missionary Society employed a missionary named O'Brien to attempt to "save" the Irish Catholics from their Roman Catholicism. The Native American party held a rally on Fort Hill in the midst of an Irish slum in 1847 hoping to provoke a riot, but the Bishop ordered his flock to stay off the street and frustrate them, so nothing happened. The Boston City Council prohibited burials in the Catholic burial grounds in South Boston for "health" reasons, and the church had to get relief from the courts. In 1851 when the first Irishman of a long line, Bernard McGiniskin, was appointed to

the Boston Police, he was discharged, reappointed, and finally re-discharged all because of prejudice. The Hannah Corcoran riots of 1853 in Charlestown which attempted to destroy St. Mary's Church, the visit of the insane "Angel Gabriel" in 1854, and finally in 1855, the year the Know-Nothings won control of the State Government—these were all depressing instances of this Protestant hostility, as were the shenanigans of the Joint Special Committee on the Inspection of Nunneries and Convents, amusingly satirized in the cartoons of D. C. Johnston.

During this outward turmoil, Bishop Fitzpatrick continued to build churches for his increasing flock, using the talents of the New York architect Patrick C. Keeley. In the last half of the century, Keeley designed and built more than two dozen churches for the Boston diocese. Services were now started in such places as Brookline (1852), Brighton (1853), Medford (1849), and Watertown (1847). The start of the parochial school system dates to 1849. Planning for what became Boston College started in 1857, with the first students entering a building on Harrison Avenue in the fall of 1864. The enormous number of immigrants, many of them "poor beyond poverty," swamped the facilities of

243

Directors of the Holyhood Cemetery Association pose for their picture about 1904. James Driscoll, superintendent of the cemetery, is on the right. Archbishop John Williams (1866–1907) is the fourth man from the left. (Courtesy of *The Pilot*.)

the few charitable organizations in the city and required responses from the diocese. Sister Ann Alexis was judged the principal charitable worker of the mid-century. Father Haskins founded the House of the Angel Guardian in 1851 to aid young boys, an organization still doing useful work today. A Catholic layman, Andrew Carney, endowed the hospital which now bears his name, opened in 1863, three years before Bishop Fitzpatrick died.

The first years of Boston-born Archbishop John Williams' long service to his church (1866 to 1907, longest "reign" of any Boston prelate) began with quite peaceful relations with his Protestant neighbors, due in part to the Civil War uniting them in a common cause against a mutual foe. Yet it was a period of great internal activity in the diocese. Immigrants, not all Irish now, but mainly Catholic, still poured into the Boston area. Many French-Canadians were moving into Cambridge, Somerville, and Medford. After 1880, Italians began arriving in such numbers that eventually they contributed the most immigrants to America of any foreign nation. A large Polish immigration began about 1900, as did an influx from Lithuania and Syria. All these people furnished problems and recruits for the Boston archdiocese and diluted its previously almost all-Irish character.

Churches, schools, seminaries, monasteries, convents, orphanages, hospitals, asylums, societies—all these multiplied under Williams' quiet, firm direction. He had been made archbishop in 1875 and the archdiocese was cut down to

Church of the Holy Trinity
erected for the German Catholics
in 1842–43.

A view of St. Vincent's Orphan
Asylum and some of its "flock."

the five counties of Eastern Massachusetts. The same year, the new Cathedral was completed on Washington Street. Built of Roxbury pudding stone, it cost an estimated $1½ million. It had about forty-five thousand square feet of space, could seat 3,500, or stand twice that number.

In this period, Catholics were granted their long-denied rights to receive their services in public institutions. They began to elect Catholics to public office from 1857 when the first Catholic was elected to the Common Council. In 1870 they elected their first alderman, and in 1884 Hugh O'Brien was elected Mayor of Boston, reelected the next year, and twice thereafter. The change in political power was dramatized in 1887 when the mayor, the chairman of the aldermen, the president of the Common Council, the city clerk, and the chairman of the School Committee were all Irish Catholics.

The prominence of Catholics in the city's life partly precipitated the last significant local opposition to Catholicism, by supporters of the American Protective Association movement of the 1890s. Partly, the reaction was directed against the parochial schools and the attempts by a basically Protestant legislature to dictate standards, curriculum, and practices to the private Catholic school system. The "NINA" signs were one symptom of this last flare-up ("No Irish Need Apply"). But the old prejudices were less influential—not that they were not still dangerous. During the year 1895, three Catholic churches (in South Boston and Dorchester) were destroyed by arsonists, and a fourth

"The Little Red Schoolhouse" float in the July 4, 1895, parade in East Boston that ended in a riot.

William Cardinal O'Connell (1907–1944).

threatened. A riot in East Boston after a July 4th parade the same year ended in the only killing in an anti-Catholic riot (an amazing record in itself). John W. Wills, a middle-aged Catholic longshoreman, and probably an innocent bystander, was the victim.

The institution that Lowell-born Bishop William O'Connell took over from Williams at his death in 1907 was a powerful one. Archbishop O'Connell, as he soon became, quickly showed that a strong hand was on the throttle. He earned the irreverent nickname of "Bull." Thoroughly worldly and sophisticated, he proceeded to reorganize the creaking administration for maximum unity and efficiency, to intensify all activities of the diocese (he created thirty-two new churches in his first four years alone), and to readjust relationships between Catholics and the rest of the community. Catholics were now a huge majority in the area, and O'Connell saw no reason to be unmindful of that fact.

The parochial school system was extended into many parishes. *The Pilot*, fondly called "The Irishman's Bible," became the official organ of the archdiocese in 1908. (The obituary columns of local newspapers have long been known as the "Irish funnies.") Boston College, separated from its High School, became the focus of a huge fund-raising drive, and in 1913 moved out to the old A. A. Lawrence estate in Chestnut Hill, which was rechristened University Heights. There, twenty stone buildings in the English Collegiate Gothic style were soon begun to the designs of the firm of Maginnis and Walsh. O'Connell moved strongly in every field to centralize the power of the organization he had inherited. He took over control of the seminary; centralized charitable projects; emphasized foreign missions; and formed Guilds for Catholic professional men. (St. Luke for physicians and surgeons in 1910 and St. Apollonia for dentists in 1911 were two of them.) By 1911 his vigorous activity had earned him his red hat, and he became the third native American and first Bostonian to become a cardinal.

World War I did not diminish his activities, although the war virtually ended European immigration. Catholic influence was made increasingly visible as

David I. Walsh became the first Roman Catholic Lieutenant Governor (1912), Governor (1913), and United States Senator (1918), a position he held almost until his death in 1947. O'Connell put his churches squarely behind the war effort. A mission church in Roxbury, for example, had 937 stars on its service flag when the war ended. Two new American anti-Catholic campaigns during and after the war were troublesome, but their very insignificance and ineffectiveness, locally, testified to the church's dominance in Boston and the state. That roads and squares were now named after O'Connell and other priests was but the most obvious sign of change.

The period between the wars witnessed continued Catholic growth in every direction. The founding of Emmanuel College in 1919 and Regis College in 1927 marks the educational advances. The Cardinal went on radio in 1929 to begin the "Catholic Truth Period." He founded the local Catholic Youth Organization (C.Y.O.) in 1938. He was willing to take political stands by coming out early against Prohibition and opposing the proposed law against child labor. In 1935 he spoke against the proposed State Lottery bill and it died instantly. An equal match for the tough Irish politicians ruling Boston, the Cardinal never openly opposed perennial Mayor James Michael Curley, so his "personal" candidate, Frederick Mansfield, lost in the 1929 election. But the reality of his power was evident in the 1937 campaign between incumbent Curley and challenger Maurice Tobin. The editor of the Boston *Post* headlined on election day a six-year-old statement of the Cardinal's lifted out of context. It read: "Anyone who votes for a person they know to be dishonest or otherwise unfit for office, commits a sin." That was all it took; Tobin swept to an enormous victory over Curley.

Chapel Tower on University Heights, Boston College, in the 1940s. (Courtesy of George M. Cushing, Jr.)

"Irish Steppers." Richard Cardinal Cushing (1944–1970) dancing with children at St. Patrick's school in Roxbury, 1966, (Courtesy of Phil Stack, *The Pilot*.)

Holy Ghost Hospital in Cambridge, 1970. (Courtesy of Phil Stack, *The Pilot*.)

Archbishop Medeiros (1970–   ) greeting grape growers' children, 1970. (Courtesy of Phil Stack, *The Pilot*.)

The man who succeeded O'Connell at his death in 1944 was in many ways a very different personality. Fully versed in administration, South Boston's Richard Cushing for eleven years had directed the diocesan Society for the Propagation of the Faith (called "Proppy" by students), then for five years he had been O'Connell's auxiliary bishop when Bishop Spellman left to head the New York archdiocese. Made an archbishop in the fall of 1944, Cushing showed the same administrative drive as had O'Connell before him. In ten years he established fifty new parishes, led a drive to "Save the Carney," made the *Pilot* a highly readable, lively paper, rebuilt many aging institutions, started the St. Philip Neri School for Delayed Vocations (to help older men become priests) and with the ever-generous help of the Kennedy family built a Boys' Guidance Center on the Fenway. Still it was fourteen years before he received his red hat from Rome, not the four years that it took O'Connell.

Cushing was not the stern aristocrat that O'Connell was. Instead, he had a warm, witty, human touch his predecessor lacked. He was not afraid to be photographed wearing funny hats, or dancing with old ladies at his Thanksgiving dinners, or singing in barbershop quartets at his Christmas parties, or to lend himself to any worthy project. Keenly aware of the value of press and publicity, he sought to bring the church to the people, establishing the first railway chapel, the first wharf chapel (at the Fish Pier), the first airport chapel, and chapels in suburban shopping centers. St. Anthony's shrine on Arch Street was an effort to serve intown working people and shoppers. With the same intent, he conducted the first Mass ever televised and performed the first nuptial mass on TV. His gravelly voice rapidly reciting the Rosary over the radio became a cherished Boston memory.

The Cardinal, a close friend of Pope John XXIII, was a prominent member of Vatican II, fighting for the deletion of anti-Semitic references and for the

248

Schema on Religious Freedom. However, he was cautious on the matter of birth control. He became active in the ecumenical movement, preaching to some two hundred Jewish, Protestant, and Orthodox congregations, and was the first United States cardinal to speak before a Masonic Lodge. He consistently worked to overcome racial barriers in Boston life. A close friendship with the Kennedys involved the Cardinal in their triumphs and tragedies. On Sept. 8, 1970, because of failing health and age, Cushing resigned as active leader of the archdiocese, dying shortly thereafter, leaving to his successor an establishment with 401 churches, 2,511 priests, 5,915 sisters, 12 hospitals, 7 colleges and universities, 338 parochial schools, and a Catholic population of nearly 1,900,000.

The seventh head of the Boston Archdiocese is Humberto Sosa Madeiros, an activist Bishop of Brownsville, Texas. From one of the smallest and poorest dioceses in the country, he came to head the second largest in the United States. Only New York is bigger. Born in 1915 in the Azores, he emigrated to Fall River, Massachusetts, in 1931, and studied for the priesthood at Catholic University in Washington, receiving a Master of Arts degree in 1942 and a doctorate in Sacred Theology in 1947. Before he went to the Rio Grande Valley of Texas he had held several positions in the Fall River diocese. In Texas from 1966, he revealed a strong social conscience, taking part in the strike of migrant farm workers for better pay and working conditions. As a younger man, responsive to the needs of change, he comes to a diocese that may demand even more changes than the hierarchy will allow. Issues, such as lay control, that were raised early in the history of the archdiocese and once seemed settled for all time, now appear destined to change. Much rigidity is certain to disappear.

The fearful prophecies of several generations of hostile Protestants as to what would happen if the Roman church triumphed in Boston were never

realized. Indeed, in spite of surface differences, core values of the "Papists"
and the Puritans are identical; orthodoxy in Massachusetts and in Boston continues to be orthodox. In three hundred and fifty years, Boston has been much
preached at. It will surely have to listen to many more sermons, from perhaps
surprising preachers. Probably it needs them all, though in some a wicked little
voice whispers: "Once you've heard one sermon, you've heard them all." Now
they say that "God is Dead." Gamaliel Bradford encountered the same theme
half a century ago. It prompted his poem, "Exit God,"—and notice the
chummy tone:

> Of old our father's God was real,
>   Something they almost saw,
> Which kept them to a stern ideal
>   And scourged them into awe.
>
> They walked the narrow path of right
>   Most vigilantly well,
> Because they feared eternal night
>   And boiling depths of Hell.
>
> Now Hell has wholly boiled away
>   And God become a shade.
> There is no place for him to stay
>   In all the world He made.
>
> The followers of William James
>   Still let the Lord exist,
> And call Him by imposing names,
>   A venerable list.
>
> But nerve and muscle only count,
>   Gray matter of the brain,
> And an astonishing amount
>   Of inconvenient pain.
>
> I sometimes wish that God were back
>   In this dark world and wide:
> For though some virtues He might lack,
>   He had his pleasant side.

The Great Organ of the Boston Music Hall, built in Bavaria and brought to Boston in 1863. In 1885 it was purchased by the New England Conservatory and later was removed to Methuen, Mass. Lithograph by J. H. Bufford.

Organ Building in Boston

The early Puritans, like the Quakers, shared a horror of musical instruments being played in the "Lord's House." Singing with "heart and voyce," decreed John Cotton, was "moral worship" and approved; but singing with "instruments" was unsanctified. The first organ, therefore, used in Boston was by Anglicans in King's Chapel in 1714. It was a bequest of Thomas Brattle who brought it from England in 1708. The church has had four other organs since, the last a Fisk installed in 1964 and considered by many the finest organ in Boston. Christ Church, which had rejected the Brattle organ, had the second organ in town in 1736. This was replaced in 1759 by an organ that has been many times altered until the "works" were replaced in 1958 with a rebuilt nineteenth-century Stevens organ. This is not the best Stevens organ, but is very handsome.

The early organs were all imported from England. The first organ built in Boston is assumed to be the one Edward Bromfield, Jr., constructed in 1745 for the Old South Meeting House. There is some question whether or not William Claggett built the 1736 Christ Church instrument. Thomas Johnston was the first organmaker of any note in town, and he was active in this work from 1752 to 1768, though better known as a painter and engraver.

Most noted of the early Boston organbuilders was William Marcellus Goodrich, active during the years 1805 to 1833. So satisfactory were his instruments that they were preferred to foreign ones. Among Goodrich's notable disciples were Thomas Appleton, George Stevens, and the Hook brothers, Elias and George. These two worked together and later employed Frank Hastings as a copartner, forming the noted Hook & Hastings firm. This company continued to build fine organs until 1936.

By the middle of the nineteenth century, Boston, with sixty-four organs, had more such instruments in proportion to its population than any other city in the country. This musical interest is evidenced by the publication in Boston of John Sullivan Dwight's *Journal of Music* from 1852 to 1881.

The German style of organbuilding dominated at the time of the Civil War, and this was the manner of construction of the famous organ in the Music Hall. All these organs suffered from unsteady wind pressure, some of them having their air supplied by pumpers worked manually, others by water motors. The introduction of the electric motor solved this problem. The first electric action was used in the Church of Christ, Scientist, in 1895, and the first electric motor in Trinity Church in 1900.

Boston's prominence in the organ field continued in the early twentieth century with such men as George S. Hutchings, who had worked for Hook & Hastings. The chain continued unbroken into a fourth generation as one of Hutchings' employees, Ernest M. Skinner, founded his own firm, later called Aeolian-Skinner Company and still in business.

Lately a renaissance of organbuilding in the Greater Boston area has been marked by a return to the classic principles of organbuilding as advocated half a century ago by Dr. Albert Schweitzer. One of the early leaders was G. Donald Harrison, connected in the last part of his life with Aeolian-Skinner. Active in this neoclassic development are such firms as C. B. Fisk of Gloucester, the Andover Organ Company in Methuen, and the Noack Organ Company in Andover. Such leading organists as E. Power Biggs and Melville Smith have promoted this development.

Perhaps the most spectacular organist ever in Boston was Dr. George K. Jackson who played at the old Trinity Church on Summer Street, from about 1815 to 1820. Each Sunday he would appear in the full regalia of an English Doctor of Music: plum-colored coat, yellow breeches, and square cap. He played elaborate voluntaries, and when the minister, Dr. Gardiner, asked him to shorten them, he told Gardiner to shorten his sermons. The next Sunday he picked out the psalm tunes with one finger, and soon thereafter his resignation was asked for and accepted.

Oliver Holden (1765–1844), painted by Ethan Allen Greenwood. (Courtesy of The Bostonian Society, Old State House.)

A List of Distinguished Organs in the Boston Area

King's Chapel—A 1964 Fisk which, says their organist Daniel Pinkham, is "superb."

Church of the Advent—A 1935 Aeolian-Skinner. Their finest organ, says Pinkham.

"New" Old South—A 1969 Reuter, with 4 manuals and 136 stops on the gallery organ and 2 manuals and 40 stops on the chancel organ.

Emmanuel Church—A 1918 Casavant Freres with 4 manuals and 131 stops on the gallery organ, also a chancel organ. The gallery organ is now not much used as it is in need of repairs.

Old West Church—A 1970 Fisk organ, being installed.

All Saints' Lutheran Church—An 1859 E. and G. G. Hook with 3 manuals and 34 stops.

First Parish Unitarian (Jamaica Plain)—An 1854 E. & G. G. Hook, with 3 manuals and 29 stops.

Community Church of Neponset—An 1860 Hook with one manual and 9 stops, "a veritable jewel," says Barbara Owen.

IN CATHOLIC CHURCHES

St. Stephen's (North End)—An 1830 Goodrich, restored in 1967, with 2 manuals and 15 stops.

Immaculate Conception (South End)—An 1863 Hook, electrified in 1901, with 4 manuals and 59 stops, considered "hard to beat for playing French romantic music."

St. Mary of the Sacred Heart (North End)—An 1877 Johnson & Son, electrified in 1927 with 3 manuals and 45 stops.

Most Holy Redeemer (East Boston)—An 1856 William Simmons with 2 manuals and 27 stops. "Possesses a grandeur usually found only in larger instruments," says Miss Owen.

IN OTHER BUILDINGS

Harvard University, Memorial Church—A 1967 Fisk with 4 manuals and 48 stops.

Newton College of the Sacred Heart—A 1962 Casavant with 3 manuals and 32 stops, considered about the best new Catholic organ.

Museum of Fine Arts—A 1792 Avery (English) chamber organ, fully restored.

Old State House—A chamber organ of the same period, but unrestored. Once owned by Oliver Holden, hymn and tune writer.

M.I.T. Chapel—A 1955 Holtkamp organ.

M.I.T. Kresge Auditorium—A 1955 Holtkamp organ, with 3 manuals.

Episcopal Theological Seminary—A 1957 Holtkamp organ.

Busch-Reisinger Museum—A 1958 Flentrop organ with 4 manuals and 27 stops.

Symphony Hall—An Aeolian-Skinner organ of 1949.

New England Conservatory—Teaching organs by Noack, Metzler, Hammarberg, and Rieger.

St. Stephen's Church in the North End; this old Bulfinch church, once home to a Congregational Unitarian group, later became Roman Catholic and was restored to its classic design by Cardinal Cushing. (Photo by Samuel Chamberlain.)

Paul Revere Bells in the Boston Area

Bell No. 1, made in 1792, has been in the St. James Episcopal Church in Cambridge since 1901. Weight: 911 pounds.

Bell No. 25, made in 1798, has been in the Dedham Historical Society since 1894. Weight: 224 pounds.

Bell No. 154, made in 1815, has been in the Beebe Memorial Library in Wakefield since 1914. Weight: 929 pounds.

Bell No. 161, made in 1816, has been in King's Chapel since 1816. Weight: 2,437 pounds.

Bell No. 170, made in 1816, has been in the Second Congregational Church in Dorchester since 1816. Weight: 1,220 pounds.

Bell No. 235, made in 1821, has been in the Canton Unitarian Church since 1821. Weight: 1,127 pounds.

Interlude seven: Boston to 1950

Waban characters

When Mrs. Marshall Scudder and her cousin, Mr. Blatchford, resided in the Strong house on Beacon Street [in Newton], this very proper couple contributed to the legend of Waban. Mrs. Scudder wore nothing but white both summer and winter. If one met Mr. Blatchford on the street he teetered back and forth on his toes and said endlessly, "I find this a beautiful morning. Yes, a very beautiful morning." Meanwhile the accostee missed his or her train. He often referred to his throbbing heart. "Only my thumb pressed over the bunghole keeps it from bursting." Once the two heard a noise downstairs in the dead of night. They went to investigate, but on their way down the stairs they paused so long to admire a star that the burglar—and it was a burglar—became frightened and fled. But they dismissed the incident with, "Oh, well, he left enough silver for breakfast."

—*Waban—Early Days*
edited by Jane Bacon MacIntire

A schoolboy's day

I arose at 7:30 and then went to school, after which I had a good dinner. I had great fun out on the sleds with the boys, we tumbled of and on, the corp came up and said, "Who has been throwing snow on the houses over there," and we said, "Some little girls did it." As I was going to the store a team was in front of a car and the driver did not hear him ring the bell, so he didn't get of the track, and there was a policeman on the car who jumped of the car and took the man's name and address, the man said, "I didn't hear him ring the bell," and the policeman answered, "You can tell that in the court to-morrow." I went into the house and read a little from the book I mentioned yesterday ["African Crusoes"], then I studied my home-lesson and then I retired for the night at 8:30.

—Henry Seaburg (age 13)
Diary, December 17, 1907

Visit from a passing owl

About three o'clock in the afternoon of December 30, 1908, Mr. Eugene E. Caduc sent me word that there was a small owl on the Common near to Joy Street, and very kindly kept the bird in view until I could reach the spot and designate its name. It proved to be a Screech Owl of the gray phase. It occupied a horizontal bough of a linden tree which stands by the footpath from Spruce Street to Winter Street. The afternoon was evenly clouded, and against the gray sky the form of the little owl with ears erect was clearly silhouetted. It did not move in the space of an hour's time, except once or twice to turn the head a little sidewise. One could see the chilly breezes blow its feathers, and it stood apparently contented and happy, giving no attention to a little group of persons who stood wondering beneath it or to passers-by who looked upon it with an interest which the rarity of the occurrence awakened. After I had departed Mr. Caduc and his friend Mr. Potter remained and saw it take two short flights in the direction of the Union Clubhouse and then a longer flight down towards the Frog Pond. The darkness of evening had then fallen upon the Common.

Mr. William Brewster in his "Birds of the Cambridge Region" says: "Even that densely populated part of Boston known as the Back Bay district is now occasionally invaded by these daring and adaptive little owls; Dr. Arthur P. Chadbourne tells me that he heard one wailing in the trees on Marlborough Street during the evening of January 31, 1902, and late in December, 1903, my assistant, Mr. R. A. Gilbert, saw another which had just been caught on the doorstep of a house on Commonwealth Avenue."

—Horace Winslow Wright
Birds of the Boston Public Garden

Campaigning in Boston for labor unionism

The Women's Trade Union League of Boston refuses to be outdone by its sister league of New York. Two arrests and outdoor speeches to a hooting mob have started the new era in its campaign. Mrs. Glendower Evans, of Back Bay, and Miss Mabel Gillespie, a graduate of Radcliffe, at present Organizing Secretary of the Trade Union League, were the ones arrested. The speakers were: Miss Rose Schneidermann and Miss Pauline Newman, shirtwaist makers of New York.

The trouble started Wednesday with the determination on the part of the Boston League to organize the girls of the Gillette Safety Razor Company, not, as some of the papers say, as the result of picketing. Circulars were prepared. . . .

Armed with these . . . Mrs. Evans, Miss Gillespie, and Mrs. Conboy, organizer for the United Textile Workers of America, proceeded to the factory. Previous inquiry at the police station had informed them that the distribution of handbills upon public ways was against the law. To the query, "What can we do then?" the police replied: "Keep on private property." Accordingly, when they neared the factory, Mrs. Evans and Mrs. Conboy stationed themselves in doorways, but as there were not enough doors for all, Miss Gillespie decided to defy the law to the extent of occupying the sidewalk. With an eye out for the police, the three handed out their circulars to the factory girls as they went by to their work.

A policeman appeared in the distance, went into the office of the company for a moment, then advanced upon Miss Gillespie.

"Don't you know you are breaking the law?" he inquired.

"I do," replied Miss Gillespie.

"Then you are under arrest," and Miss Gillespie was marched to the police box while the patrol wagon was rung up.

Then the policeman was in a dilemma, for Mrs. Glendower Evans decided that she preferred the sidewalk to the doorway and stepped forth to distribute more freely to the fast accumulating crowd of girls. Here was a second law-breaker he wanted

to obtain, but he was hampered by the first. Miss Gillespie, observing his perplexity, offered to remain stationary while he secured Mrs. Evans, but the policeman was afraid she might escape him. Then Miss Gillespie suggested that he take her along, but he retorted that he would be no better off in that case as they would then all miss the patrol.

Mrs. Evans, however, soon came sauntering over.

"You are in trouble?" she ventured to ask Miss Gillespie.

"It would seem so," said Miss Gillespie, smiling.

"That's splendid!" retorted Mrs. Evans, "I must go and call up the papers. It's just what we need—publicity."

"No, you don't!" interfered the grim policeman. "I want you here. You're under arrest."

Then the patrol wagon came and the two prisoners were helped in while crowds of the factory girls surrounded them.

Mrs. Evans, declaring that she might as well get all she could out of the adventure, distributed handbills to the eager crowd from the patrol wagon as it jogged along.

—*The Boston Common*
June 11, 1910

Chivalry at the Chilton

Charles Adams was invited to dine at the new Chilton Club [founded 1910]. He came to the door on Commonwealth Avenue—and was told that the gentlemen's entrance was by the side door on Dartmouth Street. "I never enter by a side door," quoth the descendant of presidents, and shouldered his way in by the flunkey!! You can't spell gentleman with two A's, one d, one m, and one s. What would Charlie have said if a lady had forced her way into the Somerset Club by the men's door?

—John Torrey Morse, Jr.
Letter to James Ford Rhodes, 1911

259

A Harvard-Yale baseball game, 1913

One of the great events of Commencement, and of the year, is the Harvard-Yale baseball match. To this I went, excited at the prospect of my first sight of a 'ball game,' and my mind vaguely reminiscent of the indolent, decorous, upper-class crowd, the sunlit spaces, the dignified ritual, and white-flannelled grace of Lord's at the 'Varsity cricket match. The crowd was gay and not very large. We sat in wooden stands, which were placed in the shape of a large V. . . . The field was a vast place, partly stubbly grass, partly worn and patchy, like a parade ground. . . . I had time to observe the players, who were practising about the ground, and I was shocked. They wear dust-coloured shirts and dingy knickerbockers, fastened under the knee, and heavy boots. They strike the English eye as being attired for football, or a gladiatorial combat, rather than a summer game. The very close-fitting caps, with large peaks, give them picturesquely the appearance of hooligans. . . .

One queer feature of this sport is that unoccupied members of the batting side, fielders, and even spectators, are accustomed to join in vocally. You have the spectacle of the representatives of the universities endeavouring to frustrate or unnerve their opponents, at moments of excitement, by cries of derision and mockery, or heartening their own supporters and performers with exclamations of 'Now, Joe!' or 'He's got them!' or 'He's the boy!' . . . The Athletic Committee appoints a 'cheer-leader' for the occasion. Every five or ten minutes this gentleman, a big, fine figure in white, springs out from his seat at the foot of the stands, addresses the multitude through a megaphone with a 'One! Two! Three!' hurls it aside, and, with a wild flinging and swinging of his body and arms, conducts ten thousand voices in the Harvard yell. That over, the game proceeds, and the cheer-leader sits quietly waiting for the next moment of peril or triumph. I shall not easily forget that figure, bright in the sunshine, conducting with his whole body, passionate, possessed by a demon, bounding in the frenzy of his inspiration from side to side, contorted, rhythmic, ecstatic. It seemed so wonderfully American, in its combination of entire wildness and entire regulation, with the whole just a trifle fantastic.

—Rupert Brooke
Letters from America

Four years under the ethercone—
Harvard 1912–16

Those spring nights the streetcarwheels screech grinding in a rattle of loose trucks round the curved tracks of Harvard Square.

Dust hangs in the powdery arclight glare all-night till dawn.

Can't sleep. Haven't got the nerve to break out of the bellglass.

Four years under the ethercone: Breathe deep, gently now that's the way to be a good boy. One two three four five six. Get A's in some courses but don't be a grind, be interested in literature but remain a gentleman, don't be seen with Jews or socialists and all the pleasant contacts will be useful in later life, say hello pleasantly to everybody crossing the yard.

Sit looking out into the twilight of the pleasantest four years of your life.

grow cold with culture like a cup of tea forgotten between the incenseburner and a volume of Oscar Wilde, cold and not strong like a claret lemonade drunk at a pop concert in Symphony Hall.

Four years I didn't know you could do what you Angelo wanted, say

　　　　Marx

　　　　　　to all

the professors, for a small Swift break all the Greenoughs in the shooting gallery,

but tossed with eyes smarting all the spring night reading the Tragical History of Dr. Faustus and went mad listening to the streetcarwheels screech grinding in a rattle of loose trucks round Harvard Square and the trains crying across the saltmarshes and the rumbling siren of a steamboat leaving dock and mill workers marching with a red brass band through the streets of Lawrence Massachusetts.

It was like the Magdeburg spheres; the pressure outside sustained the vacuum within

and I hadn't the nerve

to jump up and walk out of doors and tell them all to go take a flying

　　　　Rimbaud

　　　　　at the moon.

　　　　　　—John Dos Passos
　　　　　　42nd Parallel

S. S. *Pierce gets through*

On the coldest winter Saturday nights, when the snow lay two feet deep all around our house twelve miles outside of Boston and was still falling . . . when the local tradesmen had completely given up any attempt at deliveries since the day before . . . then—perhaps while we were eating our baked beans and brown bread at the round dining-room table—the back door would be flung vigorously open, steps would stamp into the kitchen from the entry, and bang! that reassuring crash of a big Pierce's delivery box, with slot handles, onto the kitchen table would be followed by the smaller bangs of its contents rapidly being taken out and set down. "Pierce's!" the man would call with a certain hearty, unvarying cheerfulness, and we would rise from the table, napkins in hand, and rush out into the kitchen to see him, snow all over his shoulders, face crimson, taking the last things out of the box—the crock of strawberry jam, the wooden tub of butter—and preparing to depart on his long, lonely route. "Do let me give you something—a cup of coffee," my mother would cry, but he always shook his head and laughed and said,

"If I stopped going, I'd freeze to death when I went out again." Then the back door slammed, and the sound of a horse's snort, the sound of runners would be heard; for what always happened on those bitter days when the local tradesmen failed us was that Pierce's, unable to get its auto trucks through, either, hired sleighs from livery stables and got through anyway with the delivery—a standard that, for me at least, easily rivaled the dashing boasts of the U. S. Mail.

—Nancy Hale
A New England Girlhood

Beacon Hill Christmas

Beacon Hill is said to be the first locality in the United States to celebrate Christmas by illuminating windows on Christmas Eve. According to the records of the First National Bank of Boston . . . Arthur's younger brother Alfred actually originated the practice by placing a burning candle in the fourth floor window of the Shurtleff home at 9 West Cedar Street in 1893. By 1908 the custom had spread. Mr. and Mrs. Ralph Adams Cram started the carol singing by gathering groups of children at their home to practice for Christmas Eve. Mrs. Hollis French and Dr. Richard C. Cabot soon organized bands of really excellent singers. Christmas Eve on Beacon Hill around 1930 was really at its best. On the ground floor, curtains in all the houses were drawn aside and each window was decorated with special care. A Madonna, perhaps a small bas-relief, or a decorative fruit arrangement, were illuminated by a pair of handsome brass candlesticks. The little back alleys were just as much fun to visit as Mt. Vernon and West Cedar Streets. My father's house [Arthur Nichols], which faced down Mt. Vernon Street, had at least one candle in each window on the street itself, and on the front facing down the hill. The large square Sears house opposite ours was a special attraction, with its display of one hundred and ten candles in its fifteen windows, including the lookout on top of the house. . . . Singing bands wandered around in a haphazard manner and the crowds were anxious not to miss a window or a chorus. . . .

By 1924 our children were able to ring (the youngest was then nine) and on Christmas Eve we started our carol ringing standing in the front yard of 55 Mt. Vernon Street. Our success surprised us. The crowd grew and grew and applauded as loudly as they could, their hands muffled by woolen gloves. We only knew about six tunes so we rang those twice and moved on to another doorway. The crowd followed us and others joined the throng. Flashlights blinded us as cameras were snapped. We tried to get the audience to sing with us, but this did not work well as their idea of time and ours were apt to be quite different. As we switched from one tune to another, occasionally someone would hesitate as to which bell to ring. Any one of us would then point or glare at the right bell and the tune would continue. The bewildered look of a lost ringer was always a source of amusement to the audience. Fortunately we did not take ourselves too seriously. We kept up the ringing for at least two hours, by which time we were so congealed we returned to someone's open house.

—Mrs. Margaret Homer Shurcliff
Lively Days

A *novelist's view of Boston politics in the twenties*

It was an incongruous picture: the aging political boss, up shortly after dawn, preparing for the daily war of the wards by reading a volume of verse; it was a picture from which Skeffington—who was capable, at times, of great detachment—derived considerable amusement. He knew that the widely publicized habit had given rise to indignation, even fury, among his opponents; in several campaigns it had cropped up as a major issue.

Twenty years before, it had been the principal target of Festus "Mother" Garvey, a crafty little volcano of a man who, in middle life, had been given his nickname because of his habit of carrying his mother about with him for purposes of endorsement. She would appear by his side at political rallies; the opening dialogue was unvarying:

FESTUS: Good evenin', Ma.

MA: Good evenin' to ye, Festus me son.

FESTUS: Ma, I'd like to have you meet all these grand folks out in the audience who came all the way here to see what I had to say for myself this evenin'.

MA: Well, God love them all, Festus.

FESTUS: And I'd like all you grand folks to meet the lovely mother to who I owe everythin' I have and ever will have. You'll always be my best girl, Ma!

MA: Thank ye, Festus. And I'd like to tell all of yez that me son Festus has always been the grandest son in the world to me, and if yez vote for him yez'll be makin' no mistake!

The preliminaries over, Festus would leap into battle. Skeffington, who had shared many a platform with him, now recalled vividly his little antagonist racing up and down the stage, redfaced and screaming, hurling his charges of abuse, mismanagement, and corruption. Eventually and inevitably, he would come to the poetry.

"Here we are in this grand city of ours, payin' the highest tax rate we've ever paid, and the garbage hasn't been collected for weeks!" he would cry. "Our back yards are bein' turned into vertable *bedlams* of nauseous perfumes, and where is the mayor while all this is goin' on? I'll tell you where he is; he's up in his mansion on the Avenue, *readin' pomes!* The city smells to the high heavens and Frank Skeffington's got his nose in a book! Not a one of us dares to take a deep breath for fear of bein' killed off by the poisons around us, and our mayor is readin' how Louisy May Lovebreath thinks

vi'lets has a dainty smell in June! Oh, shame upon him, dear folks! Turn this shameful scoundrel out of office, him and his pomes both!"

And Skeffington recalled, too, his own rebuttal:

"I have sat here this evening and been warmed by the sight of this good mother, speaking so eloquently on behalf of her son. It was touching. Moving. Mother love is always edifying. Seeing her here tonight by her son's side, I cannot avoid thinking of those beautiful lines:

> And 'mid the cheerless hours of night
> A mother wandered with her child."

He had smiled benignly at the fierce, diminutive old lady who, hard by the side of her fifty-five-year-old child, sat glaring at him; then, in a thoughtful tone, he had added: "Still, we must not get carried away by emotion. We must remember one thing: *everybody* has a mother. Creatures of the field have mothers. The despised reptiles have mothers. The viper, the scorpion, the asp, all have mothers.

Presumably their mothers believe in them. All of us would doubtless admire their tender trust; we would not necessarily share it. And so, this evening, while I'd like to congratulate my opponent on possessing such a loyal parent, I'm afraid I can't congratulate him on much else. You heard with your own ears what he had to say. It only proves what I have long suspected: that while responsible civic leaders are preoccupied with grave and serious problems, Festus Garvey continues to think of municipal affairs in the terms of the simple device he loves so well—the garbage pail!"

He had beaten Mother Garvey handily; he had been beating him handily for thirty years; but Mother, himself motherless now and Skeffington's age, still clung on, an undying enemy whose ferocity had mounted with the years. And Skeffington knew that in the coming campaign he could depend upon few things as surely as he could upon the unrelenting, frenzied opposition of his ancient foe, coming at him from street corners, from the radio, from television.

It was a prospect which, at this stage of the game, did not alarm him greatly.

—Edwin O'Connor
The Last Hurrah

The North End in 1935

In swarming Salem and Hanover Streets, all sights, smells, and sounds are as purely Italian as Naples itself. Mandolin strains of "Santa Lucia" and "Funiculi-Funicula" come from crowded spaghetti restaurants. Here are little theaters with Italian "talkies," and Italian signs adorn all the shops, banks, newspapers, and steamer ticket offices.

Heavy odors of garlic, sour wine, and black tobacco hang in the air, and show windows are set with goat's cheese, sausages, and rows of dark bottles with bright-colored labels.

At a pushcart, chattering men eat raw clams sprinkled with lemon juice, a penny each, while getting their shoes shined. With a loud honk of horns, a wedding party circles about the quarter, stuffed white doves tied on the motor hoods, and white ribbons waving from the cars.

From upper windows fat wives look down, smiling, waving; and on lines stretched across alleys and courts flaps the family washing. Furtively, one eye out for "cops," boys match pennies and shoot craps.

—Frederick Simpich

Blackside

. . . I went gawking around the neighborhood—the Waumbeck and Humboldt Avenue Hill section of Roxbury, which is something like Harlem's Sugar Hill, where I'd later live. I saw those Roxbury Negroes acting and living differently from any black people I'd ever dreamed of in my life. This was the snooty-black neighborhood; they called themselves the "Four Hundred," and looked down their noses at the Negroes of the black ghetto, or so-called "town" section where Mary, my other half-sister, lived.

. . . Any black family that had been around Boston long enough to own the home they lived in was considered among the Hill elite. It didn't make any difference that they had to rent out rooms to make ends meet. Then the native-born New Englanders among them looked down upon recently migrated Southerner home-owners who lived next door, like Ella [his half-sister]. And a big percentage of the Hill dwellers were in Ella's category—Southern strivers and scramblers and West Indian Negroes, whom both the New Englanders and the Southerners called "Black Jews." Usually it was the Southerners and the West Indians who not only managed to own the places where they lived, but also at least one other house which they rented as income property. The snooty New Englanders usually owned less than they.

. . . Soon I ranged out of Roxbury and began to explore Boston proper. Historic buildings everywhere I turned, and plaques and markers and statues for famous events and men. One statue in the Boston Common astonished me: a Negro named Crispus Attucks, who had been the first man to fall in the Boston Massacre. I had never known anything like it. I roamed everywhere. In one direction I walked as far as Boston University. Another day I took my first subway ride. When most of the people got off I followed. It was Cambridge, and I circled all around in the Harvard University campus. Somewhere, I had already heard of Harvard—though I didn't know much more about it. Nobody that day could have told me I would give an address before the Harvard Law School Forum some twenty years later.

I also did a lot of exploring downtown. Why a city would have *two* big railroad stations—North Station and South Station—I couldn't understand. At both of the stations, I stood around and watched people arrive and leave. And I did the same thing at the bus station where Ella had met me. My wanderings even led me down along the piers and docks where I read plaques telling about the old sailing ships that used to put into port there.

. . . I began going down into the town ghetto section. That world of grocery stores, walk-up flats, cheap restaurants, poolrooms, bars, storefront churches, and pawnshops seemed to hold a natural lure for me.

. . . I spent my first month in town with my mouth hanging open. The sharp-dressed young "cats" who hung on the corners and in the poolrooms, bars and restaurants, and who obviously didn't work anywhere, completely entranced me. I couldn't get over marveling at how their hair was straight and shiny like white man's hair; Ella told me this was called a "conk." I had never tasted a sip of liquor, never even smoked a cigarette, and here I saw little black children, ten and twelve years old, shooting craps, playing cards, fighting, getting grown-ups to put a penny or a nickel on their number for them, things like that. And these children threw around swear words I'd never heard before, even, and slang expressions that were just as new to me, such as "stud" and "cat" and "chick" and "cool" and "hip." Every night as I lay in bed I turned these new words over in my mind. It was shocking to me that in town, especially after dark, you'd occasionally see a white girl and a Negro man strolling arm in arm along the sidewalk, and mixed couples drinking in the neon-lighted bars.

—*The Autobiography of Malcolm X*

Two episodes of Boston chivalry, 1938

The second time I arrived in Boston, nearly twenty years later, I was prepared to dislike it. But I soon took a fancy to the place. Possibly it's because I was now full of culture. And for another thing, I got all around town without getting lost. Boston is famous for being the easiest city in America to get lost in; the streets are so twisty and cut up that you can make one turn, suddenly find the afternoon sun in the east, and swear that somebody must have pushed you. What's more, I encountered a couple of pleasant little incidents out of Boston life: one to uphold the cultural New England tradition, one to destroy it. I'm always happy when things reach an impasse like that.

The first came from a policeman. I pulled up to one at a corner to ask the way to Cambridge. (I wasn't lost—just slightly confused.) The policeman said I'd have to turn right. Since I was already halfway across the street, I asked if I could back up, then turn. The policeman was gruff, but no typical cop language came from his lips. What he said was exactly as follows, so help me: "Reverse promptly. I wish to use the street."

There weren't any words at all in the other incident. I simply saw a nice-looking couple about thirty years old come out of a cocktail lounge. The woman fell flat on her face twice within fifty feet. She fell down because she was (shhhhh!) d-r-u-n-k. Each time she fell, the man calmly picked up her purse and handkerchief, waited until she had sprawlingly staggered up under her own power, and then handed them to her. Do you suppose that somewhere, through those dim years between 1620 and 1938, the cold chivalry of New England could have crept silently around a corner and died?

—Ernie Pyle
Home Country

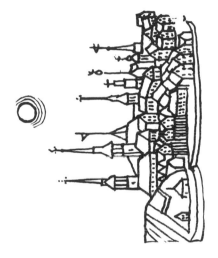

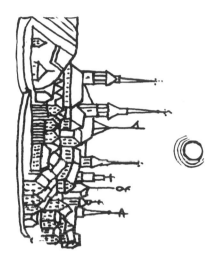

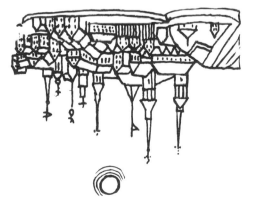

CHAPTER EIGHT

The Shape of Something Larger

The Boston that was a hamlet of houses on a sea-washed peninsula has long since passed into history. Vanished too is that contentious port town of 1775 that rebelled against its lawful king. Disappeared is that burgeoning little merchant city of the early nineteenth century. To adapt Gov. William Bradford's comment on Plymouth in 1631: out of these small beginnings, a greater Boston has been produced.

What has shaped this newer Boston has not been the politics of the larger swallowing the smaller, but a pragmatic growth, a natural outcome of the improvements and developments of the last century and a quarter. Transportation, waste disposal, water, parks, economics—these have created the commercial, industrial, and suburban metropolis we now live in, one different from any former Boston.

Better transportation initially enlarged Boston. The bridges built after the Revolutionary War linked the isolated peninsula to the mainland. There were four of them—Charles River Bridge, 1786; West Boston Bridge, 1793; South Boston Bridge, 1805; and Canal (or Craigie's) Bridge, 1809—enabling people to live outside the town limits and yet still walk easily into town.

The first stagecoaches were used more for long distance travel—Salem, Providence, New York—than for regular commuting from the surrounding villages and towns. Later, omnibus lines served as local stages running through the streets, but these were limited both in the number of runs they made and particularly in the number of passengers they could carry. They did not serve to spread the population out into the adjacent towns to any great extent.

The steam railroads were the first to do this. Other cities in the nation were well started when Boston began to explore the medium. The three principal lines were the Boston & Lowell (1830), the Boston & Providence (1831), and the Boston & Worcester (1831). This last was the first to begin limited operations, in 1834, quickly followed by the other two. Other lines were soon chartered: the Western railroad opened in 1841 to Albany; the Eastern from East Boston to Salem, in 1839; the Boston & Maine in 1841, and the Old Colony line in 1845. Meanwhile branch lines were being established, such as the Charlestown Branch Railroad of 1836, incorporated into the Fitchburg railroad six years later. By 1846, Boston had seven distinct stations serving these lines as the city terminals.

Aerial view of expanding Logan International Airport, the only airport so close to a major city. Downtown Boston is just across the inner harbor. (Courtesy of Massport.)

271

The steam railroad enabled well-to-do commuters to live in the pleasant Boston countryside, but they did not serve the masses of people. Street railways did this. After their introduction in New York in the early 1850s, Bostonians clamored for similar facilities here. The wonder is they had to wait so long. The Quincy Granite railway in 1826 used the identical system of horse-drawn wagons on rails to move granite. Here in principle was the street railway, seen daily by countless Bostonians, yet nobody suggested using the same method to move people. It was an odd lapse of that fabled Yankee ingenuity.

Once street railways were allowed by the legislature, there was a scramble to be the first to introduce them. The Metropolitan and the Cambridge Horse Railroad companies were both chartered in 1853 and operating by 1856. The same year saw the Broadway, Dorchester Avenue, and Chelsea lines begin operations, all three chartered in 1854. These lines were immediately successful and prosperous. They quickly multiplied and went through consolidation battles. By the early sixties, Scollay Square had become a traffic bottleneck as it was a great center for the streetcar lines, as were Haymarket and Bowdoin squares.

In 1860 there were 88.8 miles of streetcar lines in the city, increasing to 222.5 in 1880 and to 470.2 miles by 1887. By that time the lines had been consolidated into five companies: the Metropolitan, South Boston, Boston Consolidated, Cambridge, and Boston & Lynn. All but the Lynn line joined in 1887 to form the West End Company. The next year, electrification of these lines began following the example of a small company in Richmond, Virginia. By 1899, the line to Cambridge was completely electrified. The "trolley car," or "broomsticks" as they were sometimes called, had become a familiar sight to Bostonians.

Significantly, the street railways developed the "streetcar suburbs," since the rapid spread of horsecars through the city and surrounding towns and their frequent and inexpensive service enabled many people to move to a better life in these suburbs, while continuing to earn a living in the city. Each year after 1856, more and more middle-class families trekked to the suburbs. Dorchester, Roxbury, Malden, Somerville, Chelsea, South Boston, and Cam-

Three ways to "get out of town": —take a bridge, take a stage, take a train. (Top opposite) Bridge across the Charles River to Charlestown as it appeared in 1789, three years after it was built. (Bottom opposite) Mail coach in 1826 (courtesy of The Bostonian Society, Old State House). (Above) Anonymous watercolor of Somerville station, ca 1840 S(?). (Courtesy of Boston Athenaeum).

273

Idealized version of the last run
of the last horsecar in Boston
on the Marlborough Street line,
December 24, 1900. (Courtesy of
The Bostonian Society, Old
State House.)

bridge all experienced large population increases. Real estate promoters quickly came along to develop these pastures and fields into streets and housing developments. The old neighborhoods were utterly transformed. In these unplanned suburbs, community life became fragmented and focused on the center city. The result of this by 1900, said one observer, was that the metropolis "lacked local communities that could deal with the problem of contemporary society at the level of the family and its immediate surroundings, and it lacked a large-scale community that could deal with the problems of the metropolis."*

Meanwhile, transportation continued to expand and improve. A subway, built under Tremont Street and opened for service in 1898, was not only the first American subway but also the second in the world to be built just below the surface of the street and not in a deep tunnel. Opposition to this underground plan—because of health and economic objections—led to the building of elevated structures in several sections of the city. The success of this tunnel, however, led to the building of others: East Boston (first part completed in

* Sam B. Warner, Jr., "Streetcar Suburbs" (Cambridge, Mass., 1962) p. 160.

274

Busy, crowded Washington Street where Summer and Winter meet, about 1901. (Courtesy of The Bostonian Society, Old State House.)

1904), Washington Street (1908), Cambridge (1912), Boylston Street (1914), and Dorchester (1918). All these early lines have been further extended and improved.

The legislature created the Boston Elevated Company as a private corporation and in 1897, by legislative fiat, leased the West End Street Railway Company to it. In 1918, the state took over the Elevated Company, and later bought out the stockholders. Presently, this system is run by the Massachusetts Bay Transportation Authority (MBTA) and is supported by assessments against some seventy-nine cities and towns in the larger metropolitan area on the premise that citizens of all these communities are benefited by the rapid transit system. The Authority is now vastly expanding its system to the north, west, and south, as well as improving existing lines.

Two other Authorities coordinate transportation needs of the metropolitan community. One is the Massachusetts Port Authority (1956) which operates Logan International Airport in East Boston, the Mystic River or Tobin bridge from Charlestown to Chelsea, and several docks and wharves along the water-

The old Providence Depot, once in Park Square (above) (Courtesy of The Bostonian Society, Old State House) and old North Station (below) on Causeway Street.

South Station before the elevated tracks marred its appearance, in the late 1890s. (Courtesy of The Bostonian Society, Old State House.) (Below) The gaudy interior of South Station, circa 1915? (Courtesy of Shaw Studios.)

(To the right) Waiting to be employed on the subway construction at Charles & Boylston Streets, 1895. (Courtesy of The Bostonian Society, Old State House.) (Below) Overhead view of the building of Park Street subway station, about 1895.

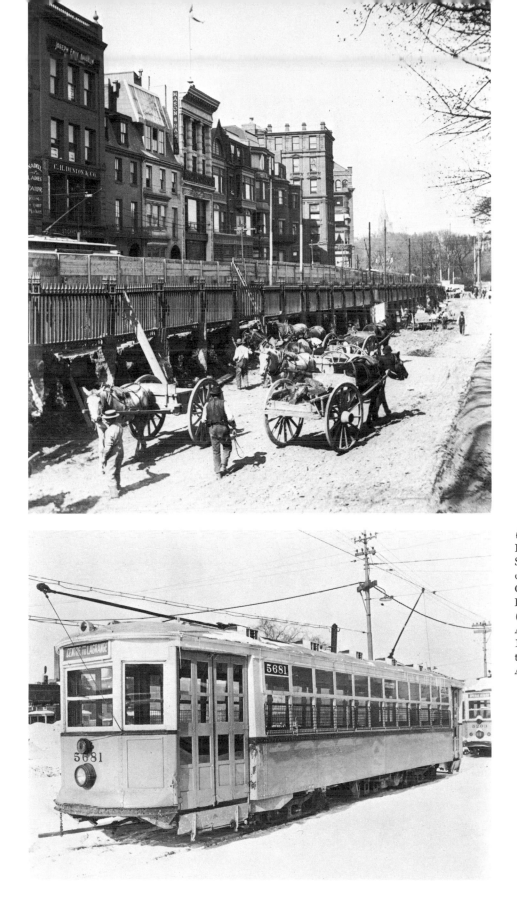

(Top) Construction along Boylston Street for the Boylston Street subway in 1895. (Picture courtesy the Bostonian Society, Old State House.) (Bottom) Picture of trolley car 5681 (Centre to LaGrange), taken at Arborway Carhouse, circa 1950. (From the collection of the Boston Street Railway Association.)

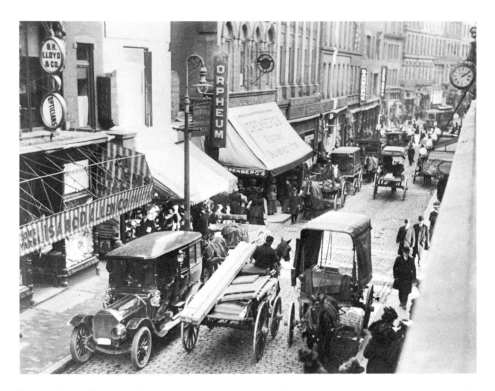

Heavy traffic on Lower Washington Street. (Courtesy of Shaw Studios.)

front. The other is the Massachusetts Turnpike Authority which manages the turnpike from Boston to the New York state line as well as the Callahan and Sumner toll tunnels from Boston underneath the harbor to East Boston.

Like all other major metropolises, the problems of good, rapid transportation into and out of the core city are essential to its economic viability. Happily, the decline of the railroads is more than matched by the up-grading of the rapid transit system. Large public reliance on automobile transportation has created major headaches for city planners, however. Too many cars come into Boston, highways need too much space, there is too little room for parking areas or garages, and pollution from exhaust contributes to the smog that hangs over the city—problems only gradually being solved. But better and faster transport has undeniably contributed toward making one community out of the many towns and cities around Boston.

The disposal of waste was the second step toward a larger Boston. Litter is always with us. The Indians living in the Boston region left their litter behind them, now considered better than gold by the archeologists. From the arrowheads, pottery shards, axe helves, tobacco pipes, and other discards they have constructed a fragmentary picture of the life of these first Greater Bostonians. The natural litter left by their existence, heaps of oyster and clam shells, food and human wastes, have usually disintegrated. Their litter was no great problem, because they constantly moved on.

The second wave of settlers, those from Europe in the early seventeenth century, stayed, and their litter quickly became a problem. True to their

280

Charlesgate Interchange from the air. The 2500-foot overpass and interchange, built by the Metropolitan District Commission, links heavily traveled Storrow Drive and the Fenway parkway system, carrying vehicles above Beacon Street and Commonwealth Avenue. (Courtesy of MDC.)

English custom, they dumped their rubbish and waste indiscriminately into the streets. Natural decay or the wind took care of some of this; free-roaming hogs scavenged more of it. But such "garbage disposals" were something of a nuisance: they tripped up the gentlefolk for one thing, so in 1634, selectmen voted that swine should be "kept up in yards." When neither hogs nor citizens observed the good intentions of this law, the selectmen (two years later) appointed Richard Fairbanks hogreeve to impound all the hogs he could catch.

Rubbish left on the shore early proved a danger, and in 1636 two men were appointed water bailiffs to see that such annoyances as fish, wood, or stone not be left about on the seashore. Seven years later, the job was delegated to one man who was instructed to clear the shore of "all offences to boats or the like" between the high and low water mark.

Cleanliness and sanitation were not matters uppermost in the minds of colonial Bostonians, however. Wooden planks, timber, or bricks would be left lying in the streets or public highways, though people might bump into them by day or trip over them by night. Holes were dug where the diggers chose. These were small offenses compared with the matter of garbage. Dumped as it was indiscriminately, the noses of Bostonians protested loudly and in 1634 the selectmen prohibited fish and garbage from being thrown from the town dock. Ordinances, however, were good to read, but not always followed, and in 1652 the selectmen voted to fine anybody who threw "any intralls of beast or fowles or stinkeing thing," on the streets or the Common. This was not to be the last time they would make this complaint.

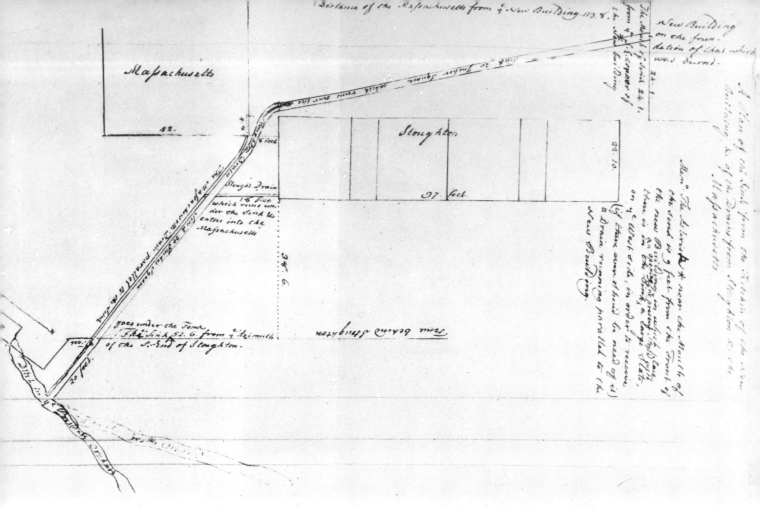

The handwritten notes on the sketch include:

(Distance of the Massachusetts from ye New Building. 113.8.)

Massachusetts

42.

Stoughton

97 feet

New Building Stoughton

Stough's Drain

which runs under the sink to enters into the Massachusetts

goes under the Tame

The Sink 52. 6. from ye Azimuth of the S. End of Stoughton.

Ditch in ye Common or Lane

Harvard Presidents once worried about the plumbing. A sketch from the notebooks of Harvard President Holyoke (1754–1775) giving the plans for the drains from the kitchen of Harvard, Stoughton, and Massachusetts Halls. (Courtesy of Colonial Society of Massachusetts.)

Butchers were particular offenders in this regard and were constantly instructed where to discard their animal wastes. As late as 1710, the selectmen of the time were telling "Mr. Richard Sherrine Butcher" that he could not kill cattle at his slaughterhouse on Wood Lane and would have to remove his "filth and Grarbage" as it was "very Noysom and Offencive to ye Inhabitants." Other odorous establishments, tanners, brewers, distillers, limeburners, blubberboilers, chandlers, curriers, were frequently advised to build their establishments away from people's homes.

Privies, of course, were so necessary that they were often euphemistically called Necessary Houses or Houses of Office. Early Bostonians might mingo (from the Latin "I make water") where they wished and they often did, but a Puritan of 1640 who was at the office, was not where a Bostonian of today would expect to find him. Necessary odors went with these Necessary Houses. By 1652 the Bostonian nose had had it, and privy builders were ordered not to put up or keep one within twelve feet of the public street unless it was vaulted six feet deep. By 1701, when there were many more people in town, the rule was altered to require privies be forty feet away from streets, shops, or wells unless they be vaulted six foot deep "and sufficiently enclosed."

When the first house drains were built is not known, but certainly before 1660. These only dumped the waste problem outside the house. Then some local inventive mind conceived the idea of linking these house drains together into what we would call a sewer, carrying the waste down to the shore, and venting it into the sea. Typical of these drains was the one Francis Thrasher, "Clothworker," built at his own expense in 1704. It was described as

a large Stone drain in the Street or highway Leading toward the Neck, extending in length from his own present dwelling House down to the Flats or water side at the Southerly end of the Town.

It is not clear whether this drain was square or round; both types were common then. The selectmen agreed that nobody else could connect to this drain without first getting Thrasher's approval and paying him something toward his cost of construction.

This practice soon became so common that the nuisance of digging up streets to lay new sewers or to repair old ones prompted both state and local action. In 1711, John Bucanan built a 160-foot sewer in Wood Lane for a group of neighbors which cost them £23. This linked up with two sewers built the year previously, making a common sewer 207 feet long. James Packer joined up a Salem Street sewer with a Prince Street sewer in 1715. So the process went on in a random, independent fashion, making a maze of drains of good to indifferent quality without an over-all pattern or plan.

By 1736, the selectmen had issued permits for over 650 sections of sewers to be laid, always requiring that work be speedy so that the street would not long be obstructed and that the pavement be carefully replaced. Still, by the middle of the century, Boston had perhaps the best drainage system in the New or Old World—all built by private initiative.

Laying the dust on State Street in 1849. (A lithograph by N. Currier, without Ives.)

As time went by some of these drains began to fall in from poor workmanship or natural erosion. The selectmen decided in 1767 that before granting new sewer permits they must approve the builders. Some sewers had become clogged and had never been cleaned out. When yellow fever hit the town in 1798, action became imperative. The Board of Health, established that same year, took several corrective measures in 1799: house drains connected with sewers should be fixed with valves to prevent backup of sewer odors into the house; carts were provided to clean out privies; sewers were ordered cleaned out. By May 1799, 113 cartloads of noxious matter had been carted away from one sewer in Market Square alone. Others were equally bad.

Special carts were provided by 1800 to haul off on a regular basis what was euphemistically called "nightsoil"—human excrement. A newspaper complained that year that the carts spilled "their filth" in Middle and Fish streets as they made their way to Hancock's Wharf where it was all dumped into the harbor water. How long, they queried, would the inhabitants continue to be annoyed by the "unwholesome effluvia" dropped by "these nocturnal goldfinders"? Relief was just a decade and a year away. In 1811, Jeremiah Bridge was given a monopoly in this field, having special equipment for the task. But his high prices offended many, and some hired other people to remove their nightsoil, or simply ignored the whole matter. The sewers were no help to this problem, because in 1799, the Board of Health had forbidden any connections between privies and sewers.

As the town grew and the flats along the shore were extended outward and built upon, the old outlets of the sewers were gradually cut off. When and where extensions of these sewers were made, problems were encountered: in some cases there was an insufficient drop for proper sewer drainage—some actually ran uphill—and new outlets that were below the high-tide level had to be provided with tide-gates to prevent backing up.

The combination of the drainage system growing old and the rapid population increase, caused the legislature to establish a State Board of Health in 1868 to eliminate unsanitary conditions in the whole Boston area. Expanding suburbs aggravated the waste problem, for everybody was dumping their wastes into the rivers flowing to Boston. Two drainage systems were recommended, each with a main and branch intercepting sewers. One, called the Northerly system, was to serve Charlestown, East Boston, and parts of Somerville, Cambridge, Everett, Chelsea, and Winthrop. This was not immediately constructed because of the difficulty of getting agreement among so many localities. The second, the Southerly system, which was to handle the city proper, and much of Brookline, Roxbury, Dorchester, and South Boston, was begun in 1876. Completed in 1855, the Boston Main Drainage System was the first construction of its kind in the United States. A series of intercepting sewers was built along the waterfront which picked up the waste from all the old sewers that had formerly been emptied into the tidal water.

This greatly relieved the unpleasant odors, but still did nothing about sewage from surrounding communities. Again, the legislature intervened, and in 1884

MOON ISLAND WHERE RESERVOIR WILL BE LOCATED

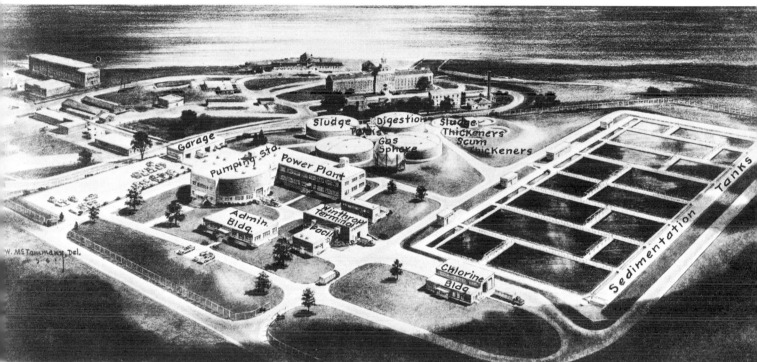

W. McTammany, Del.

Garage
Pumping Sta.
Power Plant
Admin. Bldg.
Winthrop Terminal Facilities
Sludge
Digestion Tanks
Gas Sphere
Sludge Thickeners
Scum Thickeners
Chlorine Bldg.
Sedimentation Tanks

created the Massachusetts Drainage Commission, which spurred the legislature to authorize the State Board of Health to produce a remedial plan. In 1889, the legislature formed the Metropolitan Sewerage District to implement the plan, and the first unit of today's Metropolitan District Commission came into existence.

The Board of Health's basic design is still used by the metropolitan sewerage system today. Divided by the Charles River, there is in the Mystic Valley a North Metropolitan Sewerage System which, after treatment at the new Deer Island plant, discharges its effluents into the harbor south of the island. Communities in the Charles River Valley are united in the South Metropolitan Sewerage System and connected with the Boston Main Drainage System, discharging into the harbor at Moon Island. Recent construction has brought both outlets far out into the harbor.

Forty-two towns are served by this sewerage system. There are some 225 miles of metropolitan sewers which connect with over 3,700 miles of town and city sewers with many more than 315,000 house connections. The sewerage

(Above) Moon Island, in 1880, where the reservoir for the "new" main drainage system was to be located. (Below) Design for the sewage treatment plant on Deer Island. (Courtesy of MDC.)

"Summer Showers," a painting by Allan Rohan Crite, painted in the 1930s in the South End, showing Ruggles Street youngsters enjoying a moment of coolness under the hydrant. This area has now all changed. (Courtesy of Allan Rohan Crite.)

division of the Metropolitan District Commission operates twelve pumping stations, two treatment plants, and three headworks. The men of the division maintain metropolitan sewers and their general plants, while the cities and towns care for their local lines. Well over five hundred men are daily involved in keeping the Metropolitan District Commission veins flowing and the metropolitan area of Greater Boston cleansed.

The need to preserve the natural environment was the third step toward a larger Boston. Bostonians had bought their first public park in 1634 when they paid William Blackstone thirty pounds for most of his local property including the forty-eight acres now called the Boston Common—that is, something owned in *common* by all the citizens. For almost two hundred years this sufficed Bostonians for a playground, park, and pasture. The extensive vacant land in and around the city served quite naturally as unorganized playgrounds. Subtly, as the tide of immigration swept over the city, houses, tenements, warehouses, office buildings, and factories ate up these open spaces. The rapid suburbanization destroyed many of their vacant spaces, too. Greenness was going as the urban landscape threatened to become one endless grid of housing and pavement.

When Boston became a city in 1822, it had no public lands except the Common and its Mall and the various burying grounds. Mayor Quincy's administration acquired land on Dorchester Heights in South Boston for park and reservoir purposes. With the filling in of the Back Bay, the state gave twenty-four acres to the city to use and this became the Public Garden, adjacent to the Common. It made for seventy-two acres of greenery in the heart of the city. The broad vista created down Commonwealth Avenue added a hundred-foot-wide stretch of trees and walkway through the Back Bay to the Fens area.

In 1875, after seven years of agitation of the matter, Boston was authorized to create the Board of Park Commissioners. The report of this group the next

Canoeing on the Charles River reservation, 1904. (Courtesy of The Society for the Preservation of New England Antiquities.)

year recommended the development of ten parks and connecting parkways affecting over 1,100 acres of land. Lack of money, however, prevented any action until 1877 when an appropriation of $500,000 permitted development of the fen section of the Back Bay. Frederic Law Olmstead, who had planned New York's Central Park, was called on for help. By 1881 the Fens were being developed in a natural fashion and land for parks was being purchased along Muddy Brook, the Charlesbank, in what became Franklin Park, and in East Boston at Wood Island. The next year Harvard College leased Arnold Arboretum to the city for a dollar a year for a thousand years (renewable for succeeding thousands of years at the same price!). Olmstead's plan tied much of this property together into a wandering ribbon of green landscape, given the public-relations name of the "Emerald Necklace."

Local Boston development of its parks and playgrounds received its greatest emphasis in the decade between 1885 and 1896, promoted vigorously by Joseph Lee and Charles Eliot. At the end of that period, the city could count 2,162 acres of park land. By 1930, even with the addition of the Strandway with its Columbus Park and its famous L Street Baths, the acreage had increased only to 2,446. Yet it could be said that perhaps 10 percent of Boston land was devoted to park and recreational purposes.

Boston's system of parks favorably impressed neighboring towns, and under the prodding of the Trustees of Public Reservations, a commission was appointed by the state in 1892 to plan for similar open spaces in the metropolitan area. This temporary body made a series of extensive recommendations, including that the commission be permanent. So the legislature in 1893 established the Metropolitan Parks District, consisting of Boston and thirty-six suburban communities. Within four years this group had acquired nearly seven thousand acres of land, with such prime territory as the Blue Hills Reservation (now expanded to 5,700 acres), the Middlesex Fells, Stony Brook, Beaver Brook, and Revere Beach.

BRRRRRRR-RR

F. W. Dahl cartoons have daily delighted readers of *The Boston Herald* (now the *Herald-Traveler*) for years. They speak for themselves, but postwar youngsters may need to know that this cartoon dates from the Second World War years when fuel oil was rationed to New England residents by coupon. (Courtesy of F. W. Dahl.)

A view of the Hatch Shell on the Esplanade before the roadway was widened, biting off much of the greenery for traffic—and bringing traffic noises that much closer to the ears of those trying to enjoy the melodious strains of an Esplanade Concert. (Photo by Shaw Studios.)

Children skating at the MDC's Cleveland Circle Skating Rink in 1966. (Courtesy of MDC.)

A fleet of boats waiting in the lock at the Charles River dam to be released to the Atlantic Ocean. (Courtesy of MDC.)

After this rapid acquisition, the metropolitan park area expanded slowly until presently it contains over 12,500 acres of park land and 1,500 acres of parkways. Individual communities would have found it impossible, financially and politically, to have put together such a large recreational area or to build and maintain the parkway network. Much of the District's work in late years has been in improving this property and providing varied recreational facilities for urban citizens. There are now six major reservations, twenty artificial ice-skating rinks and sixteen natural ice areas, seventeen salt-water beaches and four fresh-water beaches, two golf courses, dozens of playgrounds with varied activities and playing fields, picnic areas, observation towers, foot trails, bridle paths, ski slopes, boating and fishing areas, two zoos, museums, and historic sites, the Hatch Memorial Shell on Boston's Esplanade, and a dozen neighborhood bandstands—the first metropolitan park system in the country.

Looking ahead, a Bay Circuit of Parks has been proposed. This would be another series of reservations outside the inner metropolitan ring, perhaps starting with Plum Island on the north, swinging around through the Ipswich, Concord, and Sudbury rivers on the west, and concluding at Duxbury beach on the south. Involvement in development of the islands in Boston harbor is also foreseen. The principle is that these are regional problems, and only regional action can meet them satisfactorily.

290

Water was the fourth step toward a larger Boston. Since they first arrived here, Bostonians have been drinking water. It seems safe to say that that includes their Indian predecessors. Some Bostonians, it is true, have always preferred something stronger, settling for water only as a last resort. The statistics to prove that can be found in the court records.

Turning his tap for a glass of water, a resident of Greater Boston releases both history and politics along with his H_2O. As the water rushes into his glass from far Quabbin, sixty-five crow-flight miles from the State House dome, he is tapping into a great circulation system which undergirds the whole region's body like some huge metallic network of arteries. And he is performing an act repeated frequently by the nearly two million people living in the present Metropolitan Water District. Some 250 million gallons of water are used every day by Greater Bostonians for a daily per capita consumption of 157 gallons. Not everyone *drinks* that much, of course; manufacturing processes actually use the bulk of it. Still, the water flooding into the metropolis each day is an unimaginable deluge.

In the formative days when such a vast quantity of water was not required, springs and wells were sufficient, providing they were of good quality and regularity. It was the lack of good fresh water which prompted the first settlers to leave Charlestown for the Shawmut peninsula, then inhabited only by William Blackstone living monastically beside a good spring on the west side of Beacon Hill. The most famous early spring was the Governor's Spring, so called because it was near Winthrop's house on the northeast corner of Milk Street. Spring Lane today marks its approximate site. Wells supplemented these early springs, and by 1643 permission from the selectmen had to be secured before wells could be dug. Owners had to be careful when pumping their wells that the "wast water" did not cause "annoyance to the street." They also had to protect the wells so no danger would come to children. People who paid for these wells and pumps could refuse the use of them to any neighbor unwilling to contribute to their cost and upkeep.

For the benefit of poor people, the town paid for an occasional well and pump, the most famous being the Town Pump sunk at the head of present State Street, then the market place. Cattle as well as men required water, and a "watring" place long used for cattle was the pond adjacent to Thomas Wheeler's land on what was to become first Pond Street and later Bedford Street (north side). It would thus be beneath the present Jordan Marsh annex.

Fire protection was another reason for an abundant water supply. William Franklin and his neighbors set up a cistern in 1643 near their houses "to howld water for to be helpful in case of fier." By 1649 another group set up what they called a conduit or reservoir to hold water for the same purpose at the corner of North and Union streets. Twelve feet square and topped with planks, it was fed by pipes from nearby wells and springs. Some historians call this Boston's first waterworks department. Neither proved adequate for the purpose, but at least gave nearby housewives sufficient water for their laundering.

By the end of the seventeenth century, Bostonians were adequately supplied with springs, wells, pumps, and watering places. Even as early as 1709, some people had laid pipes from the cisterns into their houses and furnished themselves with indoor running water; others had pumps in their cellars. Enlargement of the wells often meant digging on the streets and the selectmen permitted this, requiring only that the work be done expeditiously and that the well be covered and made safe. But the increasingly crowded town meant that drain water became a problem from so many wells and springs. A primitive sewer system, already described, developed to meet this problem.

Bostonians, even as early as 1727, began worrying about the water quality. The New England *Journal* advised them that year how to avoid "Noxious" water, claiming that pumps produced dangerous gases and that even sunlight playing on wells might cause "fatal damps." Five years later, a newer pump attempted to "deliver more Water and with less Strength" exerted by the pumper. It was also claimed that it was not "at all liable to Freeze," even in "the most Bleak Places." It was not until 165 years after its founding that the town attempted to replace these individual or neighborhood arrangements with a common water supply. In 1795 and again in 1796, "The Aqueduct Corporation" was permitted to bring water from the Town of Roxbury into the Town of Boston. Its source was Jamaica Pond. Construction began in 1796, and Salem quickly followed the Boston lead and began a similar project. The advantages of such a communal supply of abundant water were obvious: shipowners would benefit as well as private individuals, for their ships could be cheaply and easily furnished with good water for their long voyages. Housewives would save soap (so the Corporation told them), cut washing time, quench fires more readily, and no longer have to fetch and lug water up several flights of stairs. Too, it would be guaranteed pure—already some wells in Boston rose and fell with the tide. Firemen need no longer complain about stagnant, ill-smelling cistern water ruining their clothing, nor people worry that a neighbor's privy sat too close to the well, nor fear his new-dug well might cause another well to run dry.

Fifteen miles of specially bored pitch-pine logs were laid from Jamaica Pond into the center of the city and many families connected themselves to the system. A "tube" ran to a subscriber's home and he agreed not to "draw or suffer to be drawn, any water except for the use of his family only." Under penalty of "having his communication with the Aqueduct cut off immediately," the subscriber also agreed not to "suffer any waste of water." For its part, the Corporation agreed to "keep the tubes in repair, except the drawing or perpendicular stand," that was the faucet inside the house. If they failed to maintain a steady supply of water, they would refund in proportion "provided that the deficiency shall not be in consequence of frost in the perpendicular tube." Aqueduct water was also hawked in the market place at moderate cost—a pail for a penny, eight cents for a barrel.

The Corporation continued for more than half a century, though it received no return on its investment for the first ten years and less than 4 percent for the next thirty years. By 1842 it reached its greatest number of customers, supplying fifteen hundred houses in the city, some with the old pine logs, some with newly laid iron pipes. Several large breweries in Roxbury were good customers of the system, so that many Bostonians who were not otherwise connected with Aqueduct water drank it in an agreeably modified form. In 1851, Boston bought the water system on a stand-by basis.

As early as 1825, Mayor Quincy had decided that Boston needed its own water system, publicly owned and operated. He secured Professor Daniel Treadwell who surveyed several possible sources of supply and recommended Spot Pond in Stoneham or a reservoir of some five acres built above the Watertown Falls of the Charles River. From either of these sources water could be brought to a reservoir on Beacon Hill and then distributed by gravity flow to secondary reservoirs on Fort Hill and Copp's Hill and thence throughout the city. The river scheme, however, required expensive pumping.

As frequently happens in Boston, this was but the first of several reports that had to be made before action would be taken. Loammi Baldwin, Jr., made a survey in 1834 and found problems with both of Treadwell's proposals and favored going westward to ponds in Framingham. This provoked controversy since the Middlesex Canal drew its water supply from this general area too, and it was feared if the city took its water from this source, there would not be enough for the canal.

A third report by Robert H. Eddy in 1836 recommended the use of Mystic Lake and Spot Pond in Medford and Stoneham, steam pumping the water from the Mystic to a reservoir on Bunker Hill for distribution to the city. Other proposals from various people were to dig a giant shaft six hundred to one thousand feet deep from which colossal well the whole city could be, it was claimed, supplied. An 1837 commission favored: (1) Charles River with a reservoir on Corey Hill in Brookline, or (2) Mystic Lake with a reservoir on Walnut Tree Hill, or (3) Spot Pond using the same Walnut Hill reservoir, or (4) Long Pond in Framingham with the Corey Hill reservoir. Commission member James F. Baldwin gave a minority report strongly supporting the last solution. Before a decision could be made, the Middlesex Canal, now losing money and business to the railroads, suggested that the city take it over as a water supply system.

The twenty-one years of discussion finally brought a solution by 1846. Long Pond was selected for the site of Boston's water supply, and the search for potable water headed west as Baldwin had recommended. On August 20 that year, ground was broken for a conduit and Mayor Quincy, son of the man who had appointed Professor Treadwell twenty-one years before, suggested using the original Indian name of the pond, so Long Pond became Lake Cochituate. The aqueduct was quickly built the fourteen miles to the Brookline reservoir, two tunnels were blasted in Newton and Brookline, and a three-arch granite bridge at Newton Lower Falls carried the water over the Charles River. With a capacity of 20 million gallons a day, it could fill the distribution reservoir at Brookline in four and a half days. From here cast iron pipes took the water to a reservoir on Beacon Hill, located about where the Brigham Extension of

The Beacon Hill reservoir shown in this wood engraving stood on Derne Street, between Hancock and Temple Streets from 1849 until it was completely taken down by 1885.

the State House now stands, and to other reservoirs on Telegraph Hill in South Boston and Eagle Hill in East Boston. (The Beacon Hill reservoir was first filled in 1849, discontinued in 1870, used thereafter for winter skating, and dismantled in 1882.)

On October 25, 1848, water from Lake Cochituate was introduced into Boston with great ceremony. The day began with a hundred guns saluting the sunrise and church bells pealing bronze hosannas on the air. (Human ceremonies always seem to involve a maximum of noise.) A monster parade of some fourteen thousand people marched through the streets to the Common and listened to an ode of James Russell Lowell's sung by children, which concluded on a typical moral teetotal note:

> I come from far o'er hill and mead,
> And here, Cochituate's envoy, wait
> To be your blithesome Ganymede,
> And brim your cups with nectar true
> That never will make slaves of you.

Politicians orated, Mayor Quincy lifted his hand, a valve was turned and the waters of Lake Cochituate via the Brookline Reservoir shot some eighty feet into the air to sparkle and fall glistening back into the Frog Pond. A suggestion that the Frog Pond also have its name changed—to Quincy Lake—was immediately given a decent burial. More shouting and rockets had greeted the fountain of water, and fireworks wound up the eventful day. It would not be reasonable to suppose that *nobody* lifted a bumper of ale in honor of the liquid occasion.

294

By 1851, every part of the city was supplied with water. The project had cost over four million dollars, ninety-six miles of pipe had been laid, and there were some 13,500 families relying on the city for their daily water if not their daily bread. It was an astounding and completely unnoticed triumph for socialism. But within eight years the system began to run into trouble. Restrictions had to be placed on the use of water during dry periods and attempts were made to stop wastage. By 1864, demand for water almost exceeded the supply.

Already a corps of engineers had been investigating every water resource within fifty miles of the city as a potential supplement, some looking longingly at Lake Winnipesaukee in New Hampshire as a permanent solution. Two seasons of drought back-to-back in 1870 and 1871 brought the situation to a head, and the next year the legislature authorized the city to take water from both Farm Pond and the Sudbury River to supplement the failing resources of Cochituate. Temporary dams were immediately thrown up and the permanent work finished by 1878. It consisted of four additional reservoirs and a connection to the Chestnut Hill reservoir. This was the sixteen-mile long Sudbury River aqueduct, having a drop of only one foot to a mile. It crossed the Charles River at Newton Upper Falls on a beautiful seven-arch, 425-foot-long Echo Bridge, seventy-nine feet above the river bed.

Introduction of the Lake Cochituate water into the Boston water system was celebrated on Boston Common on October 25, 1848.

The source of Boston's water was now steadily moving westward as the population and demand of the metropolis and the nearby communities increased. The State Board of Health recommended impounding the Nashua River and creating an artificial lake near Clinton. This was done and the Wachusett reservoir with its Weston aqueduct went into service in 1898, although it wasn't completely filled until 1908. It earned its builder, Frederic P. Stearns, a gold medal at the 1900 Paris Exposition, and kept the metropolitan area supplied for about a quarter of a century. It also resulted in the creation of a third metropolitan agency, the Metropolitan Water District, in 1895. This established a district that towns and cities could join, and a water board that both built and operated the new reservoir and aqueduct. It was required, too, to take over the rest of the city's water system. Water consumption increased enormously until metering was introduced and then consumption dropped drastically.

Beyond this area, the planners had their eyes on the Ware and Swift River watersheds as possible sources of city water. By the 1920s, several investigations led the General Court in 1926 and 1927 to appropriate $65 million and create a commission to add the waters of these two rivers to the system. A new reservoir was impounded in the area, razing the towns of Enfield, Dana, Greenwich, and Prescott—their 2,500 inhabitants and the 7,561 bodies in their cemeteries being relocated. Two huge earth dams with concrete core walls were constructed (Winsor Dam and the Goodnough Dike), creating the vast Quabbin reservoir covering forty square miles and holding 412 billion gallons of water. This is the run-off from 284 square miles of the watersheds of these two rivers. The lake formed is about 18 miles long with a shore line of some 118 miles excluding the shorelines of the 60 islands that appeared in the lake. The Quabbin began filling in August 1939 and was not completely filled until June 1946.

Quabbin water flows to the Wachusett reservoir through a nearly twenty-five-mile-long horseshoe-shaped underground aqueduct excavated through solid rock. At Coldbrook, part way down this aqueduct, provision is made to switch the flow of flood water from the Ware River either way as need may determine. This arrangement makes the best use of the available water.

Wachusett reservoir impounds 65 billion gallons of water at peak, yet one year of drought would empty this reservoir. From here, the eight miles of the Wachusett-Marlborough tunnel and the twenty-three miles of the Hultman Pressure Aqueduct carry the water beneath the Sudbury reservoir to the City Tunnel at Weston. The Sudbury reservoir, which holds some 7 billion gallons of water at maximum capacity, is kept ready for emergency use. The first portion of the City Tunnel goes to the Chestnut Hill reservoir where water is distributed in three systems called the Low Service, the Southern High, and the Southern Extra High. The second portion of the City Tunnel continues on underground about seven miles to a point in Malden where the water is distributed in the rest of the Low Service and the Northern High, and the Northern Extra High services.

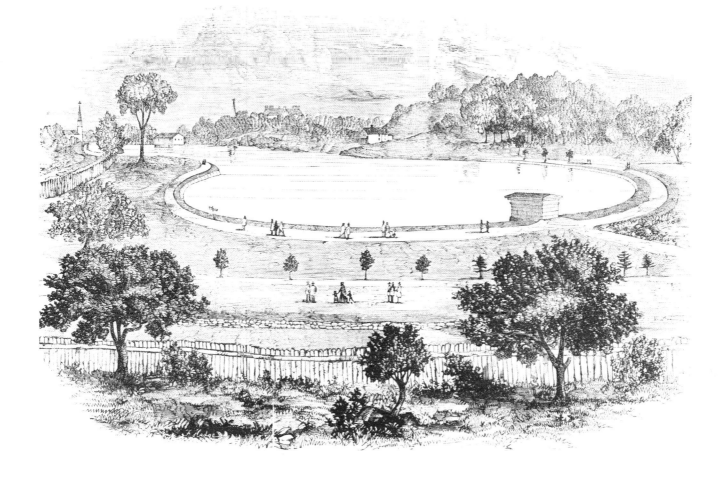

The system continued to grow until in 1948, twenty cities and towns were taking 167 million gallons of water from the District. In 1970, thirty-two cities and towns took 250 million gallons of District water. The Quabbin reservoir system is the largest domestic water supply reservoir in the world. The high quality of the upland water together with the strict enforcement of sanitary regulations on the watersheds provides Greater Boston with an excellent and ample supply of water. Expansion of the watershed area to include the Northfield Mountain and the Miller River area should assure the metropolis of an abundant supply of water until the year 2000.

In 1919, the three separate districts which were dealing with sewerage, parks, and water were consolidated for economy and efficiency into the Metropolitan District Commission, the familiar hybrid political agency serving all together some fifty-two cities and towns. More than 2.3 million people within 544 square miles are served. It is a strange hybrid because it is a creation of the whole state, yet deals only with about 40 percent of the state's population. Its chairman is appointed by the governor, but there is no direct popular control over the agency. It has acquired a police force of more than five hundred men for patrolling territory within its jurisdiction. A construction division builds and maintains its various projects. Lately it has ventured into flood-control (the Amelia Earhart Dam and Locks at the confluence of the Mystic and Malden rivers), recreational development, antipollution efforts, and land reclamation. This extensive domain's administrative headquarters is at 20 Somerset Street in Boston.

In 1963, the legislature formed the Metropolitan Area Planning Council as the official regional planning agency of the Boston metropolitan area. This group works with the Metropolitan District Commission and other state agencies and represents ninety-nine communities of 2.8 million people. It has issued many excellent reports, but it has no implementing authority.

Fragmentation of the metropolitan area into cities and towns is compounded by the overload of five county governments. Yet there is a distinct unwillingness to form one large city out of all these parts as Sylvester Baxter dreamed back at the turn of the century when he created the phrase "Greater Boston." Home rule is too strong for that. Yet there are many conglomerate problems that these old solutions of piecemeal agencies, authorities, and commissions are poorly equipped to handle. Sensible economic growth, equal educational opportunities, proper land use, a more even assessment of taxes, and orderly urban development of the larger circle of towns enclosed by Interstate Route 495—these are some of the problems of the new Greater Boston.

Something larger will undoubtedly take shape here. It may develop into a Greater Boston Regional Council which would merge the various transportation, recreational, and utilities commissions with the Metropolitan Area Planning Council to form an organization made up of some kind of elected representatives. Nashville, Tennessee; Dade County, and Jacksonville, Florida, already have such area-wide government. Local matters, such as property assessing and school construction, would be left to home communities.

Whatever the solution, it had best be guided by the principles laid down in 1893 in the original Metropolitan Parks study commission which declared:

> While divided by political lines into a large number of cities and towns, socially this district is, to all intents and purposes, essentially one community. It must therefore be considered when such questions present themselves arising from needs developed by the growth of such a community. For, if the various cities and towns forming this great urban composite are in the future, as they have been in the past, to be treated separately, these needs can be met only in the most unsatisfactory manner, and in a way that cannot fail to impede the healthy growth and hamper the proper development which should characterize a community of this class.

And Boston, lesser or Greater, has always been a community with class.

Quabbin Lake, looking northeast, in 1969—where Boston's drinking water begins. (Courtesy MDC.)

A Cluster of Independencies

Boston began greedy. In less than two years it took over "the neck of land betwixte Powder Horne Hill & Pullen Poynte," that is, some of Chelsea and Revere and all of Winthrop. Another two years and the colony records declared that "Boston shall have convenient inlargement att Mount Wooliston." So now it had swallowed up more than the present Braintree. The same year (1634) it was decreed that "Wynetsem^t shall belong to Boston" which meant the rest of Chelsea. The next year Boston was laying hands on the harbor islands, while adjusting its boundary on the north with Lynn. In 1637 it took possession of "Nodles Iland," two centuries later to be called East Boston.

This consumption caused a reaction. Roxbury, Dorchester, and Charlestown were not then part of Boston, nor inclined to be. They were frequently fretting with Boston about mutual boundaries, watchful that that town not encroach upon them. And as early as 1640 Braintree succeeded in disentangling itself from Boston's clutches. Much later (1705) Brookline followed suit. Chelsea became independent in 1739.

Then came a counterreaction. Dorchester was nibbled at in 1804, Thompson's Island acquired in 1834, part of Roxbury taken in 1850, more of Dorchester five years later, the rest of Roxbury in 1867, the rest of Dorchester in 1869. Part of Brookline was added in 1870, part of West Roxbury in 1872, Charlestown in 1873, Brighton and the remainder of West Roxbury the same year, and more of Brookline in 1874. Now came a pause while the city digested its gains. Then in 1911 Hyde Park was annexed. Here, the process has stopped temporarily at least, though Boston has always looked longingly on what remains of Brookline, protruding like a sore thumb into the city's side.

Though the towns and cities around Boston have steadily resisted absorption into the core city's body politic, they have long effectually been components of it. These satellite suburbs include at least forty-eight communities, depending on where the line is drawn. Walking distance originally "drew the line." The stages and horse cars of the early nineteenth century slowly extended the "bedroom" boundaries; later the railroads greatly helped, and finally the automobile and rapid transit system considerably enlarged the area. It is generally agreed that the circumferential highway (Massachusetts Route 128) fairly well defines the immediate suburbs of Boston. Highway construction and

This 1871 print by E. R. Howe shows that confusing traffic patterns are not limited to super-market parking lots. The title is: "Leaving Brighton Hotel for the Milldam: Summer."

This drawing by M. Swett of the Norfolk House, a popular hostelry in Roxbury in the middle of the last century, shows a different Roxbury than present inhabitants would recognize.

extension of the rapid transit system combined with the population explosion are extending the boundaries toward the larger circle drawn by Interstate Route 495.

A picture of contemporary Boston is incomplete without a word about the "bedrooms" and subsidiary centers of the core city. The following capsule descriptions, in alphabetical order, include those areas encircled by Route 128 in its swing around the Massachusetts capital. In one or two cases, towns beyond have been included because convenient highway access ties them closely to Boston.

ARLINGTON, the second most populated town in Massachusetts, was once part of Cambridge. It was set off in 1732 as the Cambridge Northwest Precinct, became independent in 1807 when incorporated as West Cambridge, and in 1867 took its present name. For many generations one of the popular names for it was Menotomy (or 'Notomy) after the brook flowing into the Mystic River. From earliest times, alewives were taken in abundance from this stream, but after the Civil War pollution eliminated the fish. The stream is still visible from the parkway of the same name which runs beside it.

The town's moment in history came the afternoon of April 19, 1775, when British soldiers retreating from Concord were caught here in heavy crossfire. Arlington had always been a place of highly cultivated farms, and after 1850 its market gardens were famous throughout the East. As late as 1907 its fields produced more value per acre than any other town in the United States. Sucker Brook, later Mill Brook, furnished waterpower for several small mills. Later minor industries were developed and for a number of decades ice was harvested from attractive Spy Pond. Cyrus E. Dallin, a sculptor from Utah, resided here; local examples of his work are "The Indian Hunter" in the park by the Arlington Library and the "Appeal to the Great Spirit" in front of the Boston Museum of Fine Arts. Today Arlington is largely a residential town of

302

under 55,000 people, 5.18 square miles in area, and six miles northwest of
Boston.

The Shawsheen River rises in BEDFORD, a community established in 1729 from
parts of Concord and Billerica. The 14 square miles of this town, fifteen miles
northwest of Boston, have been settled from at least 1640. Twin rocks on the
banks of the Concord River on the north side of the town are called the Two
Brothers or the Brother Rocks in remembrance of a land agreement concluded there in 1638 between Governors Dudley and Winthrop who were
related by marriage. Fine old houses abound in this developing residential
community of about 14,000 inhabitants. In one of them William Stearns Davis
wrote the once-popular "Gilman of Redford." Three mineral springs brought
Indians to the area, and later were promoted by pharmaceutical companies and
others for their curative effects. Although the town streets were early lighted
by electricity, for years the thrifty burghers shut them off promptly at 1:00
A.M. Now the lights burn all night both in the streets and at the Veteran's
Administration hospital and the enormous Hanscom Air Force Base, with its
associated research laboratories of the Massachusetts Institute of Technology.

BELMONT, named after the estate of a wealthy China merchant, John P. Cushing, was taken from parts of Watertown, Waltham, and Arlington in 1859
after much bitter controversy. Seven miles west of Boston and 4.6 square miles
in size, the town of 28,000 has always been a favored residential community.
The Massachusetts General Hospital established a convalescent home here in
1876 in the Waverley Highlands and nineteen years later moved its McLean
Hospital to the same location. James Russell Lowell called the Waverley Oaks
section one of the loveliest spots in the world. It became a state park in 1893,
but few of its trees remain, having been cut down earlier to build clipper ships
or smoke bacon.

Originally called Mount Wollaston, BRAINTREE was named after that English town and settled from 1625. It was a section of Boston until 1640, and twenty-five years later, to clear its title, the town purchased its land from the Indians for slightly more than twenty-one pounds. The Indians reserved fishing and hunting rights, and presumably if any descendants could be found would still be entitled to them. Its present 13.7 square miles are a small part of its early territory, land having been taken for Quincy, Randolph, and Milton. A local poet sang of it:

> O town, close-nestled at the Blue Hill's feet,
> And fronting eastward to thy hoary sea,
> Thy river winding through the meadows sweet
> Shall sing a pure glad song to thee!

The Manatiquot River (Indian meaning "abundance") rises in Randolph, flows through Braintree taking water from Great Pond and Sunset Lake, and empties into Weymouth Fore River.

Excellent mill sites along the river stimulated many small industries. The town was a great shoe-manufacturing center during the mid-nineteeenth century. Nails, leather, rubber, and woolen goods were other products made at various periods. Both coal and iron were found in small quantities, and local quarries were once known for their red granite. Trilobites found in rocks along a streambed attracted Harvard scientists and prompted the establishment of the college's geology department. General Sylvanus Thayer (1785–1872), for sixteen years West Point Academy superintendent, returned here in his later life and gave the town its library and founded the still-thriving Thayer Academy. Ten miles southeast of Boston, the town's population is over 35,000.

The parsonage and church in Braintree a century ago.

Harvard Square in Brookline, circa 1915.

Formerly the part of Boston called "Muddy River," BROOKLINE was incorporated as an independent town in 1705 and has since, although almost surrounded by Boston, declined all attempts at reannexation. Other names applied to it encapsulate some of its history: Boston Common ("simply Boston's back cow pasture," said John Gould Curtis), Boston Cornfield, the Punch Bowl Village (after the tavern frequented by the Sons of Liberty and later the rebel soldiers besieging Boston), and in the twentieth century, "the town of millionaires." Always an exclusive suburb, once noted for its elegant country seats and showplace estates of the Boston gentry, Brookline today has yielded its reputation as Boston's richest suburb. The championship tennis matches at its Longwood Cricket Club and the horseshows and races at the Country Club (established 1882) remind it of its gilded past. Increasing urbanization and new luxury apartment houses are signs of change in the 6.6 square miles of this largest town in Massachusetts with over 58,000 residents. Coolidge Corner, Cottage Farms, Longwood, and Beaconsfield, are well-known sections of this town. The Christian Science sanitorium and the Lars Anderson Park with its antique automobile museum are both here.

The quiet residential community of BURLINGTON has known an amazing population growth in recent decades thanks to the outward expansion of Greater Boston and the presence of Route 128. Thirteen miles northwest of Boston, this town of 11.84 square miles was incorporated in 1799 from part of Woburn, although settled since at least 1641. Its Old Meeting House dates from 1732. Although old farms of this once agricultural community are disappearing, some notable ancient homes as well as the pleasant Pinehurst Park still remain. Population is well over 22,000.

Ice-cutting at Fresh Pond in Cambridge.

CAMBRIDGE, the county seat of Middlesex County, was founded in 1630 as Newe Towne, the name was officially changed to Cambridge in 1638, and incorporated as a city in 1846. It is on the Charles River with a fourteen-foot channel to Boston's inner harbor. Peak population was reached in 1950 with nearly 121,000 residents. It has steadily declined to the present high 90,000s (including dormitory students). There are three distinct sections in the 6.25 square miles of the city: Old Cambridge, with Harvard University, oldest (1636) and richest (one billion endowment) university in the United States; Cambridgeport, on the northwest bank of the Charles River with industries and the Massachusetts Institute of Technology (there since 1915); and East Cambridge, in the Lechmere area, seat of the county courts.

The universities and colleges of Cambridge with their great libraries, varied museums, splendid laboratories, broad-ranging research centers, world-renowned scholars, and highly selected students make this city a great educational center. Harvard Square, five miles from Boston but only ten minutes by the subway opened in 1912, is packed with people traveling back and forth. The city is also a great commercial and industrial center. At various times glass manufacturing, printing, soap and candy factories, electrical products, slaughtering and meat-packing plants brought wealth to the area. Much of the scientific skill of the universities is drawn upon by establishments now located on Route 128. The city is indebted to the generosity of Frederick Rindge for its city hall, public library, and a technical training school.

When CANTON was incorporated in 1797 from part of the town of Stoughton, it was so named because people wrongly claimed it was on the exact opposite side of the earth from Canton, China. Fourteen miles southwest of Boston, this 19-square-mile growing residential town is reaching 18,000 population. Its industrial history is connected with Paul Revere who had a powder mill here during the Revolution and the War of 1812, operated a copper mill from 1808, and also cast his famous bells here. Other manufacturing included textiles, fishlines, leathers, and radio equipment. Remains of the massive hewn granite viaduct built for the Boston and Providence railroad in the 1830s is still a startling sight.

Older than Boston, CHELSEA was settled in 1624 when young Samuel Maverick's fortified trading post was built about where Island End River meets the Mystic. In 1634 it formally became part of Boston and was generally known as Winnisimmet until it was incorporated as a separate town in 1739. In 1857 it became a city, rising to its largest population in 1930, and since declining as highways have taken more of its land space. Its area now is 1.86 square miles and its population 30,000. Originally it was a town of a few large farms. Gradually it became what the twentieth century would find difficult to imagine—a summer resort. When its extensive real estate development was undertaken in the 1830s, it rapidly became an important industrial center with hundreds of factories drawing on its teeming tenements for low-paid workers in such industries as lithography, hats and shoes, rubber products, and elastic webbing. As the junk and salvage center of Greater Boston, many a canny dealer has gotten rich on others' discards. The United States Navy Hospital has a fine site on its three miles of waterfront.

"Quonahasit" was the Indian name for the town of COHASSET, and is said to mean "a long rocky place,"—certainly an accurate description of the coastal section of this town on Massachusetts Bay some sixteen miles southeast of Boston by water, twenty by land. Once part of Hingham, this area became a district in 1770 and five years later was incorporated as a town. It was a small fishing village for many generations with some boat building, farming, and a few mills run by tide-water power. The fine beaches gradually attracted a small summer colony as early as the first part of the nineteenth century. Jerusalem Road along the shore had elaborate estates of the wealthy. The Whitney Woods, seven hundred beautiful acres, is held by the Trustees of Public Reservations. Nearly 7,000 people live in its 9.86 square miles. Offshore, Minot's Lighthouse (1860) warns ships off its dangerous ledge. Since 1894 the light has flashed a 1–4–3 code, interpreted by the romantically minded as I–LOVE–YOU.

Chelsea was much more rural when this artist viewed it from East Boston in the middle of the last century.

CONCORD was the first inland settlement in the Bay Colony neither on the ocean or a tidal river. It is situated 19 miles northwest of Boston where the Assabet and Sudbury rivers join to form the Concord River which flows northerly to the Merrimack River and the sea. Indians lived on the hill where the streams joined and called the river the Musketaquid, or marsh grass river. Incorporating Concord in 1635, the first settlers made their title more secure the next year by purchasing the land from the Indians for the customary trinkets and a suit of clothes. The original six-square-mile grant has gradually been increased to the present twenty-five-square-mile area where about 16,000 people now live.

Though the name Concord means peace and harmony, the town is most famous for the battle that began the Revolution. Literature vies with history in this town, and visitors to its Sleepy Hollow cemetery will see the graves of Emerson, Thoreau, Hawthorne, Alcott, and other notables and can inspect their various Concord residences where still preserved. On the west side of town is the Concord Reformatory. In 1854 Ephraim Bull developed the Concord grape here, still widely cultivated. It is estimated that three-quarters of all grapes grown in this country are either the Concord or a hybrid of it. Daniel Chester French (1850–1931), the famous sculptor, is represented in his hometown by the bronze Minute Man, and memorials to Melvin and Emerson. The Walden Pond reservation and part of the Minute Man National Park are in Concord.

DEDHAM, the county seat of Norfolk County, is ten miles southwest of Boston, and has about 28,000 residents. Founded in 1636, its Indian name was "Tiot," and its settlers wanted to call it "Contentment," but the General Court decided otherwise. The town has many firsts: Mother Brook, said to be the first canal dug in America (before 1640), which connects the Charles and Neponset rivers; the Fairbanks House (part dating from 1636), said to be the oldest frame house in the country; and the first free public school in America, supported by taxes in 1649. It has been a prosperous industrial and residential town, albeit with, as a lady visitor once remarked, "the quiet of the grave but not its peace."

DOVER was part of Dedham until it was made a district in 1784 and became an independent town in 1836. Pine Rock Hill is the highest point in town, and the Norfolk Hunt Club occasionally meets here for hunt breakfasts and runs. That fact underscores the wealthy residential nature of the town, with less than 5,000 inhabitants spread over fifteen square miles, a sixteen-mile drive from Boston. A Paul Revere bell (1839) rings out from the belfry of the Dover church over the untroubled neighborhood.

Although settled at least as early as Boston, EVERETT was a part of Malden until incorporated in 1870. Its growth was so rapid that it became a city in 1892. Named in honor of Edward Everett, Unitarian minister, Harvard College president, governor of the Commonwealth, and United States Senator, it has been primarily a manufacturing center since 1850. Before then it had been a fairly prosperous farming community. Its manufacturing interests include chemicals and paint, petroleum, electric and gas utilities, and machinery and metals. Large sections of its waterfront are used for oil and gas storage tanks. A large fruit, produce, and grocery center is now located here. Mount Washington, a glacial drumlin, once yielded Indian relics. The population is slowly declining, and now about 42,000 people are packed into its 3.36 square miles.

A pleasant town on Boston harbor is HINGHAM, eleven miles southeast of the core city by water and fifteen by land. First settled in 1633, it was incorporated two years later when its original name of "Barecove" was changed to the present one. Cod and mackerel fishing and coastal trade were its early businesses, along with considerable shipbuilding and coopering. Steamboats from Boston opened the town as a resort in the nineteenth century and several large hotels were built to accommodate "summer people." The Old Ship Church (1681) with its pyramidal roof and belfry, is the oldest and oddest operative meetinghouse in the country. This town was once as famous for its smelts as Ipswich for its clams, but that was before the days of pollution. Derby Academy, founded in 1784 by Sarah Derby, is in this town. In its 22.5 square miles live some 19,000 year-round residents.

Old Ship Church, Hingham.

A rapidly growing suburb of Boston is HOLBROOK, approximately sixteen miles distant. It was incorporated in 1872 from part of Randolph, though the area (now 7.3 square miles) had been settled with farmers by 1710. It was one of the earliest towns to manufacture shoes and boots, though this has long since ceased. The Nathaniel Belcher house (1754) is a reminder of the old; the population increase of the last decade, up sharply to about 12,000, is a reminder of the new.

HULL was settled by people from Plymouth about 1624 who developed a small fishing industry. Originally called "Nantascot," it was given its present name in 1644 and incorporated in 1647. The town comprises the whole peninsula with its beautiful four-mile-long Nantasket Beach and the hilly area reaching out to Point Allerton one way and to Pemberton the other. Nearly 10,000 people live here, joined by thousands more in the summer. Exposed to the Atlantic's occasional fury the shoreline and cottage area is annually damaged. Soon the area will undergo its greatest change since its settlement three and a half centuries ago as renewal plans indicate much construction including high-rise apartments, marinas, boatels, shopping centers, a new Nantasket Pier, roads, and a community hospital. The town (2.5 square miles) is nine miles southeast of Boston by water and about twenty miles by land.

Six-sided Follen Church (Unitarian) in Lexington from 1835.

Colonized half a dozen years after Concord, LEXINGTON is inseparably connected with that town by the events of April 19, 1775. More than two dozen counties, cities, and towns throughout the United States have been named after Lexington in honor of its role that day. The admired Minute Man statue (dedicated in 1900) on its town green, was made by Henry H. Kitson, whose model was Arthur G. Mather of Medford. Settled and known as Cambridge Farms from 1642, it was made a district of Cambridge in 1691, and became an independent town in 1713. Agriculture was its first support, followed by some small manufacturing in the early nineteenth century. The town, eleven miles northwest of Boston, is primarily a residential community today of about 32,000 inhabitants. At least four seventeenth-century houses are still to be seen here, as well as part of the Minute Man National Park.

LINCOLN was formed in 1754 from parts of Concord, Lexington, and Weston. Its neighborhood has been inhabited from at least 1650. It was for several centuries an area of small but good farms, a bountiful fish pond, and for a time some small manufacturing. Now it is an uncrowded suburb of about 16,000 residents in an old-fashioned country-town atmosphere—a delight to the eyes and nerves of city-pent people. The DeCordova Museum, housed in a Victorian edifice overlooking a lake, has perhaps the most scenic spot for its treasures of any such institution in Greater Boston. The town is 14.5 square miles and is thirteen miles from Boston.

310

LYNN began life with an Indian name of Saugus or Saugust, depending on which ancient clerk's spelling you accept. It was first settled by Europeans in 1629 and two years later was a plantation. In 1635 it became a town, changing its name in 1637: "Saugust is called Lin," after the English hometown of its pastor, Lynn Regis. It became a city in 1850. Although Lynn was originally much larger, Reading, Lynnfield, Swampscott, Nahant, and the present Saugus became separate towns during two centuries. It reached its peak population in the 1930s and has since slightly declined to its present 88,000 residents living in a 10½-square-mile area. This includes the 2,000-acre Lynn Woods, one of the largest municipal parks in the country.

The city is eleven miles northeast of Boston and lies on a plain with high ground to the north and west. The Saugus River flows through the city that rejected its name and empties into Nahant Bay on which the city has 3½ miles of beach frontage. Lynn is famed for its shoe manufacturing, though it is not a major industry today. Shoes were made here as early as 1635. The specialty manufacture of ladies shoes began before the Revolution as a cottage industry. Later it moved into small factories and by 1837 over two and a half million pairs a year were being made. At its peak it was considered the second largest shoe manufacturing center in the country. A great shoe strike in 1867 began the unionizing of this trade. Lynn is now a city of diversified industries, one of the most prominent being the General Electric River Works in West Lynn, here since 1883. Thirty-one acres of the business section were destroyed in a $5 million fire in November 1889. A local personality was Moll Pitcher, better known as "The Fortune Teller of Lynn." Here, on Broad Street, Mrs. Mary B. G. P. Eddy lived and wrote the initial edition of her influential *Science and Health*. High Rock with its observation tower stands 275 feet above sea level and affords remarkable views of the surrounding countryside.

Waves not high enough for surfing crash upon the sands of a rock-littered Lynn Beach. The carter might have been collecting seaweed for a pre-organic garden.

High on a plateau is LYNNFIELD (area 10.22 square miles), 12 miles out of Boston. Settled in 1639 by farmers, it developed a few mills on its Ipswich and Saugus rivers turning out woolen cloth and such items as ploughs and bar iron. Serpentine marble was once quarried here. Established as a district from Lynn in 1782, it was incorporated as a town in 1814. Route 128 and the Newburyport Turnpike intersect in this town, bringing concomitant industries, eating places, and shopping centers. The town of about 11,000 is also favored for its golf courses.

Five miles north of Boston is MALDEN, settled from 1640 and known then as "Mystic Side." It was established as a town in 1649 with its present name, and made a city in 1881. Its current population, slightly declining, is about 56,000 persons, living in an area of 5.08 square miles. Both Melrose (1850) and Everett (1870) were set off from Malden reducing its original territory by two-thirds. Beginning with farming, this residential community developed diversified manufacturing, which still plays a substantial part in its life. Famous Maldenites include such dissimilar people as Kenneth Roberts, Erle Stanley Gardner, Ed Ames, the missionary Adoniram Judson, William T. Grant of the store chain, James B. Upham (author of the pledge to the flag), and much earlier Michael Wigglesworth, the poet who wrote the "Day of Doom." Its public library was designed by Henry H. Richardson. Among its various claims to grateful recognition by mankind is that the ice cream cone was first made here. In 1967 it was named an "All America City."

For many years MEDFORD was known for good rum and good ships. Alas, both have departed from the 8.22 square miles of the present residential suburb five miles northwest of Boston with its less than 64,000 inhabitants. Today, their rum comes from "foreign parts" and only pleasure craft churn the waters of the Mystic River—now locked behind the Amelia Earhart Dam, named after the famous Medford aviatrix of the 1930s. The town was founded in 1630 and

Medford Square looking up High Street on the right. The town watering trough has long gone, along with the trees and the lone high-wheeler riding serenely along in the almost deserted square.

became a city in 1892. Its early occupations were farming and fishing. Serious shipbuilding began later, rose to a peak in the early nineteenth century and was over by 1873. Distilling lasted longer. Begun by the Hall family whose spring supplied the water giving distinctive flavor to the spirits distilled from West Indian molasses, it continued until 1905. When the distillery closed, its special formula was destroyed.

Tufts College began classes in Medford in 1854 and became a university in 1955. Presently it counts a faculty and staff of four hundred and a student body of nearly five thousand. A good part of the 2,063 acres of the Middlesex Fells Reservation is in the north part of this city, where stands the Lawrence Observatory, 310 feet above sea level. Tufts House, thought to be the oldest brick house in New England, dating from 1668, and Royal House dating from 1732, are unique examples of colonial architecture. A French professor experimenting with silkworms accidentally released the gypsy moth here in 1867. Twenty years later it had become a serious pest feeding on deciduous and evergreen trees. Stringent control measures have confined it largely to New England.

The 4.73 square miles of MELROSE include part of the Middlesex Fells, the Lynn Fells, the Sewall Woods, and Mount Hood Park with its observatory and golf course. The region has been settled since 1638. The 33,000 residents of this suburb named after the Scottish city obtained their separation from Malden in 1850 and became a city in 1899. Originally it had been the part of Charlestown known as "Pond Feilde." The town is seven miles north of Boston. Some small industries were prominent here, especially a large rubber and shoe factory. Distinguished residents have included soprano Geraldine Farrar, the historian Samuel Adams Drake, the librarian William Frederick Poole, and writer-lecturer Mary A. Livermore. Melrose in 1878 was one of the first places to lay cement sidewalks. Long called "the spotless town," Melrose is a dry and nearly debtless city.

Most of northern MILTON is bounded by the Neponset River, that furnished valuable mill sites and attracted settlers by 1634—though Indians were located here long before the English. It was established as a separate town in 1662 from the part of Dorchester the Indians called Uncataquissett, meaning "head of tidewater." Seven miles south of Boston, the 13.2 square miles of this town contain a large part of the 5,700 acres of the Blue Hills Reservation. This includes the first weather research observatory, established by A. Lawrence Rotch in 1885, where kite-borne instruments were first sent aloft to record upper atmosphere weather. In 1935 this observatory sent up the first radios in weather balloons. The Blue Hills are 635 feet above sea level and now provide sites for television antennas.

Paper mills were early built, some paper being made from the abundant marsh grass. The first chocolate mills in the colonies were set up on the Neponset in 1765. Bass viols, artificial legs, pianos, drugs, and dyestuffs were among

The Fairmount section of Milton with a New York Central train steaming along by the Neponset.

the varied items made in the tidewater mills. Milton Academy, founded in 1797, was dedicated in 1807, closed in 1866, and reopened in 1885, becoming one of the country's outstanding private preparatory schools. Milton did not permit the electric street railway to be built until very late (1898), as rich residents worried about bringing Boston too near, explaining "What would become of our coachmen and horses if such a measure should be adopted?" By 1928 they were fully tied into the rapid transit system of Boston, yet absorption by the concerns of the metropolis is steadily resisted and there are still less than 28,000 people living in Milton. It is also proud of its continuous tradition of town meeting government, now modified into representative town meetings.

For many years NAHANT was the celebrated watering place for (in Thomas Gold Appleton's equally celebrated phrase) "Cold Roast Boston." The town, incorporated in 1853 from part of Lynn, is a peninsula jutting out about five miles into Massachusetts Bay, fifteen miles northeast of Boston. Occasionally inhabited from 1630, it was sold by the Indian Chief Poquanum to a Lynn farmer as a cattle pasture. After the Revolution it became increasingly frequented in the summer for its cooling breezes, its seaside activities (beaches, fishing), the chowders of its few Quaker residents, and such natural wonders as Pulpit Rock, Swallow's Cave, Natural Bridge, and Spouting Horn. In the early nineteenth century it was developed as one of the earliest eastern summer resorts. For several decades it had an exclusive summer colony of wealthy Boston families, but a less affluent floating population was drawn by such attractions as the Relay House and the Maolis Gardens. After the 1920s, it slowly subsided into the present quiet, uncrowded suburb of less than 4,500 people living in its 1.04 square miles. In 1876, the first lawn tennis court in the country was built here.

314

The Nahant Hotel, built by Col. Thomas H. Perkins in 1823, stood prominently on a promontory of the peninsula, later to be occupied by the estate of Senator Henry Cabot Lodge.

The Indians called NATICK "the place of hills" and it was long a favorite resort of theirs. In 1651 the Indians were granted by the General Court a 2,000-acre "plantation" here—a "gift" of their own land. Now, that would be called a reservation. The first Christian Indian church was established here in 1660 with forty members. English settlers began to move into the area about 1718 and the Indians gradually elbowed out. By 1781 Natick was incorporated as a town. For most of the nineteenth century it was essentially a village with some small manufacturing, particularly boots and shoes. During the first part of the twentieth century it became a small suburb, and after World War II it began to expand to its present under 32,000 population because of its propinquity to both Framingham and Route 128. The 14.88 square miles of this town are seventeen miles and 17 minutes southwest of Copley Square via the Massachusetts Turnpike.

NEEDHAM is practically outlined west, south, and east by the Charles River. Route 128 snakes through giving it an industrial spine. Twelve miles southwest of Boston, settlers began moving into the area about 1680. It was divorced from Dedham in 1711, and in 1881 part of it separated to become Wellesley. Industry was established here early with six paper mills on the Charles River, and manufacturing continues to the present day in such varied items as surgical instruments and knit goods plus the esoteric operations of the Route 128 plants. Thirty thousand people live in its 12.5 square miles. Much of Needham is actually not in Needham but at the bottom of Boston's Back Bay. Many hills were leveled in East Needham after the middle of the last century to provide fill for this expansion of Boston. Gravel was transported by railroad and the filling work continued for more than twenty years.

Seven miles southwest of Boston is NEWTON, the Nonantum of its Indian for-bears. The local League of Women Voters graciously styles Newton, "the Garden City." Built on seven hills like Rome, it is divided by the trough of the Massachusetts Turnpike. The sale of air rights and subsequent building upon these, it is hoped, will bring together what the turnpike has split asunder. Once accomplished, the just under 90,000 residents will again know "rejoicing," the meaning of the Indian word Nonantum. Originally part of Cambridge, this area was incorporated as Newtown in 1691 and its name shortened to the present form by the town clerk in 1766 on his own authority. In 1873 it became a city containing 17.4 square miles of which less than 3 percent is used today for industry.

Fifteen villages developed on and around the seven hills of Newton: three grew up on highways (Newton Corner, Newton Center, West Newton); three developed because of water power (Upper Falls, Lower Falls, Nonantum); eight sprang from railroad crossings (Newtonville, Auburndale, Newton High-lands, Oak Hill, Waban—pronounced "waugh-ban"—Eliot, Woodland, River-side); and one was settled and named by the Lee family in 1854 when they turned their "Uncle Joe Farm" into Chestnut Hill. These villages have always been an important part of life in Newton. Six colleges are located here: Boston College, Andover-Newton Theological School, Lasell Junior College, Mount Ida Junior College, Newton Junior College, and Newton College of the Sacred Heart. Echo Bridge was built over the Charles in 1876. Norumbega Park dates from 1897. Hawthorne wrote his "Blithedale Romance" while living in Newton.

The name NORWOOD was chosen for this town when it was created in 1872 from parts of Dedham and Walpole, after a contest in which seven other names were suggested: Montrose, Ames, Neponset, Oakland, Nahatan, Glenwood, and Elmwood. Norwood won on the third ballot for reasons unknown, and Nahatan and Neponset ended up as streets in the new town. The town seal was designed in 1906 by a high school pupil, George L. Boyden. Over 30,000 people now live in this town of 10.3 square miles, fourteen miles southwest of Boston. It boasts a racetrack, an airport, and a mixed residential-industrial climate.

Adams and granite are the two words that sum up QUINCY, eight miles southeast of Boston and about that driving distance in minutes on the Southeast Express-way. The Adamses—John and John Quincy—partook of the soil's granitic nature, and Quincy is distinguished as the only city in the country to supply the United States with two Presidents. The granite and the men joined forces in the Adams Temple, or First Parish Unitarian Church designed by Alexander Parris and built in 1828. The tombs of the two men lie here.

Back of the bay area the land rises to heights of 600 feet, and it is from these hills that the Quincy granite was dug, from about 1825 on for over a century. Now, bits of the original Quincy are scattered around the world in tombstones, buildings, or paving blocks. The quarries that it took men 125 years to excavate will be filled in a decade, if recent proposals to use them as dumps are acted upon. Thomas Morton arrived here in 1625, when the area was known as Mount Wollaston, and set up a trading post with the Indians. It was so successful that it took business away from the Pilgrims. Those pious businessmen raided Morton's establishment under the guise of putting down another Sodom and Gomorrah, shipped him back to England, and got their customers back. Today, the Pilgrims would probably be hauled into court for violating the Sherman Anti-Trust Act.

Up until 1792, the 16.51 square miles of Quincy were part of Braintree. That year it became a town and in 1888 a city, the only one in Norfolk County. Its extensive coastal area (28.9 miles long) attracts fishermen, bathers, yacht clubs, and commercial shipbuilding. The over 88,000 residents of this residential industrial complex enjoy more than 2,600 acres of park and playground. The Crane Memorial Library was designed by Henry H. Richardson in 1880. In West Quincy can still be seen the site of one of the earliest railways (1826) on this side of the Atlantic Ocean.

Also part of the original Braintree was RANDOLPH, called Cochato by the Indians, but taking its present name from Peyton Randolph, first President of the Continental Congress. It was established as a town in 1793, and early in the nineteenth century turned to manufacturing when its farmers were unable to compete with the more fertile western lands. By the end of the century, however, these factories declined and Randolph became principally a residential suburb of Boston. It is home for about 27,000 people on its 10.08 square miles, ten miles south of the core city. The Manatiquot River rises here, and a portion of the town is taken up by the Great Pond Reservoir.

Established from part of Lynn in 1644, READING or "Redding" as it was first spelled, is twelve miles north of Boston with a population of nearly 23,000. Its land titles were confirmed by the heirs of Wenepoykin, the Indian chief of the area. Shoe and furniture making prospered until the 1860s. At one time, organbuilding was a thriving business. Another ancient name for Reading was "Beantown" because of its popular baked bean suppers. The old stage coach between Boston and Reading was nicknamed "the bean pot." Lake Quanna-powitt is a lovely body of water in the center of the township. Route 128, with its cluster of firms bringing employment and taxes to the town, swings by the lake.

REVERE, keeping alive the name of the Revolutionary patriot, is better known for its crowded beach and carnival attractions in the summer. It was part of Chelsea until 1846 and was still called North Chelsea until in 1871 it honored the patriotic horseman. Perhaps it would have been more fitting if Revere had ridden a dog, since all of the local dog-track, Wonderland, is located here, while only a small part of the horse track, Suffolk Downs, is in Revere. In 1914, Revere became a city which has continued to grow from its 25,000 inhabitants to its present population of nearly 45,000 people contained in 5.95 square miles.

Its greatest period of growth came in the decade of the 1920s but had nothing to do with Prohibition and the use rum-runners were alleged to have made of its convenient coast.

As late as 1910, Revere was still a community largely devoted to farming. But the possibilities of its splendid three-mile beach had already been recognized, especially as the population of the metropolis expanded so rapidly and a narrow gauge railway made Revere easily accessible to them. The rapid transit lines have brought the beach even nearer. Maurice Prendergast painted many scenes on the old beachfront in his lively impressionistic style. Beachmont is a drumlin settlement at the Boston end of the beach. A large part of the city stretches inland behind the beach, where stands the Yeoman House, a typical seventeenth-century farmhouse, and the Slade Spice Mill where spices have been ground on an old colonial site since the 1830s.

The name of SAUGUS comes from the Indian name of the river, passing through this Essex County town. It is said the Indians originally called the river "Abousett." Early residents often spelled the name of this town with a final "t," thus "Saugust," and some today pronounce it as if the "t" were still there. Ten miles northeast of Boston, this town (incorporated in 1815 from part of Lynn) is a growing suburb of about 25,000 people spread over 10.57 square miles. Through its first two centuries it was largely agricultural. Its most famous industry was the old ironworks, said to be the first in the colony, though this is disputed by Quincy for one. The restored ironworks attracts many visitors each year.

One of the oldest houses in the Boston area is the Scotch-Boardman House, remarkable for having been in two counties (Suffolk and Essex) and four towns (Boston, Lynn, Chelsea, and Saugus) in its career. Chocolate was made in Saugus from 1794 and was still famous in the early part of this century. Snuff and cigars were made at Sweetser's Corner (now Cliftondale) and Sweetser was known in the trade for introducing "short sixes" and "long nines" to the business. When planes first came in, an aviation park was started at the old Saugus Race Track and for two or three days mail was sent by flying machine to the Lynn boundary where it was dropped to waiting messengers who rushed it to the Lynn post office. One of the first airmail flights in the country, it was abandoned after a few days.

SOMERVILLE was praised in 1912 by its Board of Trade as "the beautiful city of seven hills." Today its eight squares are more prominent: Union, Davis, Central, Powderhouse, Ball, Magoun, Teele, and Gilman. The change marks the effect of urbanization. Settled from 1630, it was part of Charlestown until made a town in 1842. Twenty-nine years later it became a city. Part of the front line in the siege of Boston, the command headquarters of the rebels was on its Prospect Hill.

After a century or so of being a thinly settled farming region, first the Middlesex Canal and then railroads opened Somerville to commercial development.

Its busy brickyards were followed by heavy industries and then meat-packing plants, once handling 75 percent of the slaughtering in the state. In the 1920s and 1930s a factory of the Ford Motor Company assembled three hundred cars daily. Its industrial base and its population have both declined, the latter down from a peak in the forties of 102,000 to the present approximately 87,000. Only its tax rate has steadily grown.

STONEHAM contains one of the great bodies of water in the Metropolitan Boston area, Spot Pond, part of the region's water system. The town's 6.6 square miles also contain the Sheepfold recreation area, part of the Middlesex Fells reservation, an observation tower on Bear Hill which has an elevation of 317 feet, and the Walter D. Stone Memorial Zoo. The town, once part of Charlestown, was established in 1725. The area, eight miles north of Boston, was unsuitable for extensive farming, and a shoe industry developed employing half the inhabitants by the 1830s. Many improvements in shoe manufacturing were introduced here. Today it is a growing residential suburb of over 20,000 people.

The history of SWAMPSCOTT is a trinity: one, poverty-stricken fishing village; two, luxurious summer resort; three, middle-class suburb. Thirteen miles northeast of Boston, the area was settled by the English from 1629. Formerly Indians fished and camped here, lobsters and cod being particularly abundant in its

A. L. Rawson drew this early sketch of Tufts College (now University) on Walnut Hill between Somerville and Medford soon after the college opened in 1852.

319

The Main Street of Waltham
more than a century ago.

waters. The first summer hotel started in 1835. It became a town from part of Lynn in 1852, and was a noted watering place all through the nineteenth century. Today it is a residential community of under 15,000, in an area of 3.07 square miles. Its name is said to mean in Indian "at the red rock," and the red rock itself can still be seen offshore of the point of land on which the New Ocean Hotel stood until recently. The name Tedesco, often used in Swampscott, came from a ship wrecked on the coast whose dead were buried here.

WAKEFIELD was named after one of its leading citizens, Cyrus Wakefield, who built the first rattan factory in the world here. When incorporated in 1812 from part of Reading, the town was called South Reading and did not take its present name until 1868. The area was settled from 1639. For many years rattan and willow furniture manufacturing was its distinctive industry. The town park extends to Lake Quannapowitt. Crystal Lake is surrounded by the town. The 560 acres of hilly woodland that make up the Breakheart Reservation are shared with Saugus. The town is ten miles north of Boston and has over 25,000 residents, in its 7.36 square miles.

"Forest home" is the meaning of the name WALTHAM, though it is anything but a forest now for its over 60,000 inhabitants. Settled from 1634 when it was still part of Watertown, it became a town in 1738 and a city in 1884, with an area of 13.6 square miles. It is a city of rugged hills on both sides of the Charles River which flows through it and whose waterpower early attracted industry: paper mills, the first cotton mill (1813), bleachery and dye works, and world-famous Waltham Watch Company, with the first machine-made watches. Later industries include such skilled trades as precision instruments and electronic devices.

Prospect Hill (470 feet above sea level) gives fine views of the surrounding area. Two elegant country estates from the Federal period still remain: Lyman House and Gore Place. The Walter E. Fernald School, Bentley College, Middlesex County Sanitorium, and Brandeis University are among the institutions in this city. Chalk crayons were said to have been invented by a local dentist. In the early period of the automobile, the Metz car was built here by a former bicycle maker, and the firm prospered for more than a decade. The city is ten miles from Boston.

WATERTOWN, one of the original towns established in 1630, has shrunk greatly since then: Weston, Waltham, and parts of Cambridge and Belmont have all been taken from it. It is now cramped into 4.06 square miles around the falls of the Charles River flowing through it to the south. The Indian name for the region hardly sounds elegant: Pigsgusset. About 38,000 people live here and the town is an important manufacturing center. The Elliott Addressing Machine was invented here by Sterling Elliott, also responsible for many other curious inventions. The Stanley Brothers built their steam autos here. The United States Arsenal was located here from 1816 until its recent closing. The Perkins School for the Blind moved here to its riverbank location in 1912. Proud of its tradition as the "Cradle of the Town Meeting," representative town meetings have been held since 1919.

Almost wholly in Watertown is Mount Auburn Cemetery, a unique garden cemetery when opened in 1831. Today, about twice as many people are buried in this woodland spot (70,000) as live in Watertown. Operating expenses of the cemetery exceed $500,000 per year, backed by an $8 million investment portfolio. Numerous monuments cover the grounds and many famous names appear on the gravestones, fascinating those who, in the New England phrase, "go deading."

This statue of Sir Richard Saltonstall is part of the monument to the Founders in Watertown Square.

WAYLAND is among the claimants of having started the first free public library (August 7, 1850). First named East Sudbury, it was made a town in 1780 from part of Sudbury. In 1835, after a vote that considered such names as Waterville, Wadsworth, La Grange, Elba, and Penrose, Wayland won on the second vote. The common view that it was chosen in honor of Francis Wayland, President of Brown University, would seem erroneous since he was only eight years old when the name was picked. Shoemaking and harvesting the area's abundant meadow grass were once important occupations in Wayland. Market gardening succeeded this. Now Wayland is an uncrowded residential suburb of less than 15,000 people. The Unitarian Church here was built in 1815 after a design of Sir Christopher Wren and with a bell by Paul Revere, thus combining two attractive traditions. The town is eighteen miles west of Boston, with an area of 15.28 square miles.

WELLESLEY is as well known for being the home of Wellesley College as for being an attractive residential suburb of over 28,000 people fifteen miles west of Boston. Settled from 1660 with a few scattered farms, it grew slowly and it was not until 1881 that it was made a separate town from Needham. Named after Samuel Welles, who had developed a large estate here in 1763, the town seal shows a bible representing the College (chartered 1870, first classes 1875) and a flower, representing the Hunnewell Estate and its famed Italian Gardens on the opposite shore of Lake Waban from the college. Babson Institute, now Babson College, was founded here in 1919. Alexander Graham Bell lived here at the time he invented the telephone. The first game of golf played in the Commonwealth was on a short course here in 1892. Sabrina Lake, or "Lake Slopover" as it was once jokingly called, is one of the few reminders of William E. Baker's Ridge Hill Farm, a sort of Disneyland East that sprawled over eight hundred acres between Wellesley and Needham before the turn of the century. Land area is 10.05 square miles.

Twelve miles west of Boston is appropriately WESTON, settled when it was part of Watertown from about 1642 and a thriving agricultural and industrial center to the 1840s. "The Farmers' Precinct" as it was called, became a town in 1713. In 1746 Lincoln was set off from Weston leaving an area of 16.8 square miles. The former Post Road from Boston to New York went through Weston and the old tavern on Ball Hill was for many years a famous stopping place for travelers. In 1765, Abraham Hews established a pottery business here said to be the first such industry in New England. The excellent Hook & Hastings organs were made in Weston from 1888 when the surviving partner, Francis Hastings, moved the factory here from Roxbury. At one time peat was taken from the local meadows for fuel. Now Weston is chiefly a growing residential town of 12,000 people, not counting the fluctuating student population at Regis College. On the grounds of this institution is the Cardinal Spellman Philatelic Museum, the only such facility in the country for the study and display of postage stamps.

WESTWOOD is one of the newer towns, incorporated from Dedham as late as 1897, although the region had been settled from 1640 and long known as the Clapboardtree Parish. Originally a farming area, it is now chiefly residential for its almost 15,000 people who live fourteen miles southwest of Boston. The Clapboardtree Meeting House (1731) is still standing. For years this was a large dairy region, and even as late as 1900 long lines of milk wagons trundled into Boston every morning. The old Town Pound for penning up stray animals can still be seen beside Route 109 and imprinted on the town's seal.

WEYMOUTH was the second place settled by the English in New England. A group from Plymouth in 1622 was unable to keep it going, but two years later succeeded. First called by the Indian name Wessagusset (or Wessaguscus), it took its present name in 1635 after the English town. It is an aggregate of several distinct communities with over 55,000 people living in its 16.7 square miles (including four islands) located between Weymouth Fore River and Weymouth Back River. As indicated by the popular rhyme:

> Cohasset for beauty,
> Hingham for pride;
> If not for its herring
> Weymouth had died.

fishing played a large part in the early economic life of the town.

Formerly there were excellent dairies, particularly noted for the quality of their cheese. Industry developed along its ponds and rivers. Shoe manufacturing began early and by 1870 there were forty such factories, the Stetson shoe being perhaps the best known. This town was one of the first affected by the now-endemic pollution problem. Discharges from the mills very soon ruined fishing and spoiled the fertilizer used on the farms. Also here is the largest boulder in Massachusetts left by the glaciers. Big as a house, it is appropriately called House Rock, or sometimes the Weymouth Sphinx. The town is twelve miles southeast of Boston.

Among the names attached to WINCHESTER through the years were Waterfield, Woburn Gates, South Woburn, and Black Horse Village. Some people suggested it be named after Count Rumford, but others objected to the "rum" part. Its present name was taken from Col. W. P. Winchester of Watertown who presented the town with $3,000 for municipal works after they became incorporated in 1850 from parts of Medford, Arlington, and Woburn—certainly a bargain price for lasting fame. Shoemaking and tanneries continued in this region beside the Aberjona River many years in the last century, but even then the town was largely residential. It still is today, with over 22,000 people living just seven miles northwest of Boston on 5.91 square miles. The Myopia Hunt Club began here in 1879, but soon moved to Brookline and then Hamilton. Beautiful ponds and part of Middlesex Fells add greenness to the town, as did for many years several nurseries and greenhouses, now mostly gone. A prominent resident was the publisher Edwin Ginn who gave a million dollars to establish the World Peace Foundation.

From 1630 to 1739, the area that is now WINTHROP was part of Boston; until 1846 it belonged to Chelsea; until 1852 it was included in North Chelsea (Revere). Since 1852 it has been the town of Winthrop named either for Gov. John Winthrop or for his son Deane Winthrop (1623-1704) who lived here. People argue it both ways. While only five miles northeast of Boston, Winthrop was fairly secluded, situated on a peninsula of 1.55 square miles jutting into the Bay. Access from Boston by sea was easier than by land route, so much of its early development catered to the boat trade. The street railway in 1876 brought it into easy contact with the city. Its development first as a summer resort and then as a residential area soon followed.

The birthplace of Benjamin
Thompson, later Count Rumford,
scientist and politician, in a
delightful rural Woburn. The
house shown was built in 1714.

Great Head, a drumlin rising 105 feet above the sea, is topped with a 100-foot standpipe visible from many parts of the area. Because of its flanking position on the bay, several forts have been active here during various wars: Fort Banks, Fort Heath, and Fort Dawes. Deer Island is now connected to the mainland by a road across Point Shirley. The population, constricted as it is to the peninsula, is holding fairly firm around 20,000 but it is the most densely populated town in the Commonwealth. For some years a horse watering trough in the town was decorated with a nearly nude female statue surely more appreciated by the wagon drivers than by the horses. A lady complained about boys seeing this, and the statue was shrouded in opaque garments. When the horse age passed, the nude lady mysteriously vanished with it.

WOBURN is not pronounced "woe-burn" but "woo-burn." The 38,000 residents of this 12.6-square-mile city ten miles northwest of Boston know this, but many others stumble over it. Settled in 1639, it became a town in 1642 and a city in 1888. The Middlesex Canal provided a direct water route to Boston and stimulated much local economic growth. Leather, shoe manufacturing, machinery, glue, and chemicals were made here for years. Two famous local citizens were boyhood friends: Loammi Baldwin, an engineer who built the Middlesex Canal and discovered the apple named after him, and Benjamin Thompson, Count Rumford, a scientist whose discovery that "heat is a form of motion," not only was of benefit to scientific theory but perhaps may explain his political dabbling which did his reputation no good. A case of wife-swapping in the late 1700s amused the village for years. Once Simeon Reed traded his wife off to James Butters of Wilmington for a team of oxen. Most men claimed Reed got the best of the bargain. Butters never said.

Index

This book was set by Machine Composition Company in Caledonia, a typeface designed by William Addison Dwiggins, and was printed by the Halliday Lithograph Corporation using Novara paper made by the Mohawk Paper Mills, Incorporated, and bound by the Halliday Bindery in Arkwright-Interlaken's Pallium Vellum and Process Materials Corporation's Seafoam Elephant Hide.

The book was designed by Richard C. Bartlett. The picture research was by the author, Carl Seaburg. The drawings which embellish the interludes were made by Gobin Stair. The map on page 40 was drawn by Leo Durling. John Paul Torrey coordinated production. This book was edited by Ray Bentley, copy edited by Cynthia Bright and Lois Randall, proofread by Joseph Gadomski, and indexed by Jean Seaburg.